MIRACLES HAPPEN

The Transformational Healing Power
of Past Life Memories

DR BRIAN WEISS
AND AMY E. WEISS

SHETLAND LIBRARY
HAY HOUSE

Australia • Canada • Hong Kong • India
South Africa • United Kingdom • United States

First published and distributed in the United Kingdom by:
Hay House UK Ltd, 292B Kensal Rd, London W10 5BE. Tel.: (44) 20 8962 1230;
Fax: (44) 20 8962 1239. www.hayhouse.co.uk

Published and distributed in the United States of America by:
HarperOne, a division of HarperCollins Publishers with offices at 10 East 53rd Street,
New York, NY 10022. www.harpercollins.com

Published and distributed in Australia by:
Hay House Australia Ltd, 18/36 Ralph St, Alexandria NSW 2015. Tel.: (61) 2 9669 4299;
Fax: (61) 2 9669 4144. www.hayhouse.com.au

Published and distributed in the Republic of South Africa by:
Hay House SA (Pty), Ltd, PO Box 990, Witkoppen 2068. Tel./Fax: (27) 11 467 8904.
www.hayhouse.co.za

Published and distributed in India by:
Hay House Publishers India, Muskaan Complex, Plot No.3, B-2, Vasant Kunj, New Delhi –
110 070. Tel.: (91) 11 4176 1620; Fax: (91) 11 4176 1630. www.hayhouse.co.in

A catalogue record for this book is available from the British Library.

ISBN 978-1-78180-002-7

Printed and bound in Great Britain by TJ International, Padstow, Cornwall.

Contents

To Carole ∾

whose idea was the seed that became this book
and whose love has nourished us both

Someday, after mastering the winds, the waves, the tides, and gravity, we shall harness . . . the energies of love, and then, for a second time in the history of the world, man will have discovered fire.

Pierre Teilhard de Chardin

Introduction

On a beautiful summer afternoon in New York in July 2010, my wife, Carole, and I were driving up the tree-lined Taconic Parkway toward the Omega Institute, a rustic retreat center where we teach an intensive course on past-life regressions. We love teaching this course. Incredible events happen every day, again and again. Participants not only remember past lives but have amazing spiritual or healing experiences, find soul mates, receive messages from departed loved ones, access profound wisdom and knowledge, or encounter some other mystical and marvelous event. Carole and I have witnessed such life-transforming occurrences over the years in these workshops and trainings, and we feel blessed to be able to facilitate and observe them. Often we do not know that a particularly powerful experience has just transpired in the workshop. The person may need time to process it, and we will only hear of it in a later e-mail or letter.

At that moment on the sun-dappled highway, Carole's BlackBerry buzzed with an e-mail describing another one of these wonderful workshop healings, a message relaying such ancient wisdom yet arriving to us through this most modern technology. The timing was perfect, for we were about to reenter the very place where we had observed so many similar happenings. We never knew exactly which amazing events and changes would transpire—only that they would. Carole turned to me and observed in her wise, understated way: "Sometimes miracles happen."

Indeed, sometimes they do. The miracles may be large ones that affect the entire group. They may be small and silent. No matter their scope, the transformation is permanent. Relationships are repaired. Souls are nourished. Lives acquire newer and deeper meaning. Miracles happen.

A miracle happened for me on the day that a patient named Catherine walked into my office and introduced me to an entire spiritual universe that I had never believed to exist. My earlier books contain a very detailed account of her experiences, and they describe how her life was permanently altered for the better as a result of them. My own life was affected at least as much. Before uncovering her amazing past-life memories, I had been a left-brained, obsessive-compulsive academic. I had graduated magna cum laude, Phi Beta Kappa, with a degree in chemistry from Columbia University. I earned my medical degree from the Yale University School of Medicine, where I was the chief resident in psychiatry. Completely skeptical of "unscientific" fields such as parapsychology and reincarnation, I was the chairman of a prestigious psychiatry department at Mount Sinai Medical Center in Miami, and I had authored more than forty scientific articles and book chapters in the fields of psychopharmacology, brain chemistry, and Alzheimer's disease. Catherine turned my skepticism—and my life—upside down.

Although it has been over thirty years since that day, I still remember the very first time that she crossed the invisible boundary of her current life and entered the realm of other lifetimes. She was in a deeply relaxed state, her eyelids lightly shut but her concentration intense.

"There are big waves knocking down trees," she whispered in a hoarse voice as she described an ancient scene. "There's no place to run. It's cold; the water is cold. I have to save my baby, but I cannot . . . just have to hold her tight. I drown; the water chokes me. I can't breathe, can't swallow . . . salty water. My baby is torn out of my arms." Her body had tensed; her breathing accelerated.

Suddenly, her body and her breathing relaxed completely.

"I see a cloud . . . my baby is with me. And others from my village. I see my brother."

My skepticism needed more time to erode, but the process had begun. Catherine's severe symptoms began to disappear as she remembered more scenes from this and other prior lifetimes. I knew that imagination could not dissolve such chronic symptoms; only actual memories could. Catherine would go on to remember many historical facts and details from her past lives, which we were sometimes able to confirm. She was also able to relate private truths from my own life, truths that she had no obvious way of knowing or discovering. She would tell me these personal facts while she floated in that beautifully relaxed state in between physical lifetimes.

Those powerful evidential encounters with Catherine began to open my mind and to erase my doubts. I found other reputable clinicians conducting regressions and research, and I became further convinced. Ever since *Many Lives, Many Masters,* my first book, was published in 1988, I have treated over four thousand individual patients using past-life regression therapy and many, many more in large groups during my experiential workshops. Each case validates and confirms, teaches and expands. Each case reveals more of life's mystery. In that time, I have met with past-life pioneers and luminaries from all over the world. Where there was once disbelief, there is now carefully collected knowledge and wisdom. The stories in this book will propel you on the very same path and lead you from doubt to discovery. Just open your own mind and let this miraculous journey begin.

In the workshops that I conduct, approximately two-thirds of the audience successfully remembers episodes from previous lives. Their memories and recollections frequently heal emotional and physical maladies. Symptoms resolve even though the memory may not be absolutely accurate, for an error in recall does not negate the truth and importance of the memory. As an example, in a regression you may recall the trauma, chaos, and even the entire emotional reaction of your mother when you were three years old and ran into the street, almost getting hit by a black Buick. When you check with your mother, it turns out that the car was a navy blue Cadillac. Otherwise, everything else in your recall was accurate. This slight degree of distortion is acceptable. Memory is not literal time travel. And if, in describing the memory of the near accident, you used a word that you did not learn until you were twelve, this is also fine. Your observing and describing mind is your present-day consciousness, not your three-year-old brain. You never actually stepped into a time machine. Hypnosis is the tool I use to help people recall such childhood events—and more. Many of my patients and the people who have attended my workshops are able to remember events not only from their childhood but also from when they were in their mothers' wombs, from that mystical state when they were in between lives, and from past lives.

Throughout the years, I have encountered people whose preconceived notions about past-life regression therapy have compelled them to dismiss the concept entirely. They argue that the memories are distorted or inaccurate, as I have addressed above, or that its therapeutic effects can be ascribed to wishful thinking, or that everyone who has a regression erroneously identifies themselves as a famous historical figure in a past life. Such critics are vocal but misinformed. This book contains numerous stories of people who have undergone or performed their own regressions, and together they present a catalog of an incredible diversity of experiences that definitively challenges such assumptions. Its pages contain far more recollections of paupers and peasants than people of prominence. Imagination or fantasy does not cure deeply entrenched physical or mental conditions, yet this book is brimming with examples of how remembering our past lifetimes does—and neither the patient nor the therapist even needs to believe in this concept for the healing to occur, just as neither Catherine nor I did at first. The stories in this book, like a microcosm of the entire field of regression therapy, illustrate a widely varying range of past lives, yet they also point again and again to the fundamental commonalities in our soul's journey and evolution. To open your mind to their truths—that we are immortal and eternal beings who have lived before and will live again, that we are all one, and that we are all here on Earth to learn lessons of love and compassion—is, to borrow from that well-known quote, to take one important step for a man and one giant leap for mankind.

Whenever my patients and workshop participants successfully remember one of their past lives, a direct avenue to divine wisdom and to physical or emotional wellness is established. The awareness that we have had multiple lifetimes, separated by spiritual interludes on the other side, helps to dissolve the fear of death and to bring more peace and joy into the present moment. Sometimes, just the remembrance of past-life traumas leads to incredible insights and healings. This is the rapid route.

Those who have not had a past-life memory can attain understanding and an enhanced perspective by witnessing or reading about the experiences of others. An empathic identification can be a powerful transformative stimulus. This is an alternative route, where the direction of progress is more important than the speed. We will all eventually reach a state of enlightened awareness.

Reincarnation, the concept that we have all lived past lives, is the door through which I entered a greater level of understanding. Catherine opened the door for me, and I have subsequently held it open for many more.

But there are many doors. People have accessed the higher realms through near-death experiences, through mystical encounters, or through meditation. Others have had a sudden insight or "aha" moment. All doors lead to the same place: a transcendent recognition that our true nature is spiritual, not physical. There often is a simultaneous awareness that we are all interconnected and that we are somehow manifestations of one energy.

The author Paolo Coelho writes: "Life is the train, not the station." On our soul's journey home to a state of infinite love and wisdom, a journey filled with mystery and miracles, we rest, recuperate, and reflect at the stations, in between lifetimes, until it is time to board again: another train, another body. There is only one home and eventually we will all return there, sooner or later. It is a place of bliss. This book will help you find its shores.

The treasure of this book lies in the stories carefully nurtured and harvested by readers and workshop participants over the past twenty-three years. Shared here, the experiences underlie and honor everything that I have written about and taught. In a thousand voices, these stories validate not only the phenomena of past-life regressions but the entire psychospiritual universe. You will read of souls and soul mates, of the life that is found after death, of present lives being utterly transformed by encounters with the past. The stories share how mind and body can be profoundly and permanently healed. They tell how grief can be changed to comfort and hope, and how the spiritual world interpenetrates and enriches our physical world at all times. These stories are filled with wisdom, love, and deep knowledge. They are humorous and serious, brief and extensive, but always wise and instructive. Gleaned from all over the world, the shared experiences will help many thousands of souls toiling through their current lives. Helping others to heal, to understand, and to progress along their spiritual paths is the soul's noblest duty.

Reading the stories and reflections in this book is like experiencing a hundred vicarious regressions. Powerful resonances to the reader's own latent past-life memories stimulate the subconscious and elicit a heightened awareness. The deeper mind discovers new possibilities of physical and emotional healing. A comprehension of our higher nature—that we are the soul, not the body or the brain—leads to profound shifts in our core values and aspirations. And then the most important transformation of all begins. Our consciousness awakens, opens its divine but dormant eyes, and discerns its spiritual path. The stories that have been selected to be in this book do not merely describe these gentle wake-up calls, they provide them. To read them is to be changed in some ineffable yet indelible way.

At that moment of awakening, when we discover our inherent nature as eternal beings, doubt disappears. As if an ancient alchemist sprinkled his magic dust on us, fear is permanently transmuted into inner peace, despair into hope, sadness into joy, hate into love. At the level of the soul, anything can happen.

Words have their own alchemical power. This book is not a collection of stories; it is a collection of transformative possibilities. By reading about and empathizing with the regression experiences of others, we gain a deep connection to their immense wisdom. A link to an incredibly wise and loving cosmic process is established and gradually strengthened, story by story. Each one that has been chosen for this book facilitates those empathic connections and provides accessible insights into the deeper nature of our souls, our purpose on the earth, and our healing potential. My commentary, I hope, helps to clarify these themes even more. As you read of others' mystical encounters, the likelihood of having one of your own becomes increased. The stories set the table, and now the special guest can enter. They shine light on an entire metaphysical philosophy. The concepts of reincarnation and past-life regression demonstrate the reality and essence of our higher self and our higher purpose. The techniques and teachings found in the following chapters can be used by all to improve your lives, to endure along your spiritual path, to experience more love and happiness right now, and to understand that there is no need to fear, as we are all immortal. We are all souls.

My daughter, Amy, is a therapist as well as a writer and an editor. She and I collected hundreds of submissions from people who had a meaningful memory to share. We carefully read and reread each one, selecting those that we felt would highlight an important point, provide a platform for teaching, and, most of all, illuminate our shared life lessons. Their beauty and their insights were frequent topics of discussion around the family dinner table. Amy and I worked as a team to write this book. Sometimes, my words give poetry and purpose to her thoughts; sometimes, her words give form and finish to my thoughts; but at all times, both flow into each other seamlessly. It has been such a pleasure and a blessing to be able to work with her on this project. Yet the most important collaborator by far consists of you, the authors of its stories. Without you to truthfully, bravely, and eloquently share your experiences, this book would not exist. Without you, there would be no words. You are the inspiration for its creation and the conduit for its healings.

This book is not necessarily designed to be read in one sitting, for its stories are rich and layered with lessons. Wander leisurely in their wisdom. Linger with them awhile. Feel their emotions and textures. You might find parallels with your own life experiences, and these are worth taking the time to explore. Reread the stories as many times as necessary. Each time that I do, I unfailingly discover new and deeper levels of meaning. You will also quickly notice that these stories are not just about past lifetimes. As I have mentioned, reincarnation is a doorway into an expanded consciousness and incredibly rich vistas of spiritual knowledge and wisdom. What is on the other side of the door is more important than the door, even though the door itself is fabulous.

The stories that you are about to read are examples of our inexorable progress toward spiritual perfection. They point the way; they illuminate the steps. They are like multifaceted jewels that we have collected but that are meant to be shared. The facets of one seem to reflect all of the others. Although I have created chapters, the jewels really mirror one another and so could be located anywhere and everywhere, like holographic gems.

Years ago, I had dreamed about humans as these jewels, and I described the image in *Many Lives, Many Masters:*

It is as if a large diamond were to be found inside each person. Picture a diamond a foot long. The diamond has a thousand facets, but the facets are covered with dirt and tar. It is the job of the soul to clean each facet until the surface is brilliant and can reflect a rainbow of colors.

Now, some have cleaned many facets and gleam brightly. Others have only managed to clean a few; they do not sparkle so. Yet, underneath the dirt, each person possesses within his or her breast a brilliant diamond with a thousand gleaming facets. The diamond is perfect, not one flaw. The only differences among people are the number of facets cleaned. But each diamond is the same, and each is perfect.

When all the facets are cleaned and shining forth in a spectrum of lights, the diamond returns to the pure energy that it was originally. The lights remain. It is as if the process that goes into making the diamond is reversed, all that pressure released. The pure energy exists in the rainbow of lights, and the lights possess consciousness and knowledge.

And all of the diamonds are perfect.

Here are more diamonds.

We Are All Connected

Once, when I was teaching a large group workshop, I noticed a little card. On it was a poem or prayer that read: "Buddha nature pervades the whole universe, existing right here and now. I dedicate the merit of this practice to all sentient beings. Together, we realize liberation."

As I read these words, I realized that this is true for everyone and everything. You can substitute, instead of "Buddha nature," if you feel more comfortable, the word *love*, or *God*, or *Jesus*, or *higher power*, or any other spiritual figure. It does not matter. It simply means a kind, wise, and loving energy, perhaps with attributes beyond which we can comprehend, that fills the atoms and molecules and energetic particles of the whole universe—an energy from which we are made and precipitated, in a sense. This energy, this Buddha or God nature, exists right here and now, everywhere and all the time. You can dedicate the practice of your daily life to bringing about in a compassionate manner the advancement of all sentient beings; that is, all things that have consciousness. Together—because every one of us is connected—we can realize liberation, which is freedom from the process of birth and death and rebirth, so that we can graduate from the school that we call Earth.

That word *together*, that one simple word, is crucial. There is such a sacred energy in the gathering of the group. As the stories in this chapter illustrate, it is no accident, no coincidence that specific people come together at a certain time and for a collective purpose. Some of the authors of these stories are able to divine the intricate, infinite threads that tie each one of us to another. Others who call themselves strangers find that they have been intimately linked throughout their lifetimes. There are no strangers. There is no separateness. No one stands alone.

For example, any particular group of people who are attending one of my workshops is not truly random. They are already connected to each other even before they have assembled, pulled in by some greater coordinating force. It is as if a cosmic magnet attracts those specific souls that are needed for that workshop. Soul mates and others, some of whom have shared past lives but have not yet met in the present one, are brought together. These unions are actually reunions.

As I looked at the card, I remember thinking, *How important this little prayer is.* Then as I was teaching the course, with the words of this prayer still resonating in my mind, I understood that the 130 people who had come to this intensive course were assembled not just for their own purposes, and not just to experience a past life. What if God or a higher power had assembled these 130 people to heal three or four? What if the intention was, "Well, let's get these particular 130 people and their unique energy to heal these three or four among their group who are in need?" What a privilege, what an honor, and what a blessing it would be to be included among those 130 people.

That gave a different perspective to me and to the entire group. We realized that miracles were happening. We merely had to open our eyes.

. THE FABRIC OF CONNECTION .

In 1993, I was given *Many Lives, Many Masters* by a stranger who knew nothing of me but said that it was "for" me. It made everything in my life prior to that finally make sense—not so much my experience with past lives as much as personal conflicts that I felt with the common perception of grief. For the first time in my life, I felt validated for not feeling completely stricken with loss when someone passed away. I had a resonating knowing that if I could only work with you and learn from you, I could help others to shift their perspective from pain back to connection.

More than ten years later, my husband, a California highway patrol officer, was killed in a pursuit. Two years after that, I saw you on *The Oprah Winfrey Show,* and that same resonating feeling of knowing came through me as I watched. With your July Omega professional training only weeks away, I booked everything within minutes. It was as easy as water flowing.

When I arrived at Omega, my psychic awareness was completely blown open as never before. I was aware of my connection not only to all others there but also with the little animals and plants. You agreed to demonstrate a regression on me in front of the entire group. As you did a rapid induction, I immediately saw the word *trough* galloping through my awareness and then saw the actual trough we used for our horse's water on the farm on which I grew up. I was led through a childhood memory of being forced by circumstance to sell our beloved horses. I remembered witnessing the pain this had also brought my father, how he had related to my mother that his instincts told him not to sell the horses to that particular buyer, and how he had ignored those instincts with great regret. I had made a conscious decision to not cry, in order to spare my father any additional guilt. From that moment as a child until I sat with you at Omega, even the thought of sadness in relation to that incident remained deep and anonymous inside me. The pain came flowing up from my diaphragm with each exhalation as I described what was happening. The combination of absolute shock and relief was indescribable.

I went next to a memory of my son's birth, when my own instincts had screamed to me that something was wrong for weeks yet I allowed myself to repeatedly be convinced by the doctor that I was simply paranoid. Finally, I pleaded with him to induce my labor and he reluctantly agreed, but then I was thrown into an emergency cesarean section when arriving at the hospital. My son had needed to be resuscitated, gangrene infecting the entire placenta and umbilical cord. The next day, when he was finally stable enough for me to hold him, I looked down upon him and saw his little stained fingers. I knew that by ignoring my own intuition, which I should have trusted more than the air that I breathe, I had failed my first real test as a parent.

I had begun to cry in anger, sadness, and frustration, the same way my father had when he sold our horses. Just then, my son began to fuss and move uncomfortably, and I realized he could feel this pain coming from me. Out of concern for causing any additional pain to him, I stopped crying and forgot the guilt completely until those fourteen years later, during my session. I released the extreme pain that I was completely unaware of harboring. Absolutely relieved, I felt as if the weight of the world had literally been lifted from my chest.

I then became aware of my guides' presence, and the familiar sense of peace and belonging washed over me. They went on to make me aware that I was a part of them, just as they were a part of me, and as I felt you to my right side I realized that you, too, were a part of that "team."

You asked if my husband was there. Looking for the answer, I could feel him to my left, and I turned my head as if to bring him more clearly into my awareness. Just as I turned left, I also felt him in front of me; I turned my head forward, only to feel him to my right, yet still to my left and front. "He is everywhere!" I said as I realized what I had been feeling.

Hearing this, the entire rest of the room of 130 people let out a collective sigh. In that moment, I became aware of energy, like blue threads, that had been connecting me to each person in the room since our introductions had begun the night before, extending from my diaphragm to theirs individually. When they collectively sighed in response to their own emotions, which were stirred from sharing in my awareness of my late husband's presence, the threads shot out from each of them, from one another to one another, in a beautiful, simple yet complicated fabric of connection. I became aware of the fact that everything I would go on to do from that moment would affect all these others, just as everything that they would go on to do would affect each of the others as well. *Heal the healers* was the awareness I had, with a knowing that in our connection was our strength.

I tuned back in to hear you ask if my guides were still present. I responded that they were and that they always are, and I said, "We are a team and we have a purpose." You asked what the purpose was, and I began to see infinite flashes of scenes—only flashes—but with details and emotions attached to each. The few that I could capture involved a prisoner sitting on the side of his bunk with his head in his hands, feeling more pain, fear, and anger toward himself than any of his victims could ever fathom because even he did not know why he did the things he did, and so he could not trust his own actions. A mother holding her child, both of them starving to death. The mother choking on her own pain, knowing her child would die of malnourishment before her, fearing she would die believing her mother was selfish for not dying first. All I could verbally translate of these flashes was, "The pain, the pain, so much pain," as I cried with such intensity that I felt as if I would split into pieces.

"All of the pain is from fear, misunderstandings, fearing and being feared," I said. I knew that the purpose, as you had asked, was to reduce the collective pain through eliminating fear, and through this an elevation of all livings things would ensue. I understand now that being one is not a goal—it already *is*—and that everything that we do, even those seemingly small things that we do individually, does indeed directly affect us all.

ᘯ *Nina Manny*

In my lectures and workshops, I frequently talk about how we are all connected, how what one does affects everybody else. Nina says it beautifully: in our connection is our strength. The bonds that connect us are ones of loving spirituality. If we are of the same energy, composed of particle and wave and not blood and bone, then what we do affects one another—and not just human beings. Our thoughts and actions have consequences, all the more reason to be loving and compassionate and not fearful or harmful. They create our destiny and our future.

Nina's story wonderfully expands upon and explains the energetic cords that unite us. But there is so much more here. She perceives her late husband's ubiquitous and loving presence. She is aware of the constant eternal wisdom that grace, heaven's hand, provides us in various forms, whether through guides, angels, spiritual messengers, or in many other ways. She has recognized lifetimes filled with lessons, loss, pain, and hope. And she has reminded me of a long-ago message from a Master, conveyed through Catherine, recorded on tape, and written in *Many Lives, Many Masters*. It is one that has nourished and motivated me ever since.

> You were correct in assuming this is the proper treatment for those in the physical state. You must eradicate the fears from their minds. It is a waste of energy when fear is present. It stifles them from fulfilling what they were sent here to fulfill. . . . Energy . . . everything is energy. So much is wasted. Inside the mountain it is quiet; it is calm at the center. But on the outside is where the trouble lies. Humans can only see the outside. . . . You have to go deep inside. . . . You must get rid of the fear. That will be the greatest weapon you have.

It is what Nina reminds us: "All of the pain is from fear." Love and understanding dissolve fear.

The great teacher Jon Kabat-Zinn taught me a meditation of a mountain. I think of this often, for it helps me to understand how to stay grounded no matter what happens on the outside. I believe that it has been such a powerful image for me precisely because the Masters had mentioned it so long ago in the above quote.

Picture a beautiful mountain, perhaps with a peak covered in snow. As you look at it, you can see that it has an inner core of constant peace and constant temperature, so that no matter what happens on the outside, the inside remains unchanged.

Now imagine that the seasons come and go. Summer comes with lightning, with storms, with flooding and fires, yet inside the mountain remains completely still, tranquil, and calm. The summer becomes fall, with howling winds and leaves falling off the trees; then winter arrives with snows and freezing temperatures; and this too turns to spring, as the snows melt and avalanches occur. Yet the inner core, the beautiful space deep within the mountain, is unaffected by any of these changing seasons.

We are like the mountain. We do not have to let outside events rob us of our joy and harmony, no matter how strongly the storms rage, no matter how loudly the winds howl. We all have that inner core of calm and quiet. It is there whenever we want or need it. By going inward, we can access its powerful healing presence. The mountain, inside, is perfect—and so are we.

Envision, now, that tourists come to the mountain. They arrive by train, airplane, car, boat, and other ways. And they all have opinions: This mountain is not as beautiful as one that I have seen elsewhere. It is too small, or too tall, or too narrow, or too wide. But the mountain does not care, because it knows that it is the ideal essence of mountain.

We, once again, are like that mountain. No matter what people say about us, no matter what criticisms or judgments they may offer up and call mirrors, we are already ideal and divine. We do not have to be affected by their opinions, even those of people who are close to us, such as our family, our bosses, or our loved ones. In that sense, we are solid and grounded in the earth like the mountain. We know, deep within our hearts, that we are the perfect essence of a spiritual being. The words of others cannot rob us of our inner peace and joy unless we give them the power to do so.

I often use this meditation to remind myself and others of our magnificence and nobility, just like the beautiful mountain. Although we have merely forgotten this, we are already perfect. We have always been so.

. LOVED AND WORTHY .

The week at Omega in October 2010 touched and opened my heart in so many ways. It helped bring to my conscious mind so much that I had forgotten. There is a reawakening emerging in me that brings me to tears whenever I allow myself to sit still and realize how wondrous we all truly are.

On the first morning, Dr. Weiss guided us into a group regression. This was not my first regression, and I was looking forward to another past-life experience. I usually sense, feel, and visualize in sync with the words of the person guiding the journey. This time, however, to my surprise I saw myself as I am in this life at my current age. I was standing in a space where everything just felt hazy. I looked in front of me, and there seemed to be a curtain of fog. A bare arm came though, took my hand, and brought me through the curtain.

I found myself standing in front of an old friend, Joe, who had passed in the 1970s, when we were in our twenties. Joe and I had been very close. As a matter of fact, I had never been as close to anyone before or after him. We were friends, lovers, and confidants. We would talk for hours about the possibilities of life after death. We promised each other that whoever died first would come back to the other one and explain what it was like. Eventually, we got in our own way and went our separate ways—badly.

About a year or two later, Joe and I spoke on the phone, and it was clear that whatever had come between us was not as strong now. He invited me to visit him the next time I was in Santa Barbara. I said that I would, but I didn't. I was afraid, and I told myself that I needed more time before I saw him face-to-face.

Not long after that, I got a phone call from a mutual friend, who told me that Joe had taken his life. I was in disbelief. I became mad, and sad, and then mad again. If only I had called him when I was in Santa Barbara, then maybe this would not have happened.

Time went on, and Joe kept his word. I would get visits from him, mostly at night in vivid dreams. There were also the times, after I had spoken to someone about how angry I was that he took his life, when I would be woken up with my bed shaking, and I could hear his voice telling me not to be mad at him. I made myself stop voicing my anger out loud, and soon I realized that I just missed him. Eventually, I told Joe I no longer wanted the dreams, and they stopped too.

After that, from time to time, I felt Joe's energy around me; just knowing that he was there was so reassuring. Then one day, in the 1990s, I was in my kitchen and I could feel Joe's energy surround me. It was around me and in me. I heard him tell me that he loved me and that he was leaving this vibration and going to another dimension, where he had work to do. He told me he was going to be greeting the souls who had passed from AIDS. He showed me a quick glimpse of a space where there was so much sorrow, pain, and confusion. This was part of his debt, he said, for taking his own life. I felt his energy enveloping me and filling me with an unconditional love that I had never experienced before. Tears of joy streamed down my cheeks.

I don't know how long I stood there before I again became aware that I was standing in my kitchen in the middle of the day.

That was the last time I ever felt Joe's energy—until the group regression on the first morning of the training. There I was, standing in front of Joe. He took me to him and hugged me fully and unconditionally. He now had wings. He impressed upon me, without speaking, that he had progressed. I could feel him wrap his wings around me. It felt like there were other energies around us, also surrounding me in love. I heard the words, "You are loved. You are worthy." My jaws hurt, my throat was tight, my arms ached, and tears rushed into my eyes. Joe continued to hug me until I accepted and surrendered to the message, and at that moment the physical discomfort also stopped. A teacher came and put a "light crystal" in my heart. I followed Dr. Weiss's voice and opened my eyes. I was back. I didn't want to be back! It was lonely and cold here.

That afternoon, I volunteered to be hypnotized in front of the group so that Dr. Weiss could demonstrate a rapid induction. It worked well. While I was in hypnosis, Dr. Weiss asked me about my morning journey. I told him about meeting Joe, although I purposely did not use his name, instead referring to him simply as "a friend." I told him of the wings and of his message. I said that my friend had taken his life and that I hadn't gone to see him, as I'd promised I would. Dr. Weiss told me that I wasn't responsible and should not have any guilt for my friend having taken his life. To my friend I was, he said, "loved and worthy."

Immediately, I felt a sense of relief. I hadn't consciously realized that I had carried this burden of responsibility, but now that it was spoken I could feel a layer of sadness being lifted. I could feel the emotion of the moment, yet I still sensed that I was holding back somewhat and not letting go entirely.

Several days later, still during the training, a friend and I were on our way to the dining room for breakfast. A woman named Rachel was walking toward us on the path. She looked at me intently and asked, "Are you Jeannette?"

When I said that I was, she said, "I have a message for you from Joe. He says he loves you." She told me that she had gotten this message and was compelled to find me to relay it. I thanked her with tears streaming down my cheeks. This was my confirmation. Joe knew me too well. He knew he would have to bring his message through someone else just to make sure I would believe it.

And I do believe it. Since this encounter, I have a sense of quiet calm. I feel more comfortable with myself than I have ever been before. I now know that we are all truly loved in ways that we cannot imagine on this physical plane. And now, finally, I accept this truth.

ᥫᯅ *Jeannette*

The earth is like a one-room schoolhouse in which students of different grade levels are assembled together: first graders coexist with college seniors, remedial students with the gifted. Its courses are taught in every language and cover every subject. Students of all nationalities and all races attend this school—every human does. All are on the path toward a spiritual graduation. The lessons in this school are difficult because here we have bodies, so we experience illness, death, loss, pain, separation, and so many other states of suffering. Yet the earth also has such powerful redeeming virtues, like incredible beauty, physical love, unconditional love, soul mates, pleasure for all our senses, kind and compassionate people, and the opportunity for accelerated spiritual growth. Eventually, over the course of many lifetimes, we will learn all these lessons. Our education will be complete, and we will not need to reincarnate anymore.

Jeannette provides a glimpse into how our education continues on the other side, even after our consciousness has left the physical body. The earth is a school—a difficult and popular one, but not the only one. In those higher realms, we do not learn through bodily sensations or emotions or relationships or illness. There, our studies are more abstract and conceptual. We discover the advanced dimensions that exist beyond our human awareness, and we begin to unlock their many mysteries. There, we see and feel the sublime manifestations of what on Earth appears to be solid and material, and we acquire an understanding of these absolute energies at their most elevated vibration. There, we explore the nuances and levels of loving-kindness; compared to Earth and its physical forms, it is learning at a higher octave. Even though these lessons are the graduate-level courses, they are still part of our soul's curriculum. Our knowledge is always expanding.

Joe tells Jeannette that he has incurred a debt for taking his own life. He probably had left a healthy body when he committed suicide. His consciousness, of course, was not hurt or damaged, but without a body it cannot do its work on the earth plane. The body is essential for the soul's manifestation in a physical dimension. Joe's soul must wait for its next incarnation to continue its spiritual journey on the earth. But it is not punished with eternal damnation or obliteration. Karma is for learning, not for punishment. And so Joe is assigned to work with the spirits of people who have died from AIDS. Here are people who have suffered greatly, dying too young because their bodies have become irreparably damaged from a horrible disease. What better way for Joe to learn the value of a healthy body, of the gift of life?

While working with the souls of the victims of AIDS, Joe was not in pain or distress. He was filled with unconditional love. He was, in a sense, earning his wings, like an angelic being. He was erasing his karmic debts. If Joe, with all his debts and flaws, could make the transition from human to angel, then we all can. For truly we are all angels temporarily hiding as humans.

In her story, Jeannette mentions her encounter with Rachel, who had a special message to give her. Below, Rachel tells how she received that message.

. TELL HER I LOVE HER .

At the Omega Institute training, I was regressed one evening and taken, in my mind, to a beautiful garden with daisies. There I spent some time speaking with my guides, who watched me with love and happiness. I was given messages about my back pain and feelings of control. After a while, I was ready to leave this realm, but I had the feeling that I needed to wait. This is when I felt a spirit come to talk with me. I knew it wasn't anything to do with me. He had a message for Jeannette.

"Tell her I love her," he said to me.

I was prompted to ask his name. It was Joe. I was highly skeptical about that, as it almost seemed too generic. It may as well have been "John Doe." Nonetheless, I could clearly envision what he looked like. He appeared to me an older man with short, curly, whitish-gray hair, olive skin, and a broad chest. He danced a jig from happiness because I promised I would pass the message on.

Unfortunately, only two days into a training of well over a hundred people, I had no idea who Jeannette was.

I have received messages before, but only in dreams and nothing as clear as this. As with all the messages that I have had in the past, they nag at me until I do something about them. I didn't find Jeannette that evening, and so the nagging continued. When I was going to sleep, I asked that Joe go into holding until the morning, when he could pester me again.

I have no idea where that idea of a holding came from, or even if there is such a place, but I had a fairly restful sleep. An hour before my alarm went off I was awake, and Joe was in my ear about Jeannette.

Once I had delivered the message, confirming that Jeannette did know Joe, I asked him to leave and go to the light. He wanted to stay and help me, even though I didn't want him to. Joe explained that helping me was his way of saying "thank you," as well as part of his own spiritual healing. It was something he needed to do, and I had no intention of stopping him on his journey. By the end of that day, he was done helping my angels get messages through to me.

∽ Rachel

Our rational minds often attempt to minimize or even negate the mystical, spiritual, or psychic encounters that we have. We forget the immediacy and the power of our own experience. If we receive validation and confirmation, we are able to let go of our doubts and embrace the reality of the event.

Rachel was pushed by Joe to confirm Jeannette's reunion during her regression. Jeannette also knew that their meeting in her kitchen was not her imagination. Joe was helping her, healing her, and emanating his eternal love for her.

The messages from Joe and from the other "energies" were not only for Jeannette. They are for all of us. "You are loved. You are worthy." We all are. Do not let your own mind minimize or negate this reality.

Faith, whose story follows, also received an important message from the other side. Passing it along to its intended recipients allowed her to validate not only her psychic impressions but also the important truth that our loved ones are always with us.

. MESSAGES FROM BEYOND .

The second day of your workshop in Los Angeles in 2002 started with a regression. Microphones were scattered around so that people could talk about what they had experienced after the regression ended. Across the room, a woman stood up at the microphone and told how she had come that weekend because her daughter had recently died from cancer. As she was talking, I kept seeing a light behind her. I tried to shake it off, but each time I did, it became brighter until finally it resolved into a very pretty girl with brown hair and blue eyes who was standing just behind the woman. The girl was looking right at me.

I knew that I had to find this woman and tell her. During the break, I walked into the hallway, and even though there were five hundred people at the event, the only people in the hall were this woman and her husband.

First, I described the girl whom I had seen behind her in exact detail. The woman and her husband were both crying as she pulled a picture from her purse and showed me an image of her daughter. It was the girl whom I had just perfectly described.

I then told her that she wasn't imagining it when she thought she heard giggling as the water splashed on her while doing the dishes; that when she was making the bed and thought she felt herself being tickled, she was; and that when she was sitting and reading or watching television and thought that she felt a hug or a head on her shoulder, she really did.

The husband couldn't speak by this point. The woman told me that even though he didn't believe in any of this stuff, he had bought tickets for them to come to the weekend because he felt he should. When she had wanted to go outside during the break, he wouldn't let her leave the hallway where we now stood, so they had hung around and looked at the art. All the things that I had described to her were things that she had told her husband and no one else, things that she had been feeling happen around the house.

Of course, by now we were all crying. I smiled and said, "For whatever reason, your daughter chose me to tell you what I just did." I am not someone who sees or speaks with ghosts, but this young woman unquestionably passed a message to her parents through me.

It wasn't until I went back into the workshop room and sat down that I realized just how altered my state had been when I received those messages. From where I was seated, there was absolutely no physically possible way that I could have seen that woman at the microphone. There were two support columns in the room; I was sitting on the far left, and the microphone was placed behind the one on the far right. It was an impossibility for me to have seen her standing there. Yet I did. I needed to see her daughter, and I needed to be the messenger that day and bring a measure of peace to her and her husband's pain.

∾ Faith Susan

Every one of us possesses intuitional abilities and powers far beyond what we know. Faith is not a professional medium or psychic, but as she entered the altered state her vision became clairvoyant and unobstructed by physical barriers. She saw and heard with her heart as well as her eyes and ears. And the little girl's father trusted his intuition to get the tickets to the event and to linger in the hallway, even though he didn't yet know why.

If we do not follow our intuition we create obstacles and opposition, and oftentimes this can be dangerous. But if we follow our heart, we flow with the process; we do not force or block, much like the Taoist principle of *wu wei*. Spiritual beings strive to understand and flow with the process, not struggle against it.

The little brown-haired girl wanted to comfort her parents, to ease their grief. Because the three adults opened their minds and trusted their intuition, the comfort was received.

When in doubt, choose from the heart, not from the head.

. THE DELICATE LITTLE FLOWER .

I went to your Omega workshop in July of 2009. I want to thank you for showing a great interest in my ongoing medical issues and for taking the time to guide me through a one-on-one regression therapy session. After the regression, it took me a few days to begin processing everything. I began to make connections specifically to the lifetime where I was just a small child in the field of yellow flowers, which were poisonous and which I mistakenly ate. My mother, the same one I have in this lifetime, killed herself upon my death, for she was so distraught that she hadn't been able to save me. She was overprotective in this lifetime, as we discussed, and soon I began to remember things that she had told me when I was growing up.

I remembered that she had shared with me that after I was conceived, my parents decided to separate, unaware that my mother was pregnant. Once my mother discovered the pregnancy, the discussion began about terminating it. Her friends and family and my father tried to convince her that going through with it on her own would be a mistake. However, my mother responded that although she didn't know why, she knew she could never terminate the baby, and as hard as it was going to be for her on her own, she had to have it. She always told me that she had a strong feeling that she needed to bring me into this world.

I also remembered that my mother had shared with me that she was extremely paranoid about me while I was in utero. She would often not feel me move for a period of time, which would send her straight to the doctor in fear that I was not alive. She was constantly afraid that I wasn't going to make it. In addition, I was often sick as a child, and many times this resulted in a hospital stay. Each time I was hospitalized, my mom worried that I wasn't going to live through it.

After I was regressed, I realized that I was born into this life with my mother's preconceived notion that I needed to be taken care of, because of her fear that she was always going to lose me. Oddly enough, I recalled that while I was growing up my mother used to call me "her delicate little flower," as I was so fragile and constantly getting sick. It was somewhat eerie when I remembered this, because you and I had just discovered that in another life I had actually died as a young child from an allergic reaction to eating little yellow flowers.

I have not yet discussed all of my experience at Omega with my mom, but I plan to do so. As far as my eating, I am now up to thirty-six different foods. That's twenty-five more than I was able to eat before you regressed me. It is a slow process, but I couldn't be happier and am looking forward to being able to eat many more. I am still continuing to try new food, and I am having success after not being able to eat certain things for over three years. My body has been healing ever since that day. I also wanted to let you know that after the regression, many people approached me and told me that my regression had helped them. This made me think of your words when you said that we were all brought together for a purpose.

രു *Nikki DeStio*

We have lived before alongside many of the people with whom we live now. Our souls have reincarnated together. When a situation occurs that reminds us of a past-life trauma, the seeds of our suffering are watered and our anxieties bloom. We fear what has already happened because we have forgotten the past. We mistakenly believe that the traumatic event will happen in the present or in the future.

Whenever I encounter obsessively overprotective and controlling parents, my focus shifts to the past-life causes. Overwhelmingly, the cure to their fears lies in those buried memories. The parents' worries are allayed, and the child, now liberated, can begin to prosper. The key to the future is often hidden in the past.

At that workshop, Nikki recalled another tragic past life in which she died early. Amazingly, another woman who was attending and who had never met Nikki remembered the exact same lifetime. Her story is next.

The world works in mysterious ways.

. LOVE, LOSS, AND LIFETIMES .

In July of 2009, I was fortunate enough to be able to attend your seminar. I knew that a whole weekend with you was going to be an exciting experience, and it exceeded my expectations by far. The last day was the most profound.

In my regression, I felt a constant burning in my stomach and tightening in my chest; it was difficult to breathe. I saw a farmhouse in the distance as I walked over a fog-covered bridge. I was a young woman with beautiful features. I stood in the grass, away from the house, feeling great anxiety about entering it. The burning in my stomach and the tightness in my chest remained. And then I was taken to my last day of life. I was young, perhaps in my early twenties, wearing a crisp white dress, like a nightgown. I had long, dark hair. I was leaving someone whom I loved dearly and romantically. It was so sad, but somehow I knew that I had to leave him.

Suddenly, as I left that life, I felt Vincent's presence. Vincent is a dear friend, a man whom I was just beginning to recognize as my soul mate. Later that day, a young woman named Nikki came onto the stage for a regression with you. *How strange*, I had thought. Vincent's daughter, with whom he is very close, is also named Nikki.

As she sat on the stage with you, Nikki described a problem that she had had her entire life with swallowing and eating food. She had consulted many doctors about it, but none could find any physical reason for her problem. You regressed her to a past life in which she was a child. She was choking on a flower, and her mother had to try to pull it out of her throat. It was revealed that the flower was poisonous;

the little girl had died as a result. The girl's mother, who happened to be Nikki's mother in this lifetime as well, committed suicide over her grief.

Remember my burning stomach and tight chest, my inability to breathe well? I thought it was so odd that I had just felt those very feelings, and here Nikki was feeling them in a regression. But my mouth went dry as you regressed her to an even earlier time. I was beginning to fidget and to grip my journal; the woman next to me asked what was wrong. I asked her to read the description of the regression I had had earlier that day, which I had written down.

Nikki was describing herself as a man. She was swinging happily in circles with a girl who wore a white dress and had long, dark hair. She loved this girl very much. As you moved her forward, she described the old farmhouse that I had seen in my regression. She stood, almost like I had, not wanting to go into the house. She was afraid; something bad was happening in there. You finally coaxed her inside, and she described the girl as I had seen myself, lying on the bed, dying. She had been poisoned. Nikki felt the great loss of such love.

By the time Nikki's regression ended, I was crying, and the woman next to me had finished reading what I had written that morning. She said that I had to share this with you and Nikki, but I did not want to. Nikki had had such emotional memories; I did not want to tell her my experience. I had been such a skeptic of this whole thing, and I worried that others would find me an opportunist of some sort for seeking five minutes of your attention. Nonetheless, the woman asked for the microphone and promptly handed it to me.

"It's strange about Nikki," I started hesitantly. "She described exactly the scene I observed when I saw the farm. Nikki was a man standing at the same faraway distance. He was upset because he was going to lose his wife. She was dying and he was devastated, so sad for the rest of his life. When I was dying in my regression this morning, I was so upset to be leaving my husband. I felt like we didn't have enough time, that something was unfinished. I felt a burning in my stomach and a tightening in my chest. My throat was so tight, it made it hard to breathe."

I had a hard time relaying my regression to Nikki. I cried and, at times, choked on my words. Later, I sought her out in the crowd to introduce myself. I asked her if it would be okay to give her a hug, but she had a protective friend with her who immediately said that I could not, that Nikki had problems with hugging because it made her feel like she was choking or that she could not breathe. Nikki, however, gave me a big smile, and she hugged me tight for a good, long time.

ᔕ *Shannon*

In my recollection, Nikki's diet was extremely affected by her past-life death from eating the little yellow flowers as a child. She could only eat eleven different foods and would have severe allergic reactions if she consumed anything else. It was nearly impossible for her to go to restaurants. Her life was limited and constricted by this problem. Within days after her regression, her diet expanded to fifteen different foods; within a month, to twenty-four; and then eventually to thirty-six.

It was not by chance or coincidence that Shannon, a complete stranger to Nikki, was in the same group that weekend. Such strong confirming memories, even physical symptoms, were shared. I am sure that Shannon is no longer a skeptic.

Vincent, a soul mate whose daughter is also named Nikki, was also around, teaching about eternal love. We are not just our bodies or our brains, but expansive spiritual beings. Perhaps it was Vincent's higher self that was helping and orchestrating Shannon's experiences that weekend. Wouldn't a soul mate want to help open the mind and the heart of his skeptical loved one?

Nikki's friend, not yet realizing that the regression to those two past lives had already begun the therapeutic process, was being protective. But Nikki, intuitively aware that she was healing and feeling better, overruled the friend and was able to happily hug Shannon. These two women were both learning about soul mates reconnected, about eternal bonds of love, about transcending death. The good, long hug expressed their mutual understanding and transformation.

It does not happen very frequently that two people, often strangers, remember the same past lives. However, when it does, it provides even more validation that those lives were indeed real. They are not imagination or fantasy, not metaphor or symbol. Since we have lived hundreds or even thousands of lifetimes, it is not unrealistic to find that we have shared some of them together, just as we all share parts of this current one.

In medicine, we have a saying: "When you hear hoof beats, don't look for zebras." This means that you should look for horses—or, in other words, the most probable explanation—before considering a more exotic possibility. There are several ways to account for the occurrence of shared past-life memories, but they are zebras. For example, the memories could be attributed to the collective unconscious, Carl Jung's concept that at some deeper level everybody knows everything, even if we have forgotten how to access that bank of infinite knowledge. The American psychic Edgar Cayce, as well as others, has written about the akashic records, which is similar to the collective unconscious in that it is a knowledge of all things. But the most realistic explanation—the horse—is that these are simply actual past lives. The specificity of detail found in each regression and the healings that occur as a result lend additional support to this view.

We are not limited to regressing to our own lifetimes, whether shared or individual. In the next story, Raymond found that he was able to visualize the past life of another person, someone whom he had not even known the week prior. Miracles happen when we set our minds free.

. THE SHAIVITE SYMBOL .

At your professional training in Austin, Texas, I personally experienced "high definition" regressions that altered my life for the better. I also had an unplanned shared-consciousness event with a complete stranger. That event is etched in my mind forever. The stranger I have mentioned was another man who was attending your training at the same time I was. My wife and I had sat at mealtimes beside this very fine fellow, who was a psychiatrist from Canada. His story is my story.

As this man and I talked at supper one night, he was somewhat saddened by the fact that he was having no regressions, while I had related mine to him and had expressed to him that I was in disbelief, if not shock, from everything that I had encountered. I began to feel a strong empathy for him, and I found myself quite concerned that he find his way to an experience. Part of this was that I recognized that his ability to do so could have a great impact on his patients, as well as on himself. His situation stayed on my mind and in my heart.

During a coffee break at one of the sessions, I stumbled across Brian and Carole out back of the building and tried to excuse myself. They would have none of it, and so I told them of the psychiatrist and the good that I thought he could do should he have a regression. The next day, Brian called him up for a demonstration in front of the class, and he had a marvelous and detailed regression during which he was being trained by a holy man in ancient India, many centuries ago, in order to assume his place as a provincial ruler. He went on to have a coronation ceremony. The detail was remarkable. I was so happy that Brian had undertaken the regression for the psychiatrist, and I sat through the majority of it with my eyes shut, grateful to the extent that I guess you could call it relief. While my eyes were shut, I had the sudden picture in my head of some oddly shaped symbol, which looked like a bug. It was quite distinct and clear, but I had no idea what it was or why it would appear during this fellow's regression.

That evening, my wife and I sat with the psychiatrist at supper. I told him how glad I was for him, and he told me how he was undergoing the transitional type of thinking that I had had earlier in the week upon first experiencing a past life. As we discussed his regression, I mentioned the weird symbol that I had seen while he had been hypnotized. He asked me what it was; I told him that I had no clue but could draw it for him. I took a napkin and drew it, and he got a look on his face that I cannot describe. Somewhat astonished and serious at the same time, he stated, "That is the symbol that was on the flags at my coronation." He did not know what it was, nor did I. By this time in the week, I had resigned myself to being freaked out about my experience of being regressed, but this was too much—now I was experiencing shared consciousness with a total stranger.

I spent the next several years trying to find out what the symbol meant. I wrote to universities in India. I called people, never telling them the truth but simply saying, "I saw this somewhere and was trying to figure out what it was." No one had any clue.

My wife and I went on an Alaskan cruise and, prior to going, I signed us up for a Reiki class in Seattle. (Bear in mind, before attending your past-life regression seminar I thought that such people were nuts; odd how experience can humble and enlighten.) As we left the Reiki class, we asked the instructor if she knew where any coffee shops were in Seattle, and she said that the one she was familiar with was "kind of different," as it served Indian food and was in a unique part of town. We got directions and went. I asked several people there if they had ever seen the symbol before as I drew pictures of it for them. They had not.

As we prepared to leave, we went over to the old bookstore part of the shop, and when I checked out, the fellow at the counter said, "Did you find everything you need?"

I replied, "Everything except the one thing I was looking for."

He inquired what it was, stating that he was well versed in India's history, and asked me to draw it for him. And so I did. He knew immediately what it was: a small sect's portrayal of a Shaivite symbol. It had only been drawn by a limited number of people. Five years after seeing the symbol in a stranger's regression, I was finally led to another stranger who could explain it.

◠ *Raymond Wilson*

Raymond's fascinating story reveals how his empathic connection to the Canadian psychiatrist opened his own intuitive capacities. With his eyes gently closed during the other's regression, he rather suddenly saw the oddly shaped Shaivite symbol. The psychiatrist validated Raymond's vision at dinner that evening. Five years later, Raymond received a second validation at the old bookstore in Seattle.

After reading this account, I remembered that after returning home from that Texas workshop, I had dictated some of my own recollections of that week's experiences. I quickly found my notes about Nikhil, the psychiatrist:

Nikhil's first past-life memory was from about 2,500 years ago in ancient India. Nikhil was a six-year-old boy surrounded by other children, one of whom was his best friend. He could see the guru of the place where he lived. This guru wore no shirt but a string of sandalwood beads, which Nikhil could smell; his senses had become heightened during the regression. The guru taught the boys lessons, and later Nikhil collected firewood and performed other chores. Sitting around the fire, holding hands in a circle, he heard and was able to repeat to the entire workshop group the guru's teachings about humility, simplicity, giving, compassion, and kindness.

Nikhil had a second past-life memory in India, in which he was the prince of a small kingdom. In that life, his best friend had sacrificed his life in a battle in order to save the life of Nikhil. In his current life, this friend is his sister-in-law. This memory helped to explain much of their relationship: the immediate connection and the sense of safety, security, and deep friendship.

Raymond's journey of validation took five years until the Shaivite symbol was identified. Nikhil's transformation was immediate, especially as he remembered and incorporated the twenty-five-hundred-year-old wisdom. These teachings are age-old, yet they could not be more relevant today. They are the lessons of the Masters shared with us through Catherine, and they are the lessons of all great spiritual traditions. We are to be humble, kind, generous, and compassionate. We are spiritual beings, and this is how spiritual beings feel and act. This is timeless wisdom—and this is how we can save the world.

Raymond could see into Nikhil's past life and envision the symbol displayed on his coronation flags. While watching a female workshop participant undergo a regression, Eileen, who tells her story next, opened her own intuitive eyes to find the face of an ancient male monk looking back at her. Past-life regressions are quite literally transformative. Eileen accomplished this feat spontaneously, but in my book *Through Time into Healing* I describe an exercise called "Faces" that can enable you to experience it for yourself.

Sit a few feet across from a friend, with the lights dim and with soft music in the background. Look into the other person's face. Watch to see if the person's face changes. Observe and describe the changes you see. Features often do appear to change. Eyes, noses, and hairstyles dissolve and re-form. Headgear sometimes appears.

You can also try this exercise alone, by using a mirror and observing the changes you see in your own face. . . .

The only secret to Faces is to make sure you try it in a dimly lit room. This frees up the left brain and allows easier passage of intuitive impressions.

Faces can provide clues to many different past lives. As in other methods, meditation, visualization, and/or free association to the observed changes can fill out the memory. Let them expand and develop, without censoring the material. A face may become a group of faces, or a whole scene may unfold behind the face. You may hear a voice or an important word. Try it and see.

. A MONK'S WISDOM .

I was at a workshop in New York State in 2008. I didn't have any past-life memories, but I did experience profound meditations during those group sessions, as well as a very interesting meditation one evening with another participant. I was not a practitioner and had gone there on my own.

One of the participants, a woman named Erin, was upset about two of her past-life memories, of which I knew nothing. I only knew that she was saddened. The next day, Brian regressed Erin to a prior lifetime that was rather criminal and violent. She sensed death and corruption, firearms even. It was not a nice place to be. Another memory was of being a man in Southeast Asia, working on the land and the water, feeling lonely. Much sadness and dark shadows were in these memories, and loneliness prevailed.

The next regression was to a place that would throw light on or explain these two regressions that brought such sadness. Erin found herself in a place of great learning, an ancient library with people sitting around a huge table and writing in all languages. Books of learning and knowing were kept here; they had to be hidden away in case of attack or war. She spoke of this place as containing the truths of the world.

As the regression was occurring on the stage, I looked at Erin and stopped seeing her face and body. Instead, I saw the face and body of a monk. This monk's head was huge, and his eyebrows were very long, fine, dark, and pronounced. His face was highly intelligent and clear-skinned. I blinked my eyes numerous times to see if I was being deceived by angles or light, but he remained. He was a big man, wearing a brown monk's habit that had a huge fold-over V-necked collar running from shoulder to shoulder.

The monk, as Erin, spoke these words of wisdom: "All religions have boundaries which are causing divisions, and this is not the purpose. We must look beyond the boundaries, beyond the narrowness. We must know the truth that life is eternal and that these are important times on Earth. The truth of knowing is that we are all one. We must become aware of the knowing and the truths and seek union, not separation. Knowing is deeper, almost, than wisdom, as it is an internal shift in perception."

I knew the implication of the words. I knew that knowing is union with the deep soul and God within. There was not a sound in that room. Perceptions were extremely heightened, especially for me. I had the idea that the place where Erin was had high walls with ladders to the volumes; I think that she said this. I also had the idea that this place was ancient and somewhere on Earth. I am not sure if she said this, but I recollect the image in my mind. When she was brought back, the monk disappeared, and there Erin was again.

Brian told Erin that she had experienced the sad lives because it was necessary for her to have the understanding of those things in her life journey, that all of this was for her learning on Earth. It was important for her to know that she was highly developed.

I had sketched an outline of the head of the monk; it was nothing more than bare lines on my notepad. I felt the urge to speak with her, but we then all went into the group progressions to two hundred and two thousand years ahead, and there I was again in the stars.

I felt compelled to ask Erin about the place she had seen and if she had been with monks. I managed to speak to her by pushing in front of someone who was already talking with her—I was a bit rude! But I had to leave immediately and wanted to ask.

Erin told me that the place she had seen was somewhere between England and Scotland. I wondered if it was Lindisfarne, which is near the borders of England and Scotland, so I asked her to sketch the place on my notepad. She did. She drew the outline of the British Isles and the European continent. She showed an island to the very southwest of the British Isles, and then she drew the North American continent. This island off the southwest of the British Isles, which is Cornwall and which is around the Scilly Isles, she drew in harder outline, and then she drew some smaller islands to the east side of the North American continent. She said that what she had seen was on this island—the one near the Scilly Isles.

I was quite astounded because this is the reputed area of Avalon, beyond the Scilly Isles and where King Arthur rests. I realized that Erin spoke of Scotland and England because most people didn't know about the British Isles, which is why I had first thought of Lindisfarne. But she meant the southwestern region and those long, hidden islands west of the Scilly Isles. This I found amazing.

Afterward, I pondered all of these things and tried to recollect everything. I am aware of "knowing" being beyond earthly perceptions, and the deep truths and words of the monk were of such things. My knowledge of King Arthur and the Knights of the Round Table is such that whilst I am aware it is legend, I am equally aware that the stories come from the Druids, who were based in England beyond five thousand years ago, and that the family of Arthur was pagan (Druid) and of the "old" religions (Merlin). Arthur brought together the old and the new; when Christianity came to the British Isles, he signified the unifying force of the two coming together. Where I live now in Brittany was equally a Druid place and, in fact, the Druids are still here. Much of the land has not been developed industrially, so there are ancient places, untouched, including an area of graves and other stones from at least three thousand years ago. There are many holy wells in this area that date from before Christianity. When Christianity came, the wells were kept for religious purposes and churches were built nearby, so the link between the old and the new was a unifying force, not a separating one. Indeed, there is a chapel near me that was originally a Druid worship place; then, when the Romans came, it was turned into a chapel to Venus; and later on it became a Christian church. This fascinates me because it shows the seamless adaptation of monuments and ancient, holy places of worship from age to age, without conflict or division. And this, of course, makes me think of the profound words of the monk that I saw in Erin.

~ *Eileen de Bruin*

Eileen observed the monk in Erin just as effortlessly as she observed the metamorphosis from nature's cathedral to temple to chapel to church. I remember once visiting a mosque built upon the ruins of a Christian church, which had been built upon the ruins of a Roman temple, which itself had been built upon the ruins of an even more ancient Greek temple. Archaeological reincarnation manifested as seamlessly as the reincarnation of our souls, just as Eileen has described.

During her regression, Erin spoke, as the monk, of how religions often divide whereas spirituality unifies and connects. Whether it is Nikhil echoing his long-ago guru or Erin the primal Druidic knowledge, the messages are so similar. We must treat each other as loving family, because we are the same. Each one of us is connected.

We have walked on the moon and we have split the atom, yet we still discriminate and wage wars in the name of religion. We seem to only see the differences in our faiths and not the shared truths. We miss the forest for the trees.

There is a classic parable in which blind men were permitted to feel only one part of an elephant and were then asked to describe an elephant's form and nature. Some men felt the tail and declared an elephant to be like a rope; those who touched the trunk deemed it a snake; the ones touching its leg thought it to be like a pillar; and the ones who felt its ears and tusks had their own differing thoughts. All were correct, yet all were wrong. They were right about the particular features but not about the whole. It is as if we were those blind men. To find the spiritual core of our religions, the whole is more important than the particular parts.

Erin speaks precisely of this core when she says, "We must know the truth that life is eternal . . . the truth of knowing is that we are all one . . . and seek union, not separation."

Remembering our past lives and the mystical state after death allows such knowing. Knowing is so much deeper than belief, reason, or logic. It is the fruit of direct experience, and its power is immense. It heals and it liberates. Knowing the truth of our spiritual essence can soothe the world and bring about peace, because those who know will renounce violence and embrace compassion. Life is eternal. We are all one. To hate or to harm another is to hate and harm yourself. Violence harms us immediately, because we are all connected. Violence also harms us subsequently, because its karmic debt has to be repaid, often in a future lifetime.

And what happens when we allow religion or nationality or other similar characteristics to become the basis for such violence? We need only turn on the news to find the answer. The author of the final story of this chapter remembered a past life in the Holocaust, and her account certainly offers another example. However, and even more important, it presents the antithesis: a world where we transcend our divisions, rather than perpetuate them; where we unite together to form one loving and loved whole; and where "everyone matters, everyone is equal, and . . . where there are no barriers to separate us."

. COMMUNITY .

It took me years and the accumulation of many synchronistic moments to arrange my schedule as a parish minister in order for me to attend Brian and Carole's past-life regression therapy workshop at Omega Institute. Having incorporated hypnotherapy and Reiki into my parish ministry, I thought that it might be interesting to add regression therapy to my repertoire of skills. Needless to say, I never expected the workshop to change my life in so many different ways.

The first morning, Brian regressed the group. After going to a childhood memory and then back to the womb, he presented us with a door to our past lives. When I went through it, I wasn't prepared for what I was about to experience.

Looking down at my feet, I saw that they clearly belonged to a mature woman of fairly comfortable financial means. The shoes were burnished brown dress shoes of leather, in a sturdy but somewhat sophisticated style. The hose were a heavy nylon blend that reminded me of the kind that my grandmother used to wear. I was wearing a straight, midcalf brown wool skirt, a cream-colored blouse, and a strand of pearls and clip-on pearl earrings. My hair was brown as well, and it was drawn back in a roll that went from the sides of my head along the nape of my neck, forming a kind of "U" in the back of my head. I couldn't figure out how I got it to look that way. I was relatively slender and around five foot five—neither of which describes me now!

I was standing near a window in what appeared to be my living or dining room. It was clearly the top floor of an apartment building, as I was looking down toward the street below. The building across the street was similarly structured, and the façade was made out of stone or cement with some decorative molding along the roof line and across the window tops. This was clearly a cityscape. The room that I was in had high ceilings; the furniture was heavy but elegant in its own fashion. A crystal chandelier hung over a dark wood dining table. On the table were strewn family pictures, jewelry, candlesticks, and other small objects.

Several adult children and their spouses anxiously moved around. The kids were playing and chasing each other, but their parents seemed very agitated. We were waiting for something when my husband came through the door and announced that we needed to gather what we could and report to the train station in one hour. We were being deported to a work camp. My husband looked like my present husband, only taller and more slender.

Brian had us move forward in the regression, and I found myself waiting at the train station and then in the cattle car. There was a horrible combination of fear, physical pain, terror, and claustrophobia. I felt like I was being crushed, which coincidentally is a phobia I've had during my entire present life. As Brian brought us out of the regression, my tears came down in torrents.

On the second day of the workshop, Carole was looking for people who had had a regression experience on the first day and who would be willing to work with her in front of the group. I told her my story as I limped forward with a cane due to a chronic knee problem and a recently crippling back ailment. She chose me to be her "client," and we decided to go deeper into my first regression.

I got a bit panicky, worrying that I wouldn't be able to get hypnotized, that I would only see a blank wall, or that being in front of the group would interfere with my ability to experience anything. Quite the contrary happened. The induction was like a slide into the deepest relaxation I had ever experienced. Carole expertly guided me back to that memory of the train tracks. I learned that my husband was a doctor and that I had been his nurse. There was incredible chaos at the train station, with Nazi soldiers barking orders. People were terrified, children were crying, and everyone seemed to be turning to my husband and me for information and for calm.

When we saw the cattle cars pull up, the sheer terror of it all started to corrode my otherwise stalwart character, but I tried very hard to hold it all in. The conditions were horrific: a bucket in the corner for urine and feces, one small window to let in light and air. The soldiers crammed as many bodies into the car as possible, and everyone was screaming to hold up the children so that they wouldn't get crushed. It was impossible to sit down; there wasn't any room. My legs and back hurt terribly, just as they do in this lifetime, but I kept trying to soothe the grandchildren. I begged my children to have faith that God would protect us. I thought it couldn't get any worse. I was wrong.

The train arrived at a camp far away. We had traveled for hours, and it was difficult to climb down and walk. Everyone was disheveled, dirty, hungry, and scared. There was initial chaos and then more shouting of orders. This is when we were separated. The women began to scream when our husbands were taken from us. But nothing prepared us for the children being ripped away. They told us they would all be together in a "nursery," but by then none of us believed anything we were told.

My daughters, daughter-in-law, and I, along with some of the other women we knew, were taken to a building where we were obligated to hand over our suitcases and give up our clothes. We were naked and cold. Someone lined us up to cut our hair ("to avoid lice," they said), and we were marched into a large room for showers. The water was cold, and there was no soap. Afterward, we were given rough, scratchy shifts to put on. No towels. It was humiliating and degrading.

As Carole guided me through this nightmare, I remembered telling the officers at the camp that I was a nurse. I had heard that my husband was working as a doctor in the men's infirmary. But instead of using me in my professional capacity, they made me join the others and help move rocks to build a road. It severely hurt my back.

Carole then brought me to my death. I did not die in the gas chambers; I died in the women's infirmary. I saw my husband one last time in the distance, and our eyes locked momentarily. I learned that he had found a way to get me into the infirmary (had he bribed someone?). My lungs were filled with fluid. My hands and feet were cold, dirty, and filled with sores. I was, at least, on a cot.

Yet I also remember that the few women who tried to attend to me were kind, even though they didn't have anything to help treat my condition. I was so appreciative that they just left me alone. I had tried my best to comfort and sustain those I met in the camps, even though I always felt that I couldn't do enough. I was grateful to die with a shred of dignity. I didn't know what happened to the rest of my family, but it almost didn't matter. I knew we were connected in ways that even the Nazis couldn't destroy. Death was welcome.

Needless to say, it was a very emotional and informative session. For my whole life, I have suffered from a fear of being yelled at, scolded, or ridiculed. After such an episode, I feel like a dog that has been whipped, and feelings of guilt and shame and fear fill me. Every cell in my body responds. Just before writing this, as I was going home from church, there was a policeman directing traffic at the end of the street. It is always difficult to make a left-hand turn there, and I was thrilled that he could stop the traffic. As I was turning past him, he yelled, "Come on!" I felt sick all the way home. Why did he yell at me? I was going as

fast as I could! It made me feel terrible inside. Then I remembered my
past-life regression to the Holocaust. I could hear the guards screaming
at me to move faster, calling me names, making me feel inadequate and
shameful. It was such an incredible revelation for me.

I continue to feel a powerful healing process in my body and my
spirit. I can't wait to continue this work on myself, and I see the tremendous potential for insight and healing for others. This regression was a
great gift that was given to my life. But the story does not end there.

Early in the morning of our last day together at Omega, I asked my
guides, in meditation, to give me some names for validation. I received
the names "Ruth" and "Hiam" (or "Hermann"—I'm not entirely
sure). I asked for a last name so I could check the list of Holocaust
victims at Yad Vashem. I repeatedly got the word *gemeinschaft*. At first
I didn't even know how to spell it, yet the word flowed from my pen. I
kept coming up with different variations in my head, but *gemeinschaft*
continued flashing at me.

Later that evening, I frantically searched the database but couldn't
find anyone with that last name. I was so disappointed. I searched
everywhere but kept getting blanks. Still, the word was screaming in
my head. So at midnight, frustrated and sad, I decided to see if *gemeinschaft* was a word at all. What I discovered gave me chills.

Gemeinschaft was first coined by a German sociologist in the late
1800s. It means "community." The doctrine of gemeinschaft is about
a living organism, a real and organic community where people are
connected to one another because of beliefs, cultural ties, or other identifying markers. In gemeinschaft, everyone matters, everyone is equal,
and everyone has something to contribute to the whole. Gemeinschaft
transcends society, and when you are part of this community, wherever
you are, you are recognized as being an intrinsic member of it. It is
about the "beloved" community, one where there are no barriers that
separate us.

I felt like my guides were sending me a message that was more
important than a last name. I'd still like to do more regression work,
because I feel that there's so much more that I need and want to learn.
But in the meantime, I'm going to take this message to heart and see

where it takes me. Certainly, the community that we created at Omega was gemeinschaft to the tenth degree.

~ *Cindy Frado*

Although her pain lessened and her sleeping improved, the striking aspect of Cindy's regressions was the extraordinary level and acuity of detail. She could see, smell, feel, taste, and hear that cattle car. She was ministering to her Jewish Holocaust gemeinschaft, and in this life she is, in fact, a minister, once again tending to her flock, once again with grace and dignity.

Our souls may take on a million different forms. We can become lion or dandelion, plant or person. If we have assumed a human form, we can be any color, any race, any sex. Whichever form we choose, underneath the surface we are exactly the same. We are all connected; we are all the same substance and energy, born of the same source, composed of the same spiritual material.

It really is senseless to continue to afflict ourselves with countless wars and violence, because we harm ourselves whenever we harm one another. Nazis have reincarnated as Jews, and German Jews as American Christians, just as in Cindy's two lifetimes. We have been the murderers and the murdered, the violent and the victims of violence. If we have had a lifetime of being hurtful, then we have also had a lifetime of being the monk who would never harm even an ant, and now we are living somewhere in between, learning about balance. That is how we evolve. We are often pulled back into the bodies of our enemies to teach us the truth that skin color, nationality, religion, and gender are external trappings that do not belong to the soul. Hatred distorts reality. We have to learn from all sides. When we are born into our enemies' bodies, what choice do we have but to love them? We see their helpless little babies; we watch them tending to their aging grandparents, worrying about having enough food or shelter, and dealing with the same thousand details of everyday life that we do. We recognize that they are us. With this wisdom comes peace.

Our community, our true gemeinschaft, is the entire human community—and beyond. Once we look into the eyes of another and see ourselves looking back, we will be able to create a heaven on this earth.

· 2 ·

Validating the Memories

P ast-life regression therapists are usually working at two levels during their sessions. The therapeutic level is constantly present and perhaps most important. The validational level is occasionally possible but always fascinating. Over the years, many of my patients have been able to confirm the accuracy of their reincarnational memories through documentation of names, historical facts, or even military identification, such as dog-tag numbers. They have remembered home addresses, ship names, and numerous other details that confirm their recollections.

The Internet has made documentation so much easier. Online searches can be carried out quickly and inexpensively. Several people have used information on the Internet to confirm Catherine's brief description of one of my own previous lifetimes, which was mentioned in a few paragraphs in *Many Lives, Many Masters.* This kind of investigation was much more difficult thirty years ago, when I was treating Catherine.

Observational confirmations are also important. People who, during regressions, are able to speak foreign languages that they have never studied provide another sort of confirmation about the validity of past-life experiences. This is called *xenoglossy,* and it cannot be attributed to mere fantasy or imagination. Sometimes the languages spoken during the regression may even be extinct, such as ancient Aramaic. If the session has been recorded, the languages can be verified by a university linguistics department.

A surgeon from Beijing, who was seeing me on her first journey outside China, regressed to a lifetime in California in 1850. Because she knew no English at all, the session was carried out with the expert aid of a Chinese interpreter. As the woman recalled having an argument with her husband in that life, she began to speak very fluent and colorful English. The translator, not realizing what was happening, automatically began to translate what she was saying back into Chinese. "Stop," I had to gently instruct him. "I understand English." The interpreter nearly fainted, for he knew that the woman had never spoken a word of the language. I will never forget the look of amazement on his face.

. RETURNING HOME .

In the summer of 2008, I was part of your training seminar (I'm the director of spiritual life and the chaplain at Nichols College, and in the round of introductions I described myself as "the man with the hyphenated name—Wayne-Daniel—half Portuguese, half Jewish, a Portajew!"; it got quite a laugh). Since receiving your training at Omega, I have been leading regressions with great success. It has become a major tool in my work as a chaplain.

I underwent a series of past-life regression sessions with Dr. Sylvia Hammerman of Massachusetts, all centering on the same life in the first century C.E. The regressions began with me as a small boy, six or so years old, called Yosia (or "Yossi"). I was apparently an orphan raised by the Essenes. At that age, I escaped the destruction of my home, the Essene compound at what is today Qumran, at the hands of the Romans. During the course of my sessions with Sylvia, I experienced memories from that early age all the way to my death as Yossi in my twenties.

After my escape from the burning Essene compound, I wandered in the Judean desert for two nights. Finally, I was found by a goatherd, a woman who brought me to her home. A few weeks later, her brother appeared to take me away. With the Essenes I had begun to learn the rudiments of reading and writing, and this man, whose name was Ishmael, had a school where I could live and be further taught.

As Sylvia moved the memory ahead in time, I experienced myself as an early adolescent, the primary pupil and assistant to Reb Ishmael.

He was very progressive in his approach and teachings, utilizing not only traditional Jewish texts but also concepts from Greek philosophy and other sources. This angered many at the Torah Academy where we lived and where he taught, and at one point it was necessary for us to flee in the night. We went south, over time ending up in Alexandria.

Initially, Sylvia had requested that I not attempt any research on the memories I was experiencing; she wanted me simply to allow the experience to sink in. Although I had heard about the Essenes, I really knew little about them, and it took a few sessions before I came to understand where I had been and with whom. Eventually, Sylvia gave me the okay to start doing some research on my memories. I was astounded, to say the least, by what I found.

That night, I searched online for "Josiah," but only found things about old Puritan New Englanders. I then typed in "Rabbi Josiah" and came to a website that spoke of a second-century Talmudic master named Rabbi Josiah. Very little was known of him; he lived in the south, and the Palestinian Mishnah was largely written in the north, in Galilee. It went on to say that he was the primary disciple of a Rabbi Ishmael ben Elisha. I clicked on that name and found information on him.

One piece of scholarly speculation was that Ishmael ben Elisha was just a code name for another rabbi, named Elisha ben Abuya, apparently an infamous heretic. He was condemned and expelled from the Sanhedrin. There were a number of possible explanations: that he was too devoted to Greek thought and tried to introduce it into the assembly, that he was a Gnostic, that he was a Christian, and so forth. The article made a point of saying that all we know about Reb Elisha came from his enemies and wasn't very reliable. It is known that he was a major scholar with lots of contributions to Talmud; so much so, the speculation goes, that some rabbis didn't want to have to expunge all his teachings, and as a result they invented this code name to cover their flank. He is also referred to in the Talmud as "Akbar" and "the Other."

Well, I was bowled over! I noticed that, unlike the other names I was seeing, this Rabbi Josiah was not listed as *ben* anyone, which means "son of." Just Josiah, as if he had no parentage. I had never heard of Elisha ben Abuya and knew nothing of his background. This only confirmed for me the validity of the regressions.

In 2009, the summer following my regressions, I had the opportunity to travel to Israel. I stayed at a Christian monastery on Mount Zion, and I was determined to get to Qumran. In the company of a friend I'd made in the monastery, a teacher at a Catholic school in America who'd listened to me recount my regression experiences and didn't think I was crazy, I got on the bus and headed off.

We arrived, paid our entrance fee, and approached the ruins of the Essene compound.

"Well," my new friend said, "I suppose you know where you're going?"

"I certainly do," I answered. "We go right in through here."

"But that says 'Exit.' "

"I don't care what it says," I responded. "That's the way in."

I moved though the ruined compound easily and deliberately. I knew exactly where everything was and what it was.

"Up this lane," I said to my friend, "was the place where we ate. The men sat on blankets, and the boys served them. Afterward, we had our meal." And, sure enough, at the end of that path was a ruin marked REFECTORY, with a drawing of men seated on blankets, eating.

"Down here," I said as we proceeded, "was the place where the scrolls were written. We boys would stand to the side, and the scribes would call out for more ink or for a new writing utensil. They used short, hollow reeds, sharpened on one end." Needless to say, we turned a corner and walked into a ruin marked SCRIPTORIUM.

In my first regression session, I had seen this scriptorium with a round, raised hearth burning. It was quite distinctive. I described it to my friend, saying, "It was right around here somewhere."

"Wayne-Daniel," he said, "look down." There, at my feet, was a series of concentric circles, made of stone, pressed into the earth— exactly as I had seen.

ᔡ *Wayne-Daniel Berard*

In Wayne-Daniel's story, in which he was a rabbi around two thousand years ago and a chaplain now, we can see the continuing thread of a spiritual life. The affinities and interests of our current lives often have their genesis in past ones. Talents and abilities have been honed in previous incarnations before reappearing once again in the present one. We are the sum of our experiences, polished by our intuitional wisdom and our evolving awareness.

The most intensive validation work is generally done by the person remembering the past life, as is shown here. The therapists are busy and often have many patients, but the clients are highly motivated to confirm the memories because the experiences are theirs. Confirmation of details lends even more power to the regression. Although the early research that Wayne-Daniel accomplished prior to his trip to the ancient Essene community was important and interesting, his on-site experiences were extraordinary. The déjà vu feeling of familiarity and of knowing your way around cannot be learned from maps. It comes from actual experience. He could describe the activities, the settings, and the details, and these were immediately confirmed.

I remember my own past-life experience in Alexandria about two thousand years ago, where I wandered among the Essene communities in the desert to the north. The time period was the same as in Wayne-Daniel's memory.

Perhaps his coming to the training seminar was more of a reunion than we realized.

According to a 2009 survey conducted by the Pew Forum on Religion and Public Life, nearly three-quarters of Americans believe in life after death, and approximately one-quarter believe in reincarnation. Almost half claim to have had a mystical or spiritual experience—a percentage that has more than doubled in the past fifty years—and about 30 percent say that they have felt in touch with someone who has died. Even though the numbers of people who believe in reincarnation are higher in Asia and other areas where the concept has been accepted for many centuries, the Western world is finally catching up.

Researchers such as Ian Stevenson, M.D., the late chairman emeritus of the psychiatry department at the University of Virginia, have documented thousands of cases of reincarnation, mostly through interviews leading to identification of the family from that person's most recent past life and then that family's ensuing confirmation of the recalled details. Dr. Stevenson's work, which focused primarily on children's spontaneous past-life memories, revealed the frequency with which mortal wounds from a prior lifetime manifested as birthmarks in the child's current body.

Nearly a decade ago, the Canadian Broadcasting Corporation produced a beautiful, high-quality documentary series on past lives for which I was interviewed and acted as a consultant. After volunteers were chosen to undergo past-life regressions, a reporter named Sarah Kapoor traveled all around the world, including to tiny rural villages and gravesites, to verify the memories. She spoke to priests, village elders, and historians, among others, who were able to validate the past lives that the volunteers had experienced. I watched the compelling and confirmational video documentation and am still moved by many of the cases. In 2008, when I regressed several people on *The Oprah Winfrey Show*, that show's producers interviewed Sarah. The earlier findings were confirmed once again, and in the intervening years, additional details had emerged after Sarah had followed up with the volunteers.

In my previous books, I have extensively documented clinical cases that have validated past-life memories. There are countless confirmed stories. Jenny Cockell, a British woman, discovered the children whom she had borne during her previous incarnation as Mary Sutton in Ireland in the early twentieth century. Five of Mary's children were still alive when Jenny found them in the 1990s. They were able to completely confirm Jenny's past-life recall of even minor events in their childhoods, events that occurred more than seventy years prior to their emotional reunion with Jenny—the reincarnation of their mother, Mary Sutton.

A carefully documented account of reincarnation is found in the book *Soul Survivor: The Reincarnation of a World War II Fighter Pilot* by Bruce and Andrea Leininger. The parents of James Leininger observed their two-year-old son recalling a prior lifetime as James Huston, a man who was killed in the battle of Iwo Jima. The degree of confirmation, even of the tiniest military details, is a testament to the careful research done by little James's parents.

Whether from single-case reports, like the experiences of Jenny and the Leiningers, or from ongoing research studies by investigation of re-incarnational material, extensive confirmation of the validity of past lives has been accumulated. Validation helps minds to open to new possibilities. A closed mind cannot learn anything new. A closed mind is stuck in the past. Thanks to the tireless efforts of researchers, we can legitimately state now that reincarnation can be accepted on the basis of clinical data and not solely by belief.

Of course, truths really do not need research support. They exist above and beyond scientific confirmation, because science is constrained by the limitations of its measuring devices. It cannot prove what it cannot yet measure. When the appropriate tools are developed, the truths will be there, waiting to be discovered. Truths are independent and are unaffected by the beliefs of humans. Yet many people, understandably, find comfort and support in statistical and scientific proofs. Ideally, truth and proof coincide. For the concept of reincarnation, this has become the case.

As an example, Sir Isaac Newton described gravity, but he did not invent it. For millennia, people knew the truth: what goes up must come down. It took the development of mathematical tools to allow Newton to actually explain the phenomenon. And as the tools of physics are further refined, gravity will be even better understood. Similarly, we can describe reincarnation, even though we don't yet know its exact mechanisms. We are still awaiting our Newton.

After a training workshop, I dictated a brief experience that Claire, one of our participants, had had. From Ireland, Claire had never been to North or South America before in her life until she came to my training. There she had a past-life memory in "Chichen Itza," as she pronounced it. It was a place that she didn't know and that made no sense to her, yet she recalled it perfectly.

She began describing an apparition that was like a magnificent, large angel with changing colors. Claire was a young woman who, along with some others, was involved in some kind of ceremony. She wore a white, belted robe. There were pyramids with flat tops and many steps that led up to a temple where she meditated to purify herself before the next part of the ritual. Claire was alone in the temple at the top of the steps, the flat-top pyramids below her. Suddenly, she found herself in a large hole in the ground. She was able to explain what was around and in the hole with great detail. She had become wrapped in a large fern at some point in the ceremony. This was apparently a sacrifice, but Claire was not at all traumatized, for she felt it was an honor to be chosen. Her family felt similarly honored. The decision to partake in the ceremony had been made willingly.

Such details were later verified by another member of our training who happened to be a Mexican anthropologist and who was quite knowledgeable about its ancient ceremonies. I was impressed that in our small group, there was an anthropologist from Mexico who specialized in Mayan and indigenous cultures and who could immediately validate Claire's memories, which were far more elaborate and detailed than what I can recall or describe here.

Neither Claire nor I had talked to the anthropologist before her regression. When I contemplate the odds of encountering a professional who specialized in the very same subject matter of Claire's recall, in the same small workshop, I am reminded that there are no coincidences in life.

Jill, the client featured in the next story, discovered this same truth. The strong connections between her present and past life were far from accidental, and it was no coincidence that the details she recalled in a regression matched those that she later found in historical documents.

. WE ARE ALWAYS FREE .

My client, a white female in her fifties, relayed a story to me during a therapy session. In her present life, Jill was a social service worker who single-handedly began an inner-city soup kitchen. As a girl of about ten years old, she had gone to Mount Vernon to visit the home of President Washington. During that visit, she began to remember a past life. To her and her aunt, who had taken her on the visit, Jill's reactions to seeing the home and to viewing photographs were strange. She recognized a little girl whom she said she played with at this house. She also talked on and on about the placement of furniture in the Mount Vernon estate and how it was all wrong. I recognized this story as a past-life memory, and Jill was open to the idea of exploring it further. She came to one of my workshops and was easily regressed. There, she put all the pieces together of this haunting memory.

As Jill relayed to the group of us at the workshop, she had found herself as a ten-year-old black slave girl in George Washington's home at Mount Vernon. She had played with a little girl named Nell, and she later moved with the family to Philadelphia. She remembered that her mother was a black slave who was a seamstress, and her father a white tailor. She called herself a *mulatto*.

Later, this young woman fled on a ship to freedom and settled in Portsmouth, New Hampshire, where she married a free black sailor and had three children. She remembered living in fear that she would be found and taken back into slavery, but she remained a free woman until she died peacefully in her old age. My client was able to get dates as well as locations, and she stated that her name was "Oney Judge." When I asked what the lessons were for her in that lifetime, she responded in a very different voice, the voice of her soul: "We are always free."

Later that evening, Jill's partner went on the Internet and yelled at her to come quickly. There on the computer screen was an African American history website describing the life of a courageous young slave who had fled to freedom: Ona Judge, the runaway slave of George Washington.

All of what Jill had relayed to the group of us that night in the workshop was verified by the website. She had gotten many of the details correct. Jill has no recollection of ever studying this in history class in school, and she probably did not, as African American history was not taught in the days that she attended school. She also did not grow up in Portsmouth.

Jill is still processing and integrating this information. She finds much comfort and relief in finding out why she had these memories at a young age, around the same age that Oney was at Mount Vernon.

The regression has also been helping her to integrate parts of her personality in this lifetime, as well as to determine her future goals.

ᘯ Maria Castillo

Every so often, a geographical stimulus will precipitate the past-life memory. No hypnosis is necessary, just the visiting of the locale. In this case, Maria's client began to spontaneously recall details of furniture placement and other historical facts. Years later, her regression and some Internet research provided further validation. Interestingly, the profession and projects in Jill's current life mirror the issues found in the life of Ona Judge.

Wayne-Daniel also experienced past-life recall when he visited the archaeological excavation at the ancient Essene community. To physically return to the site of a previous lifetime is a powerful trigger and can evoke both strong emotions and detailed memories. If you visit a foreign city and feel a marked aversion or, on the other hand, a strong positive connection to the place, the origins of these feelings may lie in your past lives.

You have lived many lives and have tasted the beliefs and cultures of nations from all corners of the globe.

The possibility of verifying the details of a past life is undoubtedly an intriguing aspect of a regression, particularly for those people who might be skeptical about the memory they have just recalled. The person who wonders *Was that really a past-life memory, or just my imagination?* may find that having factual evidence that validates the data of their experience helps them to accept it as real or at the very least to recognize that the mind is capable of knowing things at a level far beyond the standard five senses. It certainly did for me when I was treating Catherine, my first patient to regress to a past life. I did not believe in this concept at all, yet I could not deny that she was rapidly healing, nor could I refute that she was able to provide me with unknowable and quite detailed personal information about my son, my father, and my daughter. Had she not provided me with this level of "proof," I might not have been so compelled to research and explore the field of past-life regression.

Most of us, at one time or another, have had a dream that may have been chronologically inaccurate, or possibly even illogical, yet moved us to a new level of understanding or insight upon awakening. A dream analyst would never think to write off such a powerfully evocative event because it is "inaccurate" or "untrue." This is also the case with past-life regression. Like dreams, past-life recollections, because they are sometimes retrieved from very deep states of consciousness, may contain symbols and metaphors as well as actual memories. Such symbols and metaphors need to be interpreted so that their meaning and message become clear. A dreamlike or symbolic past-life memory is no less powerful than a literal one. The mind sometimes displays the past-life scenes more like a poem than a history text.

Past-life recall is also subject to the same potential distortions as any other memory that we have in our regular waking consciousness. The memory may be entirely accurate, but sometimes dates and other details can be slightly blurred. Memory is like that. For example, what you are sure happened to you in kindergarten may have actually occurred in the first grade. Ninety-nine percent of the memory is correct, however, and that one mistake does not invalidate the general accuracy of the recall. Emotions and themes tend to be extremely accurate. The most common distortions are in numbers and other logical or left-brained functions. The deeper mind is more concerned with understanding and healing than it is with details and dates.

My previous books provide a more thorough exploration of the validation of cases. However, as the years have passed and as I have borne witness to so many of these cases, my focus has shifted a bit from the confirmation of the past-life memory and toward its therapeutic value. It is rarely, if ever, the facts, details, or historical accuracy of the regression that has a significant healing effect on the patient, but rather its emotional content, the feelings and relationships that are brought to the surface, the insights into life and into our deeper nature that are gleaned. The stories in the next chapter illustrate how such understandings can powerfully and permanently heal people's lives.

· 3 ·

How Understanding
Can Heal

Our bodies and our minds are the masks our real self—the soul—wears in the physical world. When we die, we remove our masks and we rest in our natural state. There is no disappearance, no oblivion. We simply take off our masks, our clothes, and other outer coverings, and we return home to the spiritual realms. Here we are renewed and restored. Here we reflect on the lessons of the life that we have just left. Here we are reunited with our soul companions across the centuries. Here we plan our next lifetime on the earth. When the time and circumstances are right, we don new masks—a baby's body and brain—and return to the physical state. With a refreshed energy and outlook, we continue learning our spiritual lessons until the need to reincarnate is no longer necessary. Then we can continue to help people from the other side.

It is important to remember that we are the souls, not the masks.

As we gain a higher perspective and understand that our present lifetime is one of a myriad of lives that our soul has experienced over eons of time, the sense of expansion, timelessness, and joy that we feel can be palpable. We can let go of guilt, of despair, of feeling trapped and rushed. We have an eternity of time to learn our lessons. Our symptoms and fears have probably carried over from previous lifetimes. There is always hope for us once we realize that we are more than just a particular body and brain.

Our greatest lesson is love. Remembering the causes of our afflictions allows us to heal them. In doing so, the recognition that we are loving, spiritual beings comes more and more into focus. This strips away our anxieties and fears. It removes the barriers to comprehending our real nature. Then we can reach our highest potential, healing ourselves and our world.

Understanding can be immediate: a sudden perception of the meaning and implications of these ideas, a clear and intuitive knowing. Understanding can also be slow and deliberate, a percolating awareness as the veil of ignorance is gently lifted. Whether with Zen-like immediacy or the gradual dawning of the sun on a foggy day, the results are identical.

Many obstacles block our clear understanding. We are often force-fed specific belief systems, both cultural and religious, when we are too young to comprehend, to reason, and to make decisions for ourselves. We may become close-minded to alternate beliefs and systems. Information cannot enter a closed mind. Nothing new can be learned.

Fortunately, personal experience can be more powerful than belief. Once you experience, then you know. For this reason, having a past-life memory, whether through regression, in a dream, while meditating, or even spontaneously, can be compelling enough to unlock a closed mind and to release it from the fetters of skepticism. Now questions can be asked. Now beliefs can be examined and reexamined, accepted or rejected. Now real learning can occur.

For Heather, who presents her own story below, understanding came strongly and swiftly. She was able to restore her voice and also to distill spiritual wisdom, which enabled her to heal her mind and to nurture her soul.

. FINDING YOUR VOICE .

My body is growing cold beneath the heavy chain mail. Choking on my own blood, I am aware of my impending death, yet I am not afraid. I look up at the wet, gray sky, knowing that the battle was fought with honor and that I will die the same way.

This is not a page from a medieval fairy tale but from a life-altering experience that led to a restructuring of everything I thought I knew. I was never seeking any answers because I had no questions, but out of sheer curiosity I decided to try hypnosis. Shortly thereafter, I found myself in a previous lifetime.

I have since realized that this life is a lesson, a school in which to learn. And each encounter we have is an opportunity to change and to help. We are all in this world together, and only love, hope, and charity will be our salvation. These are sweeping words coming from a former agnostic. Let me explain.

When I was young, I did not like anything touching my neck. I would not wear turtlenecks, scarves, or chokers. In 2000, a tumor was found on my throat that required surgical removal. The terror that I felt as the surgeon's blade lowered toward my throat was more intense than would have been normal for me. It did not conform to my predisposition for "sucking it up." Today I wear a scar across my throat from that event.

I have also had recurrent issues with losing my voice, and many days, for no apparent reason, I had absolutely no voice at all. This is despite three medical evaluations and speech therapy.

Furthermore, a few years ago I experienced a reaction to a medication that sent me into a panic, the likes of which I have never known. I became paranoid and thought my throat was closing up. I was convinced I was dying. I was fine, but it took me days to shake that emotional and unnerving fear.

I went to see Donna, a clinical hypnotherapist, on a Thursday afternoon. True to form, I had no voice that day. Donna verbally coached me to relax my muscles, using guided imagery to take me to a deep level of hypnosis. Finally, when I was completely relaxed, she had me visualize a library. I was drawn to a section of books on which "Heather" was printed on the bindings. I open the yellowed and frayed pages of one book, and on the right side of the open page was a colored plate, almost like one would find in a book of fairy tales. It was a picture of a knight standing in front of a white horse, which was kneeling low. The knight wore chain mail; he held a shield in his left hand and a sword in his right. His wavy, dark hair partially covered his right eye, and his drawn, thin face was ashen.

Donna instructed me to go into the picture, and within an instant I was no longer Heather—I became the knight. I felt the extreme weariness of battle and lack of food, yet also a deep sense of honor. I had a sworn duty to fight but an uneasy feeling that it was not a just cause. I was unafraid to die and would do so with dignity. There was no woman in my life, only a love and tenderness for my horse.

Donna progressed me in time a little further, and I was in combat. The ground was green and I was on foot, fighting with my sword tight in my right hand. Although I was lying in the therapist's chair, my right hand was clenched and raised as if holding the sword, and my left held an imaginary shield. I could not unclench my fists.

Suddenly, I was choking on blood. I had been stabbed in the throat. On the chair in Donna's office, I felt as if my throat were closing up. I gagged and coughed. Donna instructed me to pull out of the body and watch the scene as if on a movie screen. I tried, but the feelings were so real—the pain, the choking—and I could not remove myself. Finally, blessedly, the pain stopped. I floated. Peace. Peace was all I knew. My hands relaxed as I released my grip on the imaginary weapons.

This was a peace I had never known. There was no pain, no struggle, just an all-encompassing serenity combined with a lovely floating feeling. There was no tension in my body. I felt freer, less constricted, eternal. I could have stayed there forever, but Donna was talking to me. I didn't want to let go of my knight. I still felt him and didn't want to leave, but she guided me out of that lifetime and into the present.

The session ended, and I was overwhelmed. As I hugged and thanked Donna, we both noticed that my voice was clear and strong. I started out hoarse and at a whisper; now I had a hearty voice again. Could it be that reliving the knight's death resolved my vocal problems? Only time would tell. I was, however, ecstatic.

In the days following, I awakened with a clear voice. Every time I answered the phone, I was pleasantly surprised. I became consumed with a desire to learn all about knights and to research heraldry.

I finally understood why I liked certain cultures, music, art, and symbols. Why I behaved in particular ways and had specific quirks, ethics, and a code that predated me. I had a better understanding of my fears and my strengths and where they originated. And although the healing benefits were surprising and I had a greater appreciation for my specific traits, this was not the revelation over which I am still in awe.

After these experiences, I became obsessed with finding out more about medieval history. Today I am still curious, but less so. To focus on the minutiae and details is to miss the bigger picture. The real meaning, the real message, is more profound than just the knowledge that I was a knight or any other person. If we accept the idea that we are more than what this current life tells us we are, the implications are far-reaching.

One implication is that we are immortal. We will go on to experience many other lives with many of the same souls whom we have been with before. We will always find each other. So "till death do us part" is simply not applicable, for even death cannot keep us apart.

Those whom we have wronged will return to us in another life so that we are given the opportunity to transform the situation. Similarly, those who have wronged us will come back to right the damage. We will again meet our family, friends, and those we have previously hurt. It is a waste of time and energy to hold hostility and anger and to harm others. Even if we have to be presented with the same issues and the same souls a thousand times, we will learn to love and purify our relationships.

Furthermore, I am aware that I am not the person I know as "Heather." It is as if I am wearing a "Heather" suit, and next time I may be wearing a "Henry" suit. This helps me to step back and look at conflicts and crises more objectively. I am just an awareness experiencing Heather's life. I now work on detaching from stressful situations, but it is still difficult because the feelings seem so real and intense. When I experienced the knight, the feelings were also intense and seemed very real. So what is real in any situation? Are feelings made real by their quality and intensity? Are Heather's feelings any more real than the knight's? The power of experience is the same. Whose should I pay attention to? This leads me to the conclusion that none of these are real—only the awareness behind them is.

These changes of perception and perspective affect the way I look at disease, chronic illness, and crises. It has affected the way I look at Heather's body, the way I look at incidents and Heather's reactions to them. "My" chronic illness is no longer personal to me. I no longer own it. It is merely something that Heather is experiencing, and there is likely a reason for her to experience it. It is a lesson that must be learned from living with disease. This helps to remove myself from the personal impact and to detach from the emotionality of it.

We are here to learn lessons about love and forgiveness. And only when those lessons are learned can we go on to "graduate." My life is seen through a new truth. Although this has been said a thousand times before and in a thousand ways, there is nothing like the experience to really bring it home. This new perception is undeniable now that I have witnessed and felt it.

∽ Heather Rivera

Heather beautifully summarizes the profound implications of reincarnational memories. We are far greater than our bodies and our brains. We are immortal spirits that incarnate here in physical form to learn the lessons that Heather highlights. Understanding the reality of reincarnation allows our fear of dying to diminish, because we know that our consciousness survives physical death. You have lived before, you have died in that lifetime, and here you are, back again, in a new and different body. The part of you that continues on after the death of the old body and that then reincarnates as a baby is often called the soul, or the spirit, or the eternal consciousness. The recognition that we are souls or never-ending consciousness is incredibly liberating. We comprehend that we are spiritual beings, not just temporary human beings. We never die, because we are never really born. What, then, is there to fear?

If you were not taught the concept of reincarnation when you were young—and I certainly was not taught this and did not believe in it—it does not mean that the concept is incorrect. It is very important to keep an open mind and to continue learning from these events in order to reach your highest potential. Heather was able to do exactly this, and her life has never been the same.

Trauma to the throat or neck in a past life may certainly cause vocal problems in the current life, yet there are other possible sources as well. You might have been punished, or even killed, for what you said in a prior lifetime. The words themselves may have been lethal. The consequence in the present life is a powerful need to censor yourself, or even to speak faintly and carefully, in order to prevent a recurrence. Words can kill.

When the cause-and-effect link is uncovered and understood, the symptom usually dissipates. For Heather, a physical problem disappeared. For Giorgio, Mira's client and the subject of the next case, the nature of the symptom was emotional. It does not matter whether the problem manifests in the body or the mind. This paradigm of healing applies to all.

. LIFE DOESN'T HAVE TO BE HARD .

One of my sessions with a client was an especially interesting and moving story not only because of the rich details, the realizations, and the emotional healing, but also because the client spoke in two different languages, neither of which he or I knew.

Giorgio found himself in a crowded chamber in an ancient time in the Middle East. He was among a group of people who were having an audience with the king of that land; they were refugees who sought to settle there. Servants stood on both sides of the path that led to the throne. An adviser whispered something to the king. Meanwhile, the crowd anxiously awaited the verdict of what would happen to them. An important decision was to be made.

The king rose from his throne, walked down the steps, and said, *"Anan shatlan temuk."*

It was not a language the crowd understood, and no one knew what it meant. They were all murmuring nervously amongst each other. Soldiers surrounded them, and the refugees were scared that they would be killed. However, their lives were spared, and they were allowed to settle in the outskirts of the town in a separate, designated area where the land was not fertile. Not much grew there, and they mostly raised animals to survive. It was hard living. I asked Giorgio to go into his house and see where he lived.

Tears began falling from his eyes as he spoke. "I am a girl, a teenage girl. I came home, and my mother is telling me how hard life is. It always is, and it always will be for us. She loves me very much, and she is telling me that life is always hard for us wherever we go. And I believe her. I listen to her and I nod. I agree. We have to work so hard."

"Is she distressed?" I asked. "Does she have a heavy burden on her heart?"

"No. She is not distressed. She is just telling me how it is for us. This is our lot in life."

The girl, Giorgio in that lifetime, accepted and internalized these statements. She was experiencing it and seeing it with her own eyes, and she never questioned her mother's attitude.

Giorgio told me that he was an only child in that life, a girl called Anash. I asked him about Anash's mother. "She is my current mother. She is a lot tougher in this life than she is now, but she is the same soul."

Anash's father was a tall, balding man with a beard. One day, soldiers came and killed him with spears, right in front of their home. He had stolen something. The mother had known of his crime and must have suspected that this could happen, for when the soldiers arrived, she was very organized and quickly hid her daughter inside the house.

"The significance of this event is not my father's death but my mother's reaction to it. It confirmed everything that she believed in and has taught me—that life is pain and suffering. That is our lot in life. And that is what my mother still tells me today," Giorgio explained.

The girl married a man who lived in the town. Over the years, the younger people from Anash's tribe slowly integrated into the town by marrying and working there. I asked if Anash visited her mother often.

"Yes," Giorgio said. "I bring her oranges."

Tears rolled down Giorgio's cheeks, and his voice betrayed the emotions that he felt. Anash was often able to sneak away flat, round pieces of bread and oranges and bring them to her mother. Life was a little better for Anash now. The house where she lived was an actual house, not a tent or a shack. There was still no money, or very little, but Anash's husband was a miller, which gave them stable access to food. He was also Jewish, and even though he too was part of a minority group, Jews were more integrated in the society than Anash's tribe. Giorgio, as Anash, began speaking in another language and said, "There are all these Hebrew words I know now."

The next important moment in Anash's life was the death of her mother. "My mother is old. She is old and sick. I am touching her face. She is dying. I am saying that I love her. She is weak. She is bony. I was very close with her."

"How do you feel?" I asked.

Giorgio said, "I feel very, very upset. I just feel like she was right, that life is so hard."

In that lifetime as Anash, Giorgio needed to learn that the perception of life being a struggle was only an assumption, only one way at looking at life, only a belief. In his present reincarnation, he continued to believe this. But life is not all pain and suffering. Changes happen in ways one could never predict; things happen in ways one could never expect. And this is a very important lesson for both Giorgio and his mother. She continued to truly and deeply believe that life was a struggle, and consequently every situation in her life confirmed that perception. Life is full of potential. Miracles do happen, and they both needed to know that.

In his present life, Giorgio grew up hearing from his mother the very same thing she taught him when he was previously known as Anash. Giorgio carried the same attitude in him and, when describing the difficulties he had encountered before the regression, he spoke of his life as something that needed to be constantly fought and survived. This attitude—that life is a battlefield—had spilled over into every corner of his life: his career, his finances, his relationships, and even his creative expression as an artist.

After our session, Giorgio chose to dissociate from the belief of life as a struggle. He realized that the circumstances that created the belief in Anash's life do not exist in his life as Giorgio, and that he is now a different person. There was no need to be negative or to worry that things were out of his control. He understood that he had the power to choose, and that he did not need to perceive the world through his mother's eyes. The choice was made to be grateful for everything good that he had been given, instead of ignoring it and focusing on what was wrong. Giorgio decided to see life and to live life as a marvelous unfolding of possibilities and blessings.

It has been more than a year now since our regression. From speaking with Giorgio, I see that the shift in him is permanent. The understanding that our session brought him has freed him from the need to re-create constant struggle in his life. He now knows that life is full of potential and that miracles do happen.

∾Mira Kelley

In the introduction to this chapter, I mentioned that what we encounter as adults may confirm or contradict the untested viewpoints and attitudes that perhaps we were taught as children and that we may have swallowed undigested and unexamined. Giorgio's account provides an excellent example of how these early beliefs and assumptions may be distorted or even false. New understandings may seem odd or strange at first because they are unfamiliar, but with time and patience, truth prevails. Mira expertly guided Giorgio to a higher level of awareness. His life became much more fulfilling and joyful as a result.

Giorgio and his mother, in lifetimes both present and past, believed life to be hard. They are not alone. Over the years, many readers and workshop participants have asked me why we are here in this difficult physical dimension at all. Why don't we just stay on the other side, in the heavenly dimensions, and learn there, where we do not have all the burden, all the pain, of physical existence?

This is a complicated question, because it implies a much higher spiritual perspective. It is like trying to know the mind of God. My answer is incomplete, but it has helped some people.

I liken physical existence to the first day of kindergarten, when we had to leave the familiarity and comforts of home to go to school and to begin that stressful trek through the various grades and classrooms. A kindergarten student might object, saying, "Why do I need this? Why can't I just stay at home and learn there? Who needs school anyway? I was perfectly happy to be in my home. I don't want to be here!"

But the young child lacks the perspective to appreciate the purpose and value of school: to get an education, learn many subjects, prepare for a career, function in society, earn a living, interact with peers, and so on. The child does not realize that home will change, that parents will grow older and retire or move. Everything changes.

We are like the kindergarten student. We don't completely understand why we are here in this physical school on Earth, but nevertheless the reality is that we are indeed here, whatever the reasons may be. And we have to make the best of it, learning our spiritual lessons and then, just like a young student going home after a long day of school, ultimately returning to our own true home.

. FINDING PEACE .

My husband and I attended your Los Angeles seminar. I booked the trip at the last minute from Houston because of a dream. A few days before the trip, I dreamed that you shook my hand and said something in my ear. It took me a while to comprehend what you said, but when you were shaking hands with my husband, I finally understood what it was. You said that I do not have kids in this lifetime because I had lost two kids in my two previous lifetimes, and that this is why I am afraid to have children. Boy, that woke me up and bugged the heck out of me, because I am *not* afraid of having kids. I am tired of trying to conceive and am letting nature take its course. I had to find out more!

During your morning seminar on past-life regression, I had this image in my mind of a white woman living in the mountains with a husband and a son. It was a simple and peaceful life. At the end, when you asked what lesson was to be learned from that lifetime, all I felt from it was pure contentment and peace. Then it occurred to me that it does not matter what life I have, as long as I am learning to be content, peaceful, compassionate, patient, and generous. As long as I am learning all the great teachings that life, your books, and Buddhism have to offer, I am good. So be it that I don't have kids. I work with children every day, as I am a pediatric dentist, and that is happiness for me. Thank you for allowing me to discover this message.

$\curvearrowleft$ *Michelle Lin*

Michelle's story is brief but powerful. The ending may not yet be written. I am sure that she has borne hundreds or even thousands of children over the course of her many lifetimes. In her present life, she cares for children every day. The insights and treasures of the spiritual wisdom gained after her regression are compelling. What a blessing to truly comprehend the basic nature of compassion, patience, and generosity as guides and stepping-stones to our liberation. Michelle understands this at a deep and experientially derived level. She knows.

Over the years, I have had many female patients presenting with fertility issues. Quite a few were able to conceive after the past-life block (such as fear of losing a child once again) was removed, or after the tension was reduced through acceptance and understanding. If Michelle continues to live with contentment and peace, happy with what she already has, her odds of getting pregnant will dramatically increase.

The following two stories expand on this theme.

. LAST CHANCE .

A number of years ago, Brian was giving a workshop in a large auditorium in Florida. We arrived early, and Brian was busy in the front of the room checking on the sound, lighting, and stage arrangement. I took a seat in the last row and patiently waited for the day to start. Soon, a young woman came into the room, wheeling a beautiful infant in a stroller. She sat down close to me. I find babies entrancing; I love their smell, their soft skin, their fuzzy hair, and their silly smiles. They always remind me of the wonderful times when my now-grown children were that age.

The young mother and I engaged in small talk about the baby girl, and then I introduced myself to her. Realizing that I was Brian's wife, she said, "You're not aware of it, but your husband is responsible for my daughter's birth."

Now, those are not words that any wife wants to hear. Remembering the neutral demeanor that I was trained to use as a social worker, I replied, "Oh, tell me more."

She told me that she had always wanted to be a mother. Soon after her marriage, she and her husband decided to start their family. However, after months and months went by without conceiving, they consulted fertility specialists. Still they were unable to have children. The woman underwent years of treatments and procedures, some of which were intrusive, painful, and embarrassing, yet every month the couple went from hope to despair. She was scheduled to see another expert for a new treatment. As she was driving to that appointment, she decided that if this procedure did not work, she would stop trying to conceive. Enough was enough.

As the woman sat in the doctor's waiting room, surrounded by many pregnant women, she thought of *Many Lives, Many Masters* and the concept of souls choosing their parents, and she remembered that the souls may be of family members or friends who have passed on. Out loud, in front of everyone, she looked up to the ceiling and said, "Okay. If any of you want to come back, this is the time. This is your last chance with me!"

Perhaps someone was listening. The procedure was successful, and nine months later this beautiful child was born.

ᠺ *Carole Weiss*

I may have been partly responsible for this baby, but I myself have borne many children. I have been male and female over my many incarnations. I have been all races, all religions, and all nationalities. So have we all, because we are not our bodies, which are merely our temporary homes. We are the souls, moving from life to life, learning how to realize our true spiritual nature here on the earth.

This shift in perspective from identifying with the body to identifying with the soul is a fundamental step on our journey. To know one's true nature is both freeing and healing. An ego or mundane mind can be easily afflicted by daily events and problems. But at the soul level, our deep calm is not affected by the minicatastrophes of everyday life or by outer conflicts. A greater perspective allows peace to prevail and our hearts to remain open and loving.

Jennifer, whose story follows, discovered this perspective one day in a massage therapist's office, where she realized that she had subconsciously been identifying with a body that she had worn hundreds of years ago. This identification manifested itself physically as a scar, and also psychologically as a fear about starting a family. The resulting change in perspective freed her to experience the joys of motherhood, just as it had for the young woman in Carole's story and just as it may soon for Michelle.

. SCARS OF SADNESS .

I believe it is a Buddhist proverb that says, "When the student is ready, the teacher appears." I was in a bookstore in November 2004, looking for a book to read on a long flight to Las Vegas, and the newest book by Dr. Weiss jumped out at me as I passed it by. I began reading as soon as my flight departed and didn't stop until we touched down in Vegas five hours later. For some reason, this book resonated with me in a much different way than his others had. I suppose it was timing; I was ready to hear the messages and to begin to implement them in my life.

As a licensed clinical social worker, I was excited and eager to learn more about how to utilize past-life regression as a therapeutic tool with my clients. To my complete amazement, I read that Dr. Weiss would be speaking at the Miami Book Fair just a few days later, and that he would also be doing a book signing. I attended his lecture, and at the signing I told Dr. Weiss what an impression his book had on me and inquired about learning more. Dr. Weiss was so kind and took the time to talk with me, as he did with everyone who had waited in line, and encouraged me to attend his professional training in Austin, Texas, the following year. I did attend the weeklong training and began utilizing the techniques shortly afterward.

Although I had read several books on past-life regression, attended numerous workshops and seminars, and gone to several practitioners, I had not experienced a vivid regression myself. I had feelings, and sometimes I would have olfactory experiences, but the images and sensations never fully developed. My first real past-life experience happened during what I thought, at the time, to be a massage treatment for temporomandibular joint disorder (TMJ).

My husband had been in a car accident and was referred to a massage therapist for treatment. After his first session, he called me and encouraged me to see the massage therapist, as she specialized in treatment for TMJ. I had suffered from this issue for many years and the symptoms were becoming increasingly worse with time, so I quickly made an appointment.

About halfway through my massage, feeling completely safe and not having any expectations other than relaxation, I began to have visualizations that made absolutely no sense to me. I then realized that the massage therapist was no longer working on my jaw, but that she now had her hands hovering over my head. I would later learn that she was using a technique called somato emotional release. "What are you seeing?" she asked me.

Feeling embarrassed, I said, "Nothing."

"Are you sure?"

"Yes," I responded. Now intrigued with these visualizations and her inquiries, I said, "Why do you ask?"

She said, "I'd like you to describe everything that you are seeing, no matter how silly it may be." *Quite silly* is exactly what I thought it was, but I took the risk and shared my visions with her. At first they came in bits and pieces, but then they developed into an experience that I felt I was reliving.

I had begun to see an ocean with a ship sailing away in the distance. On the ship were several men who looked like Vikings. They were sailing away from me, and I realized that these Vikings had left me alone on a deserted island. The time was at least a thousand years ago, and the feeling was dark and grim. It was at that moment that I felt my stomach and realized that I was at least six months pregnant.

I then became aware of who had impregnated and left me—it was my own father in that lifetime. He was one of the Vikings on the ship, and he had abandoned me on this island. I was just a young girl. I felt flooded with a number of overwhelming emotions: shame, embarrassment, isolation, sadness, anger, and ultimately pure despair. Out of desperation, I took a sword and plunged it into my stomach on the bottom left side. My intention was to kill the baby, but I believe that it was also to kill myself.

My next memory was of delivering a baby, completely by myself, on this island. The baby was dead.

I emerged from this experience without knowing the end of this girl's lifetime, but it was clear to me that this was a vivid past-life memory. The first thing that I did was to touch the area where the sword had entered my stomach. It was the exact area that had inexplicably developed a skin irritation about six months earlier, which had left a white scar about three inches in width and an inch in length. I had been to several doctors; none could figure out what it was or how it originated. It would not go away with any treatment. The last doctor had said that if it did not disappear in a month, they would have to do a biopsy.

When I arrived home to tell my husband about the experience, I pulled away the clothes that were covering the scar to show him the site where the sword had entered my body in the past lifetime. To my surprise, the mark had significantly diminished. The next morning, when I awoke, it was completely gone. It has never returned.

Perhaps even more important, that was the turning point when my husband and I began planning to start a family. We had been married for many years and had discussed this possibility for a long time, but I had never been ready to proceed. I feared that something would be wrong with the baby, that it would not love me, and that my husband would leave me once we had a child, even though he had given me no reason to believe that this would happen. But now I understood where my concerns had come from: I had had them for a thousand years.

I realized that I no longer needed to bear the scars of that lifetime; indeed, when I uncovered their source, they disappeared. We are now the very happy and proud parents of a beautiful little girl.

ꞌ*Jennifer Williams*

Each of these stories not only echoes past-life themes but also demonstrates how much we have underestimated the power and the limits of the human mind. Jennifer's story contains so many of these consciousness-expanding elements: for example, a scar appearing and then disappearing at the very location of a past-life wound. As I have mentioned previously, researchers have amply documented a similar phenomenon in children who have significant birthmarks at the site of traumas from past lives.

We do not need to continue to carry the fears and the symptoms that we have been shouldering for thousands of years. Discovering and understanding their root causes release us from these ancient burdens. They need not scar us forever.

Karma is not punishment but rather the opportunity for growth. The Viking men in Jennifer's past life will have to repay her for leaving her to die on that deserted island. They will need to understand, at the deepest level, that killing is wrong and that life is to be nurtured, not taken. They will have future lifetimes in which this basic lesson is learned through their own experiences. And even if these experiences are difficult and painful, they are not retribution; they are simply the avenue for learning the lesson of nonviolence.

Karmic connections continue over lifetimes as relationships are reestablished, expanded, and fulfilled. Our loved ones travel with us throughout time. We learn our lessons together. Sometimes they teach us; sometimes we teach them. The earth is our school, and we are both classmates and teachers. When we remember our past lives together, a deep appreciation of our shared journey emerges. The quality of the relationship is deepened. An abiding patience is acquired, because we can see the multifaceted and eternal nature of the connection.

Understanding allows us to enter the hearts and the minds of other people. This is true empathy. We know the origin of their fears, their hopes, and their behavior. Seeing all this, we no longer take their actions personally. We can be patient and accepting.

"Understanding is the basis of love," writes the Zen monk Thich Nhat Hanh. The following story of Christy and her son, Austin, richly illustrates this lesson.

. RISING TO THE CHALLENGE .

In this lifetime, I have had one's share of trials. This must be an extraordinary learning period for me, which I try to accept willingly and gracefully. I have a son who is four years old and who has a rare illness never before found in medical literature. There was a small hiccup during certain developmental stages in utero. Children with similar symptoms have not survived. This means that he is pioneering this "syndrome," if you will, as there is no literature to draw from for future reference on his abilities.

My son's greatest challenge, aside from having a hearing loss, is his difficulty with movement and motor skills. At birth, he could not even turn his head from side to side. He needed glasses as soon as he could wear them. He has had difficulties hearing, speaking, and eating. At nine weeks, he stopped breathing as a result of bronchitis and, probably, aspiration during feeding. Fortunately, I am a nurse anesthetist, and supporting the airway is my job. (This, I am sure, was planned.) Austin has been in therapy since he was six days old. We have gone to therapy four to seven times a week, and I have learned and taught my entire family sign language. Austin now is able to run a little, he signs beautifully, and he has about fifty words that are audible. We have a long way to go, but we are moving in the right direction with him. He is one of my life's greatest teachers, and he has given me my greatest heartaches as well.

I had an amazing experience at your Tampa lecture during the first regression. I was regressed to a time of wagons and old dresses. The clothing was tattered and seemed to be made of burlap material. I was walking over a hill; many other people were walking too, but not together. I didn't seem to know where we were going, and there was no sense of community. I was looking for someone who had run off. Once I got to the top of the hill, I saw a wagon with no horse attached, which had rolled slightly and stopped on a huge rock. People were running toward it—I didn't know them—but my heart sank as I knew that it was my little boy who was hurt. He was my same son as in this life; he looked different, but it was the same spirit. The boy was under the wagon; no one could get it off him. I could see only his legs. As he cried, many people were trying to lift the wagon, but it was going downhill and they had to push it back uphill. They finally did, and I was able to hold him briefly, but he was taken from me by the men I didn't know. They were trying to help but I felt so helpless, and they wouldn't listen to me.

The time moved forward, and I was at a different building where they had taken my son. It was a brownish-orange, flat-looking building made out of mud or adobe: a hospital. I stood at the entrance but couldn't go in. He died there. I know he wanted me and I wanted to be with him; I don't know why I didn't go inside. He died with strangers, crying, and I never got over the fact that I couldn't get to him.

I can't help but know that I have been given a second chance at this. I did not do a very good job advocating for my child in that past life. I didn't speak loud enough; I didn't defend him. I was told what to do and listened without question, even though I needed to be with my son and I knew he needed me. We had no one else. In this lifetime, I have become a nurse practitioner. Austin had over two hundred medical and therapeutic appointments during his first two years of life, and he never once went without me at his side. Now I understand why I am so fearful of people touching him and why I will not allow him to have a procedure or therapy if I am not there with him. He died at the age of four in the regression, due to his leg injuries and the blood loss he sustained from the wounds; in this life, he was nearly the same age when he started walking independently. I have even created a nonprofit school, the "Hope, Achieve, Learn, Overcome" (HALO) Academy, for children with disabilities, where they can have all their therapy and sign-language needs met. The woman who was sitting next to me

at your workshop may be sending us a donation check for the school
to build our own facility. The entire story from beginning to end is
completely connected and was such a beautiful experience, a tremendous blessing that has changed my life. The depth of understanding
that I have gained has been wonderful.

~ *Christy Raile*

Christy is a graduate-level student in this great earth school. She is radiating love and giving so much to Austin and to many others. Her past life
in the time of wagons and old dresses helped her to prepare for this life's
challenges. She learned well.

And, by the way, the people sitting next to you in these workshops are
not there by accident. Divine guidance, a perfect process, is always at work.
Random events are not really random, even though we may not understand
their meaning or purpose at the time. Whether we label these events as
destiny, synchronicities, grace, the source field, universal intention, or any
other name, they are not accidental. There seems to be a reason for everything, and with time and reflection the meaning will eventually emerge.

Sometimes an advanced soul will volunteer to incarnate in a physical body
in order to teach us important lessons. Austin has done this. His birth, replete
with serious developmental abnormalities, has provided the opportunity for
Christy to master love and compassion. Her love is unconditional. She asks
for nothing in return. Her compassion is universal, the HALO Academy providing heartfelt help to so many children, not merely her own.

I have been asked many times why evolved souls would ever choose to
take on a body with a painful and debilitating condition. This question is
frequently posed by a relative of someone with autism, with schizophrenia or some other type of severe mental disorder, with cerebral palsy or
another kind of muscular impairment, or with any number of illnesses,
for these family members have personally witnessed how difficult life can
appear to be for such individuals. Too often, people think of these conditions as karmic punishments. But as I wrote earlier, karma is not a punishment; it's simply a means for learning and growth. Many souls, particularly
advanced ones like Austin's, will elect to incarnate in an impaired state in

order to learn what that experience feels like. They may have had many lifetimes in which they were the caregivers, but now they are to learn what it is to receive love. Love must be balanced. This decision is also made so as to give other people the opportunity to express love. Someone with autism will need to be nurtured and taken care of, and this provides other people with an occasion to manifest caring, charity, and compassion. Thus, the condition is not the result of punishment or of karma but rather of a tremendously loving and generous desire to help other souls progress along their spiritual paths.

Wise and loving beings are always among us. We may not recognize them at first. We may not see them as teachers. Our minds get in the way.

"How can this little baby teach *me?*"

Our hearts are already aware.

Just as with Christy and Austin, the birth of a child often provides a rich education in this school of life, but the loss of a child can be a devastating and powerful teacher too. The following story explores this idea further.

. SEARCHING FOR SUCCESS .

A client of mine, Anna Silvernail Sweat, experienced this regression in 2008. She is still enjoying the results of her work. I have asked her to tell her story, and it is as follows:

After many years of feeling like I continuously sabotage my own success, quitting or leaving one position or relationship after another just as things begin to take off, I decided to try past-life regression to determine if this issue carried over from another life experience.

Having no prior encounters with past-life regression and feeling unsure about my stance on reincarnation versus the afterlife, I attended a group session with some enthusiasm and curiosity but few expectations. When asked to state my intent for this journey in writing, I reaffirmed my determination to uncover why I always bail after a certain level of accomplishment.

Relaxed and at ease, I explored a lifetime in which I was Sarah, a widowed landowner in rural seventeenth-century England. I had three children, an older son and young identical-twin girls. It was clear to me that of all my children in that life I was closest to my son, who played an integral role in helping me maintain the bit of land that I had inherited after his father's death. My total focus and sole purpose for living was to maintain our independence as a family by keeping our land and all of us together. It was a hard, laborious existence, but I had been successful for many years and was proud of my accomplishment, a rare and uncanny feat for any single woman in that time period. Just as I began to feel confident that our fears of poverty and separation were truly behind us, my son died in battle. He was only eighteen years old. I could see myself at his wake, there on my own property, utterly devastated by the loss. I knew that he could not have died in a war fought on foreign land if his body had been returned to me. In addition, I had the distinct sense that he had not voluntarily enlisted but that he had been coerced or forced in some way.

It was the ultimate failure. I had worked so hard all those long years to hold on to our property in order to keep my children safe and with me and to provide them with a life of freedom and relative comfort. Unable to protect my son from war, I had lost not only my precious child but also my only dependable help in our pastoral endeavors. In a peculiar twist, I kept picturing this dead son in an American Civil War uniform. It made no sense to me.

As I traveled further into that life, I saw that, despite the odds, I continued to work our land and save it for my daughters, one of whom married and had a family, and both of whom remained there after my death. But I was never the same, and I died feeling that the great sacrifices I made and hardships I endured had all been for naught because in the end I had failed to protect my son.

After the session was over, I felt very emotional and grieved for a loss that had occurred hundreds of years ago. Looking for answers, I did some online research the following day. In my current knowledge, I didn't know of any wars fought on British soil during that lifetime, and while I am well aware of the American draft, I had no notion if a draft concept existed in England in that time. I was surprised to learn that there was a series of three British civil wars fought in the mid- to late 1600s. This made the vision of the boy in an American Civil War uniform, the only civil war with which I was familiar, much more sensible; it was the clearest hint my mind could give me about his death. Many of the soldiers enlisted on both sides were coerced or drafted into service by county lords, noblemen, and military officers. It seems that much of the rural English population was neutral about the war, siding with neither Parliament nor the king. The only way for the two combatant parties to keep their regiments stocked was to force or manipulate able-bodied young men into their ranks. I realized instantly that my son from that lifetime had died in the British civil wars, and that he had indeed been conscripted against his will. Although we were "freeholders," we were not a wealthy or prominent family in society; therefore, my son was just the kind of person for whom the military would have been looking, someone who would not be overtly missed, someone whose family would have no recourse against his being drafted. Historical estimates dictate that as many as 185,000 men died during these civil wars—up to one-quarter of the male population in England at that time.

In the end, I realized that the tragedy of that lifetime had continued to carry over with me through new incarnations, leaving me with a lingering sense that no matter how hard I worked or how successful I became, failure was inevitable because there are always variables that one cannot control and outcomes one cannot foresee. Sarah's devastation never left me. Knowing that this was the source of my instinct to jump ship at critical junctures, I was able to begin visualizing leaving Sarah and her family behind and meditating on my personal success in this lifetime. What's more, I was able to recognize my oldest daughter in this life as the twin girl who married and had a family; her son in that life (my grandson) was, in fact, my son in this one. I understood then that my son's and daughter's need for my attention and approval in this lifetime stemmed from their experience with me in Sarah's life. Too grief-stricken and disillusioned, Sarah had never managed to connect with her daughters or grandchildren as she had with the son who died.

Today I am working on realizing my dreams, traveling to Ireland, publishing my first novel, and enjoying a close, loving relationship with all three of my children. I am grateful for Sarah's intense work ethic, but even more so for the opportunity to relax and enjoy my accomplishments—something she never experienced. Knowing that the past was still haunting me allowed me to make a concerted effort to move beyond it, to put a face and a name to my fear of success, and to leave Sarah's grief buried in England with her son.

         ∽ *Melanie Harrell*

Melanie's client, Anna, was able to repair her grief from the old English lifetime, thus removing those blocks and freeing herself to write, to be successful, and to heal her relationships. She was also able to recognize several of the reincarnated souls from that past life, which gave her an understanding of their current fears and needs. We travel through time with many of the same souls, often reincarnating in different relationships; for example, as in Anna's case, a grandson returning as a son. Dimly remembered patterns are often brought forward and repeated in the current lifetime. Through recognition and understanding, negative relationship patterns can be repaired and improved.

Anna was wise to seek out Melanie, a therapist, to explore why she struggled with feeling successful. Over the years, and especially in my psychiatry practice, I have observed so many people who feel like they are failures. They have not achieved some goal that they felt would have made them "successful." Perhaps the goal was a financial one, a certain modicum of family approval, a childhood dream, or anything else that they had not attained. I have also treated many heads of businesses and organizations, actors and actresses, sports celebrities, and similar types of people whom many would consider to have it all, yet who nonetheless felt unfulfilled, dissatisfied, or sad.

So much unhappiness results from subjective measures of success imposed on us by parents, communities, and cultures. We are souls, not robots! We are here to learn about love, compassion, kindness, and nonviolence. Success should be measured by these qualities. Are we becoming a more understanding and empathic person? If so, we are successful. The soul clings to such learning, because these are spiritual truths.

With my clients who excelled professionally yet still felt unhappy, we worked on focusing on the core values of being a better, kinder person. At that point, their outlook began to improve. That is, after all, why they are here on Earth—and why we are all here. Our purpose in life is not to be a bestselling author, or to have a financially lucrative career, or to be a star. It is to be a more loving, compassionate person. Successes can be used to further the spiritual path and to reach many people, but they are merely one possible means and not the end. The true goal is to help others, and if you make that your goal, eventually you'll become that bestselling author, or the multimillionaire—or not. It won't matter. Once you open your heart, those other things will take care of themselves.

Money is not evil. It is simply a thing, just like any other thing. It can be used in wonderful and charitable ways. But we learn through relationships, not things. Upon the death of our bodies, we do not bring our possessions to the other side—that is a place of higher energy and consciousness, rather than another physical state. So we cannot bring our houses, cars, bank accounts, diamonds, titles, awards, status, or any similar marker of success. These are merely temporary. What exists forever, what we do carry with us when we move on, is a good heart. And, once gained, it can never be lost.

In the next story, Brooke talks about what she carried with her into this life: a two-thousand-year-old fear of being alone.

. RELAX AND RELEASE .

I was at your I Can Do It at Sea! workshop series in 2011. My profound healing came during the group workshop.

Although I am a highly successful physician in my early forties, I've been obsessed with the idea of getting married my entire life. It wasn't the normal "someday I'd like to" feeling that many people have; I used to feel like I'd die if I didn't get married. As you can imagine, that intensity pushed away long-term boyfriends and sometimes scared off dates.

In the group regression, I found myself in about 1 c.e. in present-day Afghanistan or Pakistan, wrapped in a blue canvas blanket. When you instructed us to become aware of our feet, I suddenly realized that I couldn't feel mine. They were bones, and I was paralyzed from the waist down. I was an outcast from my tribe, which had abandoned me to beg on the street. I hurt so much. I died out in the cold, completely alone.

As I floated out of my body, I began to scream at the Jesus figure that accompanied me in the garden. "That's not fair! No one should have to live like that," I cried. He told me to relax and gave me messages about that life. He also told me that I was not going to die alone again and that I should heal from that fear, because it was in the past.

I came out of the hypnosis and have never felt the same. The anxiety and fear are gone. I'm dating now, and I'm comfortable no matter what happens. My best friend, who accompanied me on the cruise, reminded me that when I was depressed I used to say, "If I don't find a man, I'm going to die alone on the side of the street." How funny that I was unconsciously referring to a past life. There's no way in this life that I would die alone; I have family all around me. But I had always been carrying that grief with me.

I've never felt better. I truly believe, just like anyone with a phobia of water or of having their neck touched from a past-life pain, that I was healed.

$\sim$ *Brooke*

It is as if we are all born with a form of posttraumatic stress disorder (PTSD), but the stress comes from a past life. A person who suffers from traditional PTSD will become anxious when something triggers a painful or disturbing memory. He or she reexperiences the trauma even though it is no longer present, a thing of the past. For example, the sound of a car backfiring might immediately and viscerally bring to mind scenes of gunfire to a soldier who has just returned home from war. Although he is now safe and hundreds of miles away from the trenches, in his mind he is instantly transported back to the battlefield, fighting for his survival. Are we not all carrying around our own phobias, traumas, fears, and baggage—as well as affections, interests, and relationships—from lifetimes past? We remember these triggers on a soul level and in our subconscious minds, and even though they are not present in our current lives, we respond and react to them as if they were. Perhaps past-life traumatic stress disorder is a very real and very common condition.

The good news is that it is treatable. It requires no medication and can be cured in as little as one dose of regression therapy. In just a day, Brooke's millennia-old phobia about living and dying alone vanished. Freed from the tyranny of her obsession and her fear, her life immediately improved.

How loved Brooke is to be given the opportunity to meet the Jesus figure and have him explain what she needed to know. We are all protected at the highest levels. Our universe is benign and infinitely caring. We will find paradise on earth when we remember our true nature and align our hearts and minds with this unconditional love.

Brooke's story reminds me that if I am reaching out with kindness, compassion, and the expertise of experience, then I should not be attached to any outcome. If I help one person, or ten, or ten million, it does not matter. The results are out of my control and are not as important as the loving intention and action. This is true for every one of us, for all our actions.

Even if nobody else in Brooke's group had an experience, a healing, or a transformational understanding, the workshop would still have been an amazing success. Brooke was healed—how marvelous is that? Each one of us is precious.

Terri, the author of the next story, experienced a reverse kind of "past-life traumatic stress disorder" in that her previous life was actually devoid of stress or worry. Recalling and recovering the joy she felt in an earlier lifetime helped bring more happiness and contentment to her present one.

. THE SIMPLE LIFE .

Due to some events that occurred in my family and personal life toward the end of 2008, I spent many days feeling very depressed. That really isn't like me, but it was understandable considering what

I had been through: a falling-out with one of my children, another child divorcing, my father dying after years of fighting cancer, and becoming very sick myself. For some reason during this period of time, I became obsessed with the idea of being single, living alone, and working as a secretary.

In May 2009, I went to San Diego to the I Can Do It! conference and attended a class taught by Brian Weiss. I purchased his regression CDs at the conference, and it was only a few weeks later that I had a rather amazing experience with one of them.

When I returned home from San Diego, I had been doing the regressions every day or two, so it wasn't unusual for me to lie down on my bed on a quiet afternoon and play one of the CDs. One day, I was feeling even more sad and depressed than usual, and for some reason I put in the CD. I was home alone and had the time, so I entered into the meditative regression. I felt so sad that I immediately began crying.

Soon, the crying stopped, and I listened more intently as Brian led me deeper into the experience. I remembered a wonderful past life in Chicago. In fact, when my husband and I had visited that city two years ago, I had felt comfortable there and liked it very much, even though I'd always thought that I'd find it too large and unpleasant.

In the regression, I found myself in the 1940s as a young woman, in her twenties or thirties, named Jenny. I was single, thin, beautiful, and professional. I had been promoted to executive secretary for a vice president, and then again for the president of the company, which was a large insurance firm in a modern office building. Although disinterested in marriage or motherhood, I felt extremely happy, content, and satisfied with my life. I didn't date often and didn't want or need a man; there was no desire for a family. I may have been orphaned and so felt used to being alone.

I remember my favorite outfit well. It was a green-and-beige plaid skirt suit with three-quarter-length sleeves. I wore hose and high heels. I saw my white '40s-style bra and my "old lady" panties and garter belt. My hair was short, teased, and heavily sprayed. On the evenings and weekends, I wore white pedal pushers and sneakers. I didn't have or need a car; I lived on the same block as the office where I worked.

I was so free. No complexities, no family! My girlfriends worked with me, and we were quite close. I lived through their breakups and pregnancies.

I loved my life as Jenny. I was so happy; there was no stress at all. I would walk along Lake Michigan and feed bread crumbs to the birds in the park and then go shopping at the corner market. My apartment was small but clean, comfortable, and uncluttered. Each promotion brought a move to a larger apartment.

I miss Jenny's life—*my* life. Maybe I died too young and what I felt, in addition to "homesickness," was a sense of incompletion. Perhaps her life, my life as Jenny, didn't end the way I thought it should have. The life as Jenny was a key to unlocking my current depression and problems. I believe I may have wanted a divorce and a life by myself because my soul was so incredibly fulfilled when I was Jenny. Only one day after the regression, I felt remarkably happier than I had been the day before. A lot of it had to do with this knowledge, this understanding of why I so strongly desired living alone even though I chose to be married and to have a bunch of children during this incarnation. Six months after having this regression, I realized that the obsession I had felt prior to experiencing my life as Jenny had vanished without my even noticing it. I was no longer fixated on living alone, being single, being a secretary, and so forth. It simply disappeared from my conscious mind, and as a result I am able to go on with my life and be much happier.

ᘯ *Terri*

The validity of the past-life experience often lies in the disappearance of symptoms. Merely fantasizing about a simpler life would not remove sadness, depression, or obsession. But an actual memory would have such a healing effect—and indeed it did. Terri's sadness disappeared, and she was able to resume her current life, despite all its problems and complexities, with more peace and happiness.

Understanding takes place at many levels, not only the conscious one. Understanding at the subconscious level can be just as powerful. Our deeper minds observe the past-life dramas and say, "Oh, that's where this obsession or fear or affinity or talent or relationship or symptom comes from. I get it. I don't need it any longer. I will let it go." And then we are healed.

Experience teaches the lesson of the temporary nature of the emotions. Being aware of why negative feelings arise, and what their roots and causes are, quickly dissolves them. Sometimes they are caused by events and circumstances in your current life. Yet they may be carried over from previous incarnations, only to manifest again in your present lifetime.

To forgive those who have hurt you and to let go of your anger are hard, but you will feel so free. One advantage of growing older and accumulating experiences is that you often become aware that you have encountered a similar situation previously. I have been angry before, and the feeling has passed. Anger arises, stays for a while, and then leaves. It is like a cloud floating past, only to disappear. All our emotions behave similarly. Sadness comes and goes. Fear arises and subsides. Anxiety ebbs and flows. Frustrations enter and leave. Hurts eventually heal. Despair floats into awareness, then diminishes. All are transitory.

The knowledge that all things pass is often enough for healing to occur. But if the emotions or symptoms continue, past-life exploration may provide the cure.

It certainly did for Tom, a middle-aged man who attended one of my intensive workshops. While participating in an energy exercise, his partner had experienced a burning sensation in her abdomen. She felt that this was connected to Tom. As the exercise ended, Tom confirmed that her impression had been correct: he had stomach cancer, and from the treatments, especially the radiation, he often felt burning in that area. To all of us in the group, he appeared extremely sad.

On the second day of the workshop, some of the answers to Tom's sadness and his depressed affect became clear. He explained that he had lost his son; shortly afterward, he lost his wife as well. The entire group gasped, assuming that both had died. Indeed, his son had—but his wife had not. She had left him once his cancer had been diagnosed. Everybody could, of course, empathize with his pain and sadness at this tragic series of events, but we were baffled as to why his wife would leave him during such a difficult time.

We would not have to wait long to find out. During the group regression, Tom himself discovered the answer to that very question. Upon emerging, he described to the group what he had experienced. Already, we could see that his face looked much brighter; it was as if a weight had been lifted from his shoulders. He even smiled for the first time.

Tom had regressed to a lifetime in the American Civil War, in which he was engaged to the woman who was his wife in his current life. The war had intervened, and they were unable to be married. Near the end of the war, he had returned home and was finally with his beloved again when a group of enemy soldiers stumbled upon them. They shot him in the stomach, in the exact area where his present-life cancer existed and where his radiation treatments had caused the burning sensation. Tom floated above his body and watched as his fiancée rocked back and forth, sobbing and weeping inconsolably. He died with his head in her lap, her tears falling on his face.

It became evident to Tom that, in his current life, his wife had not left him for someone else, or for some defect in him, or for some other unknown reason. She simply could not watch him die a second time—and perhaps there were even more losses from other lifetimes of which he was not yet aware. At that moment, Tom was able to release his grief and fear, his anger and sadness. And through this understanding, a tremendous healing occurred.

For the rest of the week, Tom seemed to be a different person. His mood was so much brighter. He was helping other people. He truly understood that his wife's departure was not personal; she, because of whatever conditions existed within her, just could not bear to lose him again.

And he also discovered that he was immortal. He had lived in the Civil War and been killed then as a soldier, and here he was back again, reunited with the same woman, the same soul. He knew, at this level, that he was an eternal being, and that therefore his son, who had died as a young adult, was also not really dead.

Tom's experience was incredibly moving to our entire group. We could all empathize with the pain and sadness he had felt, and we were amazed at the immediate shift in his mood and outlook. He was able to forgive. He became unstuck; he could move on with his life. Tom had hope again. We were so relieved to see that he had passed this crisis point and that he would be all right.

We are souls, and we are connected to one another. What happens to one affects all. When a soul regains hope, at a deeper level all other souls feel more hopeful as well.

Tom's ability to let go of his anger reminded me of a parable that I recently read about two monks who were preparing to cross a river with a powerful current. A nearby woman also wished to cross the river, but she was afraid to do so because of the power of the water. One of the monks picked up this woman and put her on his shoulders, and he and the other monk safely crossed to the other side. He put the woman down, she went on her way, and so did the two monks.

After a while, the younger monk said to the other, "I can't believe that you carried that woman across the river. You put her on your shoulders. This is against our values; it's against our vows. We are not allowed to touch women. How could you do something like that?"

The older, wise monk replied, "I put the woman down as soon as we crossed the river. You are still carrying her."

In thinking over this story, I realized that we all do this every day. After we finish with our tasks and problems, we frequently do not put them down and let them go on their way. We carry them with us far longer than is necessary, creating a burden that adds weight and fatigue to our shoulders and stress to our minds.

The cure is to live more and more mindfully, in the present moment. Of course, this is difficult to do and requires practice, but it is well worth it. It is important to learn lessons from the past and to remember them, but then we must let the past go. There is no need to carry it beyond the river.

· 4 ·

Freedom from
Emotional Pain

Fears, phobias, anxieties, and other emotional states can be as debilitating as physical illnesses. Just like physical symptoms, psychological distress can have its origin in past-life events. Once those are discovered, healing can be rapid and relatively complete. Freedom and joy can be regained.

Not all our afflictions are rooted in the traumas of prior lifetimes. Current-life events are sometimes the culprits or may even be compounding past-life seeds. And the stresses of today's competitive and overly materialistic world add their own weight to our emotional maladies. So much sadness and anxiety assail us because we are easily distracted and overwhelmed by day-to-day events. We have to juggle work, relationships, and interactions with other people at every moment. We have to deal with our daily needs. And so we forget that we are spiritual beings, which leads to emotional turmoil. Spiritual beings should think and behave like spiritual beings; that is our nature and ultimate destiny. But when the circumstances of everyday life lead us astray and we forget our true nature, that is when sorrow, worry, and fear enter. That is when inner peace, joy, and happiness exit.

All we have to do is remember: remember who we are and what we are, what we have been through, where we have come from, why we are here. As we do this, emotional healing will naturally follow, just as it did for the authors of the stories in this chapter.

As emotional symptoms are resolved, the patient's family and friends benefit as well. Their stress and responsibility are lessened. Even beyond this healing shift, relatives and significant others may indirectly experience the feelings and facts of the regression. As they hear the patients' stories, they feel the emotion and the immediacy of the memories; they react and respond to the improvement in their loved ones' lives. Often, to their surprise and joy, they find their own symptoms and illnesses disappearing. Such was the case with Mira's lover in the remarkable story that follows.

. THE LESSON OF LOVE .

The story of how I became acquainted with the powerful process of experiencing one's past lives began during my summer vacation after seventh grade. I had grown up in Communist Bulgaria, and topics of any mystical or religious nature were simply not a part of my upbringing. However, a few years before that summer the wave of the democratic revolution had swept through Eastern Europe, and spiritual information had become readily available.

That summer I was thirteen years old. I came across your book *Through Time into Healing*. Even though the concept of reincarnation was not a part of my childhood and I doubt it was ever discussed in my presence, I did not question the possibility of its existence. It just seemed so natural, so normal. As Voltaire said, "It is not more surprising to be born twice than once."

I absolutely loved the stories in the book. I loved the wisdom in it, the possibilities it presented to me. I loved it so much that upon reading the final few pages, I immediately decided to make a recording of myself reading the sample script given in the book and experience a regression for myself. As I was getting ready to begin recording, I remember thinking, *But I am only thirteen. There is really nothing wrong with me. I have no phobias, no physical ailments. Why would I do this?* But the pull, the curiosity in me was too strong to resist.

I made the recording, rewound the tape to the beginning, and even though I did not know what to expect, I pressed play. The recording guided me through a beautiful relaxation, and I felt very calm and comfortable. But at the moment I crossed through the door into a past life, that changed.

I immediately dropped into the body of a woman who was running for her life, and I became her. My heart was pounding with fear, and my inhalations of air were short, abrupt, and desperate. It was terrifying. I was running down a dimly lit hallway and knew that there were men chasing after me who would kill me if they caught me.

My gray suit consisted of a jacket and skirt made of thick wool. I wore black stockings and black shoes with small heels. My dark hair was neatly tucked in a bun on the back.

The brick walls reverberated with the sound of my steps as I ran. There were rows of doors on both sides, but upon trying to open them I discovered that they were all locked. Finally, a door handle gave in. I entered the room and saw that it was bare, with one small window with bars on it that was high up on the wall, close to the ceiling. I knew that I was trapped and that they would catch me.

It was at the time of World War II. I was a doctor who, instead of healing a German general, had poisoned and killed him. That is why these men were after me—they were seeking revenge.

The next scene was one that I looked at from above. I saw how I was put on an electric chair, how my hands and legs were strapped to it, how I was executed.

Then something truly beautiful happened. I watched as my spirit rose from my body. It slowly drifted upward. There was a trail of white light in front of it that it followed. At the end of that path, there was an open door through which a magnificent white light was shining. At the door there stood a being that glowed with love and light, waiting to greet my spirit. I felt such peace, such love, and such a sense of being eternal.

That night, I eagerly waited for my mother to return from work. I told her what I had experienced and asked her if electric chairs had really existed during World War II. Years later, I learned that they have been around since 1890.

That event was a formative experience in my life, and it is interesting that it happened at the age of thirteen. The number thirteen is believed to be the number of change. To numerologists and tarot readers, it is a number of transformation. It calls for a study of one's basic principles, what one believes in. It attracts changes in the way a person defines everything in her life, which leads to shifts in her worldview and her existence. I had certainly been transformed by my first regression.

Many years later, the story of the lifetime that I had experienced as a child developed even further at a workshop at Omega Institute led by Brian. During one of the group regressions, an image of a long road lined with birch trees began emerging in my mind. I saw myself as a young woman walking down a quiet dirt road in the country. In my hand I carried a small suitcase, and on my head I had a kerchief. I was leaving my village to move to St. Petersburg to study medicine. The final stop I made on my way was to go to the cemetery, where I paid my respects at the graves of my dead relatives. My heart was heavy. It would be many years before I could return back home—if at all.

While studying at the university, I was recruited by the secret service of the Soviet Union. There were troubles brewing in Europe, and there were even talks of a possible war. They sent me to Europe to spy for my country.

I was a very attractive woman who knew how to use her charm, and it was easy for me to gather information. I saw a vivid scene of me sitting in front of a small device that I was using to send coded wires with the information I collected.

There was a nightclub establishment frequented by many Americans. I found myself going there as often as I could, hoping to meet a particular man I had come to know. I was surprised to discover within me that I was interested in him not because of my work but because I was falling in love with him. He was in love with me, too.

The next scene unfolded on a large set of stairs in front of a big administrative building. I had received orders to move to a different location in Europe, so I had come to say good-bye. The man stood in front of me, telling me that he loved me, begging me not to leave, and asking me to marry him. Even though I loved him very much, I could not stay. I had already given my word and pledged my life, my love, and my heart to my country. I assured him that when he went back home to the family farm in America he would marry a nice woman, have children, and be happy. I said good-bye and, with tears in my eyes, rushed down the stairs toward the car that was waiting for me.

Later, I married an important German officer. It greatly facilitated my work and protected me. World War II had already begun. I had been practicing medicine, mostly treating German military men, and had received orders to terminate a high-ranking German general whom I was treating for an illness. I saw myself standing in front of a table. Next to me, sitting on a chair, was the general. There was a glass of water on the table. I held a small container with powder in it and looked up toward the ceiling, feeling anxiety within me for what I was about to do. Yet, thinking that there was no other choice, I poured the powder in the glass. Instead of giving the general his medication, I had given him poison.

This is where my first regression as a child fits in. I saw myself, again, running down that hallway and eventually getting caught. But this time, because I was much older and better able to handle the whole story, I saw the gruesome details of the interrogations to which I was subjected. Did I betray my network? No. Until the very end, I maintained that I had acted alone. I was beaten, tortured, questioned, and then many more times all over again beaten, tortured, and questioned. The only thing that my interrogators spared me from was rape. They felt that I had belonged to one of them, and that was a line they could not cross. At the end, they placed me on an electric chair and executed me.

As my spirit was rising above the scene, I knew that the lesson of that lifetime was a lesson of love, of needing to approach every situation with love and of allowing myself to be loved too. That whole lifetime had been orchestrated so that I could have the opportunity to choose love when standing on those stairs as the American man asked me to marry him. Yet I chose to stay true to my promise to serve my country. I also knew that after I left, he felt that he had nothing to live for; my leaving had broken his spirit. He died in a dirt ditch, having been shot right in the forehead during combat with the German army.

In the hours that followed this experience, I was shaken to my core and filled with an enormous sense of regret for having wasted one whole lifetime and for having harmed another person. But knowing that we are eternal, I also know that every lifetime enriches our souls with invaluable lessons.

My soul must have chosen to experience and learn the lesson of profound love in my current lifetime, because nothing gives me a greater sense of meaning and fulfillment than bringing love, light, and inspiration to people. One of the ways I most enjoy assisting people is by helping them to experience their past lives and gain understanding about the people and the circumstances that surround them. I am also in a very loving relationship with a man who, coincidentally, has two very deep-seated and irrational fears: the first, a fear of ever losing me; and the second of being shot point-blank in the forehead. It makes me wonder: Is this my second chance at love with the American man I once knew?

᠎ *Mira Kelley*

As a thirteen-year-old, Mira acted upon her intuitive wisdom and her curiosity for understanding and spiritual growth as she listened to the tapes that she had made. This decision changed her life, leading her to her higher potentiality, her healing work, and eventually to a reunion with her soul mate.

Her soul mate's fear of losing her again is typical of the underlying theme of separation anxiety. Frequently, children who seem almost irrationally frightened of being separated from their parents have actually lost them in previous lives. They subconsciously remember the loss, just like Mira's present-day lover. The cure for this type of separation fear is to recognize its root in a past-life event. The trauma has already happened. It is from another time, and it is not something to fear in the present or in the future. Her soul mate's concerns about once again losing Mira and of being shot in the head both stem from the World War II era. Knowing this, he can release them and nurture a relationship that is freer and not constricted by deep-seated insecurities.

Mira's description of the events after her physical death, when her spirit left her body, closely echoes studies of the near-death experience (NDE), studies that she was not aware of when she was only thirteen. The magnificent, restorative light and the loving spiritual being in Mira's story are universally encountered in the NDE. Their comforting presence and validation of the afterlife help people lose their fear of death and dying. We are, they remind us, immortal, and death is but a doorway to the other side.

Every so often, a synchronicity will arise and almost forcibly seize my attention. Synchronous events are apparently coincidental occurrences of related events that, to me, have a linkage at a metaphysical level. We may not understand that causal linkage, but it is there.

As I finished writing my reflections on Mira's story early in 2012, my phone buzzed with an incoming e-mail. Less than five minutes had elapsed since I wrote about releasing present-day fears because the traumas had already happened in a past life.

In the e-mail, a woman described to me how her "crippling fear of flying" had prevented her from fully enjoying life. Traveling for pleasure and for business was severely restricted. In 2003, she had attended a workshop that I was conducting in Miami. As I led the group through a past-life regression, she began to vividly remember a World War II lifetime.

"I found myself looking out of an airplane cockpit . . . I was a man, the pilot of a military personnel transport plane," she wrote. The plane crashed "due to mechanical failure, killing all passengers and crew (as well as my copilot and myself)."

The workshop ended. Within a short period of time, the fruits of her regression were ready to harvest.

"Eleven days after the workshop," she explained, "I had an emergency call and needed to fly to Boston. I felt nothing . . . zero . . . no fear . . . there was nothing. Since that day in 2003 I have flown many times and have never had a single moment of fear or anxiety. So, though this has been a long time coming, thank you, Dr. Weiss."

If I needed a cosmic exclamation point, here it was. Only moments after I had written about it, confirmation that current fears and phobias often have past-life roots arrived by e-mail. Remembering these roots can completely cure the symptoms. There is no need to be anxious or afraid anymore. The workshop that cured this woman took place nearly nine years ago, yet her e-mail came within just five minutes of a perfect bull's-eye. She could have told me her story at any time over all those years. The probability of the timing being a coincidence is remote. And, as a final connection, both stories involved traumatic deaths in World War II.

Mira shares another story with us below.

. LEARNING TO ALLOW .

This is the story of Ananachimo and the lesson of needing to allow.

In one of the regression exercises that I did with Brian Weiss during a workshop at the Omega Institute, the image of a group of people crawling up a small slope emerged. I wondered what this image could have been and if it was something I needed to brush to the side in my mind in order to get to something more valid. However, I remembered Brian saying that this might be the thread that pulled me in, and I decided to stay with it and see what developed.

The picture came into focus. The group of people was a band of Native Americans. I wondered which tribe they belonged to, and in my head popped the answer that they were with the Plains Indians. Next, I began searching for myself among the group of people. And there I was. In an instant, I knew that my name was Ananachimo. I kept on repeating the name to myself in order to remember it, as it was a name I had never heard before.

At the moment that I identified myself as Ananachimo, I fully became him. Everything that I experienced in that lifetime was as if I were fully that person, feeling his emotions, feeling what it was like to have his body.

Ananachimo was a young man with an agile, lean, and muscular body. He was tall, with long black hair and a strong, square jaw. Around his neck he wore the tooth of a white bear that he had killed in a hunting trip up north.

The band of Indians was very careful when ascending the slope. On the top of the slope was a flat area where a house was built. They were spying on the settlers who lived there and who had been invading the lands of Ananachimo's tribe.

Ananachimo was looking across a valley that was surrounded by hills as far as the eye could see. He lifted his left hand, placed his palm in front of his shoulder, and gave a solemn vow to protect his land and his people from the settlers.

He was greatly attuned to nature. Nature spoke to him. He heard the whisper of the trees when their leaves were swaying in the wind. Every flower, bush, and blade of grass carried a message that he was able to read. He was also a healer, using herbs to bring the health of his people back into balance.

An important event occurred in Ananachimo's life when he was thirty-seven years old. He had captured and bonded with a mustang that had big red-and-white spots. The name of the horse was Red Lightning. The white people had somehow taken possession of his mustang. Ananachimo tried to free it, but they caught him and accused him of stealing the horse. To punish him, the white people tied his hands above his head and whipped him. I did not experience the horror of every whip falling on his back. I only saw that as the white people began whipping him, the horse, which was nearby, watched everything and shared Ananachimo's anger and sense of injustice. It was raising its front legs, kicking, and making terrible noise as it tried to free itself.

However, it was futile. This event broke Ananachimo's spirit. He lost his horse; he also lost faith in his ability to protect his land and his people. He felt that great injustice was being done but that he was powerless to bring about any change.

As time went by, things got worse. His tribe was driven toward the northwest. They were far away from their hunting grounds. On a cold day, at the age of forty-two, Ananachimo died. He was lying down in his tepee, feeling defeated because he could not protect his people, he could not save them, when his spirit left his body. Outside, women and children from his tribe (as most men had died) were going about their day. They were cold, hungry, and completely lost.

As the regression was nearing its end, I began searching for the soul lesson of that life. The lesson was about allowing. I had to learn to allow. I blamed myself for having failed to protect and save my people, but the truth was that I could not have saved anyone or protected them from the painful historic events. I must allow for people's lives to unfold as they are meant to, because their souls need these experiences. They have agreed to go through challenges to learn their own lessons and find their own enlightenment. I had seen the big injustice caused by the white men as an evil that I had promised to fight, yet I had failed to really be of help in times when I was most needed. People do not need saving. People need love, support, and encouragement that they can withstand any trials and will always come out stronger, wiser, and more compassionate. I cannot shelter anyone from the storms of life, or they will never grow, learn, and expand.

But how do you allow? How do you maintain the balance of being loving, kind, and helpful against wanting to save people from the injustice of the world or their own silly mistakes? This lesson continued to be a challenge for me, so many years and lifetimes later. Even though I changed my gender, my name, and my appearance, I still want to rush in and shield people.

I left the class session and headed to my room that night with these heavy questions on my mind. My cabin at Omega had two rooms in it. Upon entering the hallway, I met one of my neighbors. She was on her way to the bathroom, which was shared between our rooms. A moment later, she realized that she and the other roommate, who was showering, had locked themselves out, as both their keys were in their room and the door automatically locked. It was raining heavily outside, and my neighbor was barefoot. What a situation to find yourself in! I offered to help.

As I walked in the rain trying to find an Omega staff person, I instantly recognized that this little crisis unfolded because of me. What a beautiful gift that was. It delivered to me the final piece of my lesson. I should always help people in every way I can and should spare no effort when assisting them on their path. Yet I should never try to alter the course of their lives by shielding them or trying to save them from their troubles, because doing so would impede their invaluable experiences and the expansion of their souls. I was so grateful to our lovely neighbors. My lesson had crystallized for me.

It has been almost three years now since that regression, and that understanding created an incredible transformation in me. Now I have a different perspective on needing to rush in and save people. I have learned to allow, to admire, and to see the immense value and power in the unfolding of everyone's path.

∽ *Mira Kelley*

Mira again presents a classic regression experience and important divine truths. When you are open to these lessons and you trust the wisdom that guides you on your path, you will observe the synchronicities, the manifestation of grace, the helping hand. These events are not random. They are not coincidences.

As she struggled to comprehend her regression's message of allowing without interfering, Mira was led within hours to the scene that would provide her with the insight to understand—a scene as simple as two people being locked out of their room. I know the rooms at Omega well: there are no phones inside them, so Mira could not call for assistance. The paths are unlit, and to walk such a great distance in the pouring rain takes considerable effort. This was no small gesture of help on Mira's part. With a flash of recognition, she learned the nuances of her spiritual lesson.

Great teachers have always used such examples, scenarios, parables, and metaphors to help us understand their teachings.

As did Mira, Raymond had a flash of recognition as he learned his own spiritual lesson, although to him it felt more like an electric shock. In one day, his entire world was turned "upside down and inside out." You have already read his fascinating account of shared consciousness with a stranger, but now let us regress back in time to his first-ever past-life experience.

. FINDING HOPE .

Hope. If there is one predominant outcome of your trainings and experiences, it is that one is left with a hope that may not have existed before. For whatever reason, belief systems tend to be subjective and may be shaken by global or personal events, yet your trainings offer a distinct opportunity to add actual experience to faith or belief, yielding an outcome that may be rationalized but not denied. For me, that resulting and abiding outcome equals hope.

First, a little background. I am a licensed professional therapist in the state of Oklahoma, and I have spent twenty-five years working with chronic schizophrenia patients in an inpatient setting. I designed the behavioral system and had oversight of the program. Thus, as a behaviorist and therapist, you might say that structure was my guiding principle. What follows below is the universe's non-too-subtle method of saying, "Mr. Wilson, your structure is microscopically small, and the comfort and security that you have experienced within that structure is not where it begins or ends."

Approximately five years ago, I found myself in desperate need of quite a few continuing-education hours to renew my license as a professional therapist. Like many others, I typically wait until the last minute and begin seeking them in a panic. I do not recall how I found out about the seminar; however, I saw it as an opportunity to get the hours that I needed and didn't think much about the content.

My wife and I arrived at the Crossings in Austin, and the next morning, I joined many others in the first session. I was, needless to say, quickly convinced that I was in the room with a bunch of nuts when people began to identify themselves as angel therapists, Reiki masters, and so forth (terms of which I had never heard). I had the distinct feeling that I was in the wrong place. Raised in a quite strict, conservative Southern Baptist environment and subsequently having strayed from organized religion, I had not filled that slot with anything else. The result of this "religion void" was that I considered myself moral, black and white, and strongly attached to God on a personal rather than organizational level. In other words, I had God well defined and in a box that I created for him, and I was happy as long as he stayed within my parameters.

The first hour of the seminar had me ready to run out the door and not look back. However, at the break I told my wife of my misgivings and she said, "Look, you need the hours. You are already here, you have paid for the week, and you might as well stick it out." Reluctantly, I agreed. Shortly thereafter, Dr. Weiss did a group regression. I cannot emphasize enough that I closed my eyes with trepidation and extreme disbelief and caution. I would have bet the farm that my resistance would have prevented any hypnotic state. If I were ever wrong in my life about anything, this was the hands-down winner of that category.

I immediately found myself in a seashore village as a ten-year-old boy. The homes had thatched roofs, with a dirt and rock path winding between them. There were geese and dogs here and there running loose, the grass was green as green can be, and I was running and playing along the path. There were others in the village; I knew them but paid them no mind. I rounded the corner of one of the houses, and from up the hill behind me I heard a strong male voice call what I knew to be my name: "Joar," or "Johar." I stopped, he called again, and I went running to what I knew was my father. He was at our home near the top of the path, working on a large grinding stone that appeared to be a wheel. He was sharpening axes and swords, and I knew this was his job. It was clear that this was a Norse village.

In the next scene I was eighteen years old, and my father and I, along with many other Norsemen, were in a ship, sailing to a foreign shore for the purpose of attack and plunder. I stood in front of my father and said, without looking back at him, "I don't know what to do." He responded, "You will know when you get there." In my present life, I had seen pictures before of Norsemen and what they wore; however, it was while on this ship that I had the realization of what each piece of clothing was for. For the first time, I recognized that the arm bracelet was actually for defense against weaponry.

Then we were back in our own village, and my father was lying on a stiff-looking bed. He was dying from a wound that he had received while we were in battle, as I knelt by his side. Later, I had returned from another battle, and I lay dying, just as my father had. My own young son was kneeling by my side, just as I had knelt by my father. There, in response to "What have you learned?" I remember thinking, *We have not learned anything. Here we are, generation after generation, still fighting and dying, and my son will do the same.*

At this point, we were brought out of the hypnotic state. I was, for lack of a better phrase, freaked out. In the course of probably fifteen minutes, my world was turned upside down and inside out. Doubt and trepidation turned to a feeling of bewilderment in that I had no category or place to put this, nor any means of denying it, digesting it, or hiding it (any of which I would have gladly done). While Dr. Weiss did not press for whether or not the experiences were real, there was no question in my mind that they were and that my current life and future had been altered. All of a sudden, I was far more concerned about my own mental health than that of the angel therapy folks or anyone else.

Oddly enough, while this shook me to the core, it did not shake my belief in God; rather, it began an ongoing process of taking "God" out of myself and my childhood-created box and recognizing what eternity really meant. I left at the lunch break, and my wife could tell that something was wrong with me. In a period of three hours, I went from a black-and-white thinker to basically a man without certainty of anything. My belief system and limitations thereof had been shattered. There was no question that what I experienced had been true. My hypnotic state was Technicolor and as real as my hands are to me now. My prior knowledge of Norse life did not hold a candle to what I knew in the experience. My name was Joar (pronounced "Jo-har"), and I knew that it was my name. After returning home from the training, I looked for it on the Internet and found it on a site of ancient Norse names, as I knew it would be.

The following day found me between two worlds, and I went into the seminar thinking, *What next?*, almost as if I were someone sentenced to be thoroughly kicked and resigned to it. Sure enough, the next regression was more bizarre than the first. I went on to have a cosmic experience in which I became part of human evolution; a dream that allowed me to connect to the entire universe; and a shared experience with a complete stranger in which I could see the details of *his* regression.

I have worked for twenty-five years with medically fragile children and chronic schizophrenics, and your seminar allowed me some sense of peace as to the outcomes that many of these unfortunate folks experience. Little else has made sense. I came to your training seeking continuing-education credits, and I left with proof of universal consciousness. Most of all, I came away with a hope that previously was sadly lacking. It is my belief that if others could experience that hope, their world and personal view would improve, as did mine.

                      Raymond Wilson

I am grateful to whatever universal forces conspired to land Raymond in our five-day course. He is such a gift: a big-hearted, down-to-earth man who is doing truly difficult and delicate professional work. He came for the continuing-education credits and left having earned transform-your-life credits. He also transformed our entire group.

Even though Raymond's past-life regression was joyless and taught the futility of violence and war, he nevertheless came away with a sense of hope. With each subsequent experience during the week, his hope increased. Finally, he had encountered the answer to the purpose of his life and the awareness that an expanded vision of God and eternity actually existed. Life is not just a meaningless and continuous struggle to survive. As he will continue to describe in stories throughout this book, in only one week Raymond felt connected to the stream of existence, from the very beginnings of life on Earth, through Viking and other incarnations, into the entire cosmos and all of eternity. He saw and felt himself a part of the universal evolution and the indescribable wisdom that guides the whole process. He no longer felt separated or alienated.

Many people come to my workshops with an enthusiastic wish to remember a past life. They have read the books, they recognize the healing power of regressions, and they know that miracles happen. During these workshops, I often make the point that the people who have been dragged there by their significant others or well-meaning friends, who have no expectations or even interest in having a past-life regression, are often the very people who have the most vivid and compelling ones. Raymond, who certainly had his doubts about the nature of this work, is a perfect example.

He came only for the professional credits; in fact, were it not for the gentle convincing of his wife, he would have left the seminar entirely. Yet he had numerous powerful and deeply spiritual experiences.

Why does this occur? Our own expectations and desire to relive a past life can often get in our way. We may want it so much that we try to force the process and, paradoxically, we block it. However, with practice we can overcome any such obstacles. It is important to practice without any frustration and without any attachment to the outcome of a particular session. Don't say, "I *have* to have a regression," for that will only prevent it from happening. There is no need to put this kind of pressure on yourself. Just accept whatever comes to your mind, whether you are meditating, listening to a hypnosis CD, participating in a group regression, or working one-on-one with a therapist. There is a process and a wisdom at work. As you have already read, what you call this process—whether the Tao, or the way, or destiny, or any other name—does not matter. What does matter is that you trust it to guide you to wherever it is that you need to go.

Take your time and be patient. You may not immediately remember a past life but instead have a mediumistic experience, perhaps getting a message from the other side. You may have a physical healing, a remission of a troubling symptom. Every time that you practice, you are learning how to relax and how to let go of stress. You're helping your immune system and becoming healthier. These are extremely therapeutic benefits for your mind and body, and they are valuable in their own right.

The more that you practice without becoming frustrated, the deeper and deeper you will go. It may take weeks or months, but the gains are worth it. It took me three months until I could remember a past life. One of my patients tried for eight years before ever successfully regressing, but once she did, the results were incredibly profound. She has since told me that every minute that led up to those ancient memories was worth it. If your past-life recall brings you healing or spiritual growth or a sense of oneness and peace, then wouldn't eight years—or even eight lifetimes—be time well spent?

I have had many patients or workshop participants who, like the authors in this section, were able to achieve emotional healing simply by remembering their past lives. Their stories have stayed with me long after their regressions ended, and I have interspersed some of them throughout this chapter.

One such person was Yumiko, in this life a Japanese American physician, who remembered a past life as an impoverished young girl in London, England, several centuries ago. In the past lifetime, she had been the oldest child of six, and by the age of ten she was working very hard within the family. With no father present in her life and a mother who was often away at work, Yumiko had to raise her siblings, and as just a little girl she was taking care of many other young children and babies. She could recall her one dress and how it smelled because she couldn't wash it; she could see the people urinating in the street; and, especially, she remembered not having any soap. She had to wash with only water, but without soap, clothes could never be truly clean once worn.

She was forced to become a servant in a bigger, much grander house. This family had soap. Eventually, because she was treated so poorly by the "madam," she ran away. Not long afterward, she died at a young age of hunger, starvation, and illness, and she floated above and left the past-life memories.

Yumiko's next memory was of her childhood in her present life, in which she was the oldest of three children. She recalled an incident in which her brother's nappy, or diaper, had fallen off, which she then had to wash. But this time, she had soap! Her thought was *This was a "piece of cake."* Indeed, she was smiling as she relived this moment and thought of all the things that she was able to do as a child—reading, drawing—that she could never do as a child in her past life due to her extreme poverty.

While still in the hypnotic state, she explained to the group that she had learned to be happy about the small things, like a bar of soap. As she told us all, "Be grateful for and appreciate what you have, not what you don't have."

Yumiko's story teaches us that we should not take anything for granted and that we should recognize the blessings that we do have, no matter how small they may be. If we need little but appreciate everything, we will be much happier. As Lao Tzu said over two thousand years ago: "He who knows he has enough is rich."

After remembering two prior lifetimes in which she died alone, Tong could now, in her present life, fully appreciate the blessing of being surrounded by loving friends and family. Her story follows.

. LIFETIMES OF LONELINESS .

During my stay at your five-day training course, I had several regressions. In two of them, I died in a very lonely state. In the first life, I was a teacher who taught in a hillside primary school in a primitive and poor village. I was a single woman who lived alone. It seemed that I was not intimate with my students. I died accidentally on the hill, where wild dogs bit at my stomach. Nobody was aware of my death.

In the second regression, I was a reporter, and again a single woman. I worked hard and quite aggressively, but I again died lonely, this time in a train crash. When others who were either dead or injured were picked up by their families, I was still lying on the side. Nobody came to pick me up; nobody claimed my corpse.

In both of the cases, I was cool and reserved as a person; that's why I was rather lonely during the lives, and in the moments of death as well. But in this life, I chose to be a social worker. I go to people and offer help. I adopted two girls, not just to develop my own family but also to help, in a very intensive way, these two little girls. I have learned to give and relate to others, even if sometimes I have struggled to do so. And I am so happy with all of these people nearby. I know that in this life, I will never die alone again, with nobody around me.

∾ Tong

Tong's regressions demonstrate that patterns often reveal themselves in these experiences to illuminate our spiritual paths. She needed to express and to receive love, and she is doing exactly that. Tong is learning her lessons and finding out more about unconditional love. We are never alone—even if we forget this. And her choice of a social work career preceded the regression. She had intuitively chosen the path of love and service.

These were not Tong's only experiences. She shares more below.

. HOMEWARD BOUND .

My mother and father separated when I was six years old and divorced a few years later. They often had fights in the middle of the night. One day, I woke up in the morning and found that my mom had left, and her bed became vacant from then on. She had her new family soon after, and then so did my dad. I had grown up in a childhood with lots of loneliness and anxiety, lots of neglect. I have three sisters, but we were often left at home without an adult to look after us. As the second sister, I had to take care of the small ones by providing them with food or cooking them meals (later, when I could manage the task), and by doing the household chores when my elder sister was not at home. When I was in primary school, my mom would forget to take me home. I would stand at the school gate for hours, waiting for her with loads of loneliness, helplessness, and uncertainty.

At twenty-five, I got married, which I had longed to do. My husband is a colleague of mine in the same office, so we can see each other during business hours. He is a family-oriented man who gave me a sense of security after we married. However, I still found myself lonely whenever he was not with me, as when he worked late, went out for an evening class, or had drinks with his buddies. And I worried that he was not mature enough to manage his tasks or any challenges in life. This fear haunted me in a subtle way for a long time.

I also began, rather desperately, to long for babies of my own. I thought that then I would be wanted by somebody, and that I would always be with the kids if I could just have them. However, I tried for more than six years. I couldn't have one. It made me even more desperate.

In one regression I did with Dr. Brian Weiss's CD, I went back to an ancient time. In a bare, remote countryside, I was on my way home after a long war. I was a warrior with a huge body, like Hagrid in the Harry Potter books. I was dirty, hairy, tough, and strong, and I carried a large hammer as a tool for fighting. Walking with strength and speed, as if I were banging the land with each footstep, I was on my way home to see my wife and young son. It seemed that I had been walking for a long time, tired but still strong in every step. I was alone the entire way; there were only stones and some bushes in the surrounding fields. I walked and walked with nothing and nobody around.

When I saw my home, I became extremely excited and walked even faster. I opened the door to find my wife in a wooden hut, sitting next to a baby's crib. In the crib was my young son; I recognized him as my husband in this life. I got a flash: I was so worried about him not being strong enough to stay by himself and protect his mother when I was at war and could not be with them.

I woke up in the regression and realized that it was my own problem, not my husband's, if I constantly worried about him not being strong or mature enough. From then on, I stopped feeling anxious about him; I still nag him from time to time, but not in the same manner as before.

In another regression I did during the five-day hypnotherapy training class at Omega in New York, I didn't go back to a previous life but instead to the very first time in this life that I felt lonely. I was six years old and in China. It was a school day, and the weather was turning cold as autumn stepped out and winter stepped in. School had ended, and I stood at the gate, waiting for my mom to take me home. I waited and waited, but she didn't turn up. Seeing the students leaving the classroom and being picked up by their parents or the school bus, I became anxious. When all the students had gone and the buses had set off, I was left alone as darkness came with the evening. I stood on the street in front of the gate, which had already been closed. I was so hopeless. This was the first time in my life that I knew how loneliness felt.

In the hypnosis, I thought, *Why don't I try to walk back home by myself?* It was only fifteen minutes or several blocks away from where I was; maybe I could remember the way. I took a deep breath and started the walk back home. I was so excited; I was a bit scared but also a bit happy to leave the darkness in the corner of the school gate. As I took my first big step and set off for home, the scene changed, and in the trance I saw myself running through a long movie or film tape. The contents of the film were all of those situations in which I had experienced loneliness in life—and there had been many over my thirty years. I was growing older and older, from a six-year-old girl to now, as I ran through all those times. I was so happy and lofty. I ran as if I were flying, my shirt flapping in the wind.

I came back to where I was, to the room at the Omega training course, and understood that I was not the helpless little girl of six years old. I learned that I could do something by myself and for myself, that I have the confidence to make myself free from the darkness. For more than thirty years, I have been working and learning so hard to overcome all the challenges in my life, rather than waiting and relying on others or feeling helpless.

After that regression, I have never had that kind of lonely feeling again. And after a few years, I adopted two baby girls as my daughters. I realized that I could do something to make myself happy, instead of waiting hopelessly for pregnancy. All four of us in the family, and the grannies too, are so happy and pleased with the current situation. I think it might be the best time in my life. It certainly is the sweetest.

∽ *Tong*

The regressions allowed Tong to gain a sense of control in her life. She was able to recognize the past-life origins of her doubts about her husband's maturity, which permitted her to let go of her fears and anxieties.

Not all symptom-inducing traumas are found in prior lifetimes. Tong's feeling of helplessness was rooted in her present-life childhood. As she watched her subconscious display a series of scenes of her loneliness, she became empowered to take control and to be courageous. Adopting the baby girls represented, to some degree, her conscious decision to not be so fearful and passive, but instead to be active, hopeful, and happy.

Tong, from China, also demonstrates the universality of past-life memories and their powerful healing potential. The experience of prior lifetimes and of the after-death state is remarkably consistent, no matter which culture or religion is involved. People from wildly divergent nationalities and spiritual traditions are able to remember past lives that took place all over the planet. They learn the same life lessons. They are able to heal physically and emotionally, to repair their relationships, as Tong did, and to attain more peace and happiness in their lives. Early life enculturation and conditioning do not influence the content of the past-life recall or spiritual experience. We are all students in this great earth school. Does it really make a difference where our classroom is located?

Evelyn was an African American woman in her forties. She had a severe phobia of water and of drowning; although she didn't have any real clue to where this fear came from, it certainly interfered with her life. Her husband had recently bought a boat, which only intensified her fear. It had been his dream to own one, and he did not understand the depth of Evelyn's phobia. Her husband, who was outside my office during the session, was surprised to learn later that Evelyn did not even own a bathing suit—she felt that this would bring her one dreaded step closer to the water. She was also afraid that her fear of drowning was spilling over onto her three children, and that it would interfere with their pleasure in the water and in the new boat.

Evelyn's anxiety was so severe that she had traveled half the country to see me. Whenever she put her feet in water, she told me, it felt as if hands were pulling her into it. She was very, very afraid of being around water, but even more afraid of not being able to catch her breath. These fears seemed connected, but not necessarily so. I tucked this away in the back of my mind.

As I regressed her, Evelyn first went back to childhood memories. She recalled being an infant and hearing a loud noise, which had caused her to cry. As she continued crying, she couldn't breathe, and she was overcome with anxiety and panic. She saw her aunt and uncle with her, and they were terrified. Evelyn, as a baby, felt confused; she knew that her aunt and uncle were alarmed, she could feel their tension, but she didn't understand, at that young age, what was happening.

Evelyn then experienced a past life that had taken place several hundred years ago, in which she was an African boy of twelve or thirteen years. The boy, along with others from his village, had been captured by slave traders. His mother in that life was a spiritual leader of the people, probably possessing special powers and certainly healing abilities, but even she couldn't stop the tragedy of these young children being taken from the village.

In that same lifetime, Evelyn recalled the boy being held down by two white men, a boot on his throat. The men spoke a strange language. He was then "baptized," or cleaned, in a long tub with a mirror nearby. The tub was filled with water, into which the boy was being forced down. As the water came near his face, he gagged, choked, and found himself unable to breathe. It was truly terrifying. This baptism occurred before leaving Africa, which may help to specify which cultures were engaging in that practice, as there were others who did not enforce baptisms until these slaves arrived in the new country.

Her next memory was a vivid one of the same boy, around the age of twenty now. He did not know the rules of these strange white people, and he had merely said something, something not very significant, to a white woman. Rather suddenly, he was grabbed, his arms were tied behind his back, and he was placed on a chopping block and decapitated. Evelyn could see the image of his mother's face nearby; the mother had died, apparently, sometime before he had. She was talking to him and communicating a feeling of deep peace. This allowed the young man to become calmer. Afterward, he could see his head and torso separated from each other. But he—his soul— was all right. Evelyn observed clearly the disdain and aloofness on the face of the white men and women who were looking on. They didn't care. "So barbaric," Evelyn said. "How could people do such things?"

The boy's consciousness floated up to the clouds. He was feeling free, strong, and peaceful, and he could breathe. His earlier thought, immediately before the beheading, had been *I'll never be able to breathe again.* At the end of the session, after floating above the boy's body, seeing the mother's face, and feeling this peace, Evelyn told me she felt like skipping, and that she felt so much freer, lighter, and happier.

Before emerging from the session, Evelyn had another memory from her current life, an earlier childhood memory with her older brother. He was forcing her to go down a waterslide, and she remembered her mouth filling with water as she had difficulty breathing. This confirmed even more so that her fear was not just of water but of not being able to breathe.

After our session ended, Evelyn called her mother, who confirmed that when Evelyn was about six months old, she had cried so much that she had turned blue. Her mother had panicked, not knowing what to do, and she had run to the aunt's house with Evelyn in her arms. They were able to calm her down, and her breathing returned to normal as her blue color disappeared. We were both soaked in sweat; the energy, intensity, and visual details and emotions were so profound during this regression session.

Just a few days after our session, Evelyn was able to walk in a swimming pool, wearing a bathing suit—the first she had owned in many years—with no anxiety at all. She knew that there was nothing to fear. The fear had come from a long time ago; it was not of the present or the future.

Evelyn's phobia was virtually cured in only one session. Simply recalling the traumas in her childhood and past life was enough to allow her to let go of her symptoms. Her fear of water diminished, and her breathing was much improved.

As we let go of the past's negativities, and as we regard the future with no worries, we will be released from the constrictions of time. We will live fully in the beauty and freedom of the present moment.

In her past life as the young boy sold into slavery, Evelyn experienced firsthand the terrible effects of racial prejudice and inequality. Gabriella, the subject of the next case, also had important lessons to learn about the same subject.

· EMBRACING EQUALITY ·

When I first met Gabriella, I couldn't help but notice the sparkles. Her jewelry, sequined purse, and shiny, strappy shoes caught my attention, as most doctors that I meet usually don't wear such items. A well-dressed Caucasian woman with flawless fair skin, long blond hair, and the bluest eyes, she had a bubbly personality. Everything about her was sparkly. She was excited to begin the session; it shone in her eyes.

We talked briefly about why Gabriella had come for the past-life session. She wanted to understand the test-taking anxiety that had plagued her throughout her entire life. She tended to overprepare for major tests in college and even for state boards, but when it came time to take the test, the anxiety was always there. The secondary issue was that, as an only child, she had felt that she constantly had to strive to be the best. Although she had the desire to become a doctor, there was the added pressure to excel in her chosen field.

Gabriella regressed easily into the past life, but she was startled to land in the body of a six-year-old African American child standing in the middle of a cotton field. The tone of her voice became that of a little girl's as she spoke to me. It was not the color of her skin that surprised her; it was the dirty, threadbare rags that were her clothing, and the shoes that were too old and worn to even cover her feet. She was filthy from being in the hot cotton field all day. Her hair was in pig-tails, but they were frizzy and in a terrible state of disarray. Gabriella started crying at the condition of the body in which she found herself.

She looked up and saw herself standing beside a big lady with coal-black skin, the same color as hers. She smiled, comforted by the sight of her mama's thick cheeks and peaceful smile. Mama looked at her daughter, calling her "Sugar" and commenting on the heat as she continued to pick the cotton. Gabriella had the sudden recognition that this woman, in her current life, was her paternal grandmother, with whom she shared a close bond.

It was the mid-1800s in Jamestown, Virginia. Sugar and her mama, and others like them, lived in one of the many shacks situated on the back side of the big house where the plantation owner and his family lived. Mama worked all day in the cotton fields. Sugar didn't know where her daddy was; he had never been around. She did not like living there. "Mama keeps me safe from the white people who are mean and spit on me. Not all of them are this way. The white men—they think they are better, but they're not. They ignore me and are disrespectful to my mother, but not to Lily's mother or father."

Lily Williams was the young daughter of the plantation owners. She had golden-blond hair, blue eyes, and light skin. Her favorite color was blue, so her mother dressed her in blue dresses with matching ribbons in her hair. She and Sugar were the same age. Lily wore pretty, colorful clothes that were not dirty like those of the kids from the shacks. Sugar longed to wear clean, bright-colored clothing, to live in the front house, and be accepted like Lily and her parents.

Miss Anna, Lily's mother, was kind to Sugar. She let the girls play together down by the river. They swung from the rope swing into the water and sometimes held hands, like little girls do. But Sugar was aware that she wasn't allowed to do this when the other white people were around. "We like the same things," Sugar said, crying again. "I'm just dark. Dark skin makes it like I'm not equal. Lily's parents don't make me feel bad. 'Just don't let others know,' they say."

As the girls got older, Sugar would watch Lily go to the schoolhouse, dressed in her pretty clothes with her books in hand. She wanted to go with her but had to accept that such a thing would never be permitted.

The big house was a brick Colonial set on a large plot of land. It had the bulky, rich furnishings often seen in the homes of the wealthiest families of that period. Lily lived there with her mother, her father, and the house slaves who took care of the place. Miss Anna was a nice lady, somewhat plain-looking and fragile in health. She always regarded Sugar with kind eyes. A big man, Mr. Don Williams, Lily's father, wore his thick, silver hair pulled back into a ponytail. He was wealthy and owned the plantation and the slaves who lived there. Sugar would watch from the screen door as he sat inside at the table and ate. She wasn't allowed in but would wait there patiently for Lily to come out. Like his wife, Mr. Don was nice to Sugar. He let the children play together and even helped her learn how to read.

It wasn't too long before Miss Anna's health failed completely and she died. Soon after, Mr. Don remarried to a strict, proper Southern woman who didn't believe in the races' mixing and didn't allow the girls to play together or read anymore (Gabriella recognized the stepmother as her own current-life mother). Sugar grew up with the knowledge of what it felt like to be ignored, to not be seen, to not exist. It made her angry that people treated her this way just because of the color of her skin, but she knew her place, knew the trouble she'd be in if she expressed it. She wanted to grow up to be somebody, to make a difference, to live in the big house—to be accepted. Being able to read would prove to be invaluable to her.

Mr. Don and Lily secretly educated her. She missed Miss Anna, who was so kind. The lessons were kept quiet so that the stepmother wouldn't know of them. Sugar loved learning and reported everything back to Mama, who told her how proud she was that her daughter was smart enough to learn how to read. Sugar was a spirited girl who was learning to stand up for herself, learning to appreciate being seen and heard.

As the times changed, she changed with them. She felt the power of being heard when she and many other women and girls participated in a women's march. "What's right is right, what's wrong is wrong," she demanded, no longer afraid to speak her mind. "Women deserve to be heard. They will be heard."

Mr. Don granted Sugar her freedom, and her education on the plantation granted her admittance to medical school. She graduated as one of the first black female doctors in the state of Virginia and went on to open a practice in nearby Washington, D.C. She had a house just like "theirs," and the pretty clothes for which she'd always wished. Her doors were open to anyone needing treatment, whether or not they could pay. To her, they were all the same. Equality was as important to her then as it was to my client, Gabriella, who had always fought for this in her practice: equality, regardless of gender or skin color.

Sugar married a farmer who didn't have much education. It didn't matter to her; she liked him. They raised their three children together. She lived a long life practicing medicine and fighting for the rights of people until her death at eighty-six years old. Although she did not feel ready to end that life, her body simply wore out.

When Sugar passed into the light, she was greeted by many people, including Mama, who stepped forward to comfort her. Her guide explained to her that she had done what she had been born to do, which was to stand up for fairness and people's rights. She had proved by example that women could be and do what anyone could, regardless of money or race. Her growth had come through living both sides of equality and knowing what it felt like to be discriminated against based on the color of her skin. She hadn't let discrimination stop her, for she had become an educated black woman in a society where many white women didn't even work as doctors. And in her current life as Gabriella, she continues to help people. Her patients sense her courage and feel safe when she listens to them, while others are quick to brush them off because of the color of their skin. This is helping the residual effects of racism go away.

Gabriella's guide revealed that it was time now to let go of self-criticism in her current life. Her soul lesson was one of nonjudgment, yet there was still the feeling of being judged and of always having to prove herself. This was creating the added anxiety around test-taking; it was the same way Sugar had felt judged when sitting in a classroom for the first time in medical school.

The guide gave Gabriella a quick glimpse at another life in which she was wealthy and lived in an Irish castle. Many people of all different races lived there. She had pale white skin and wore beautiful things, and she treated people as equals in her kingdom. It was important to her that the workers in her kingdom know they were not second-class citizens, that everyone was the same regardless of their skin color. This woman was adamant about fairness and equality. Gabriella was shown the contrast to know that all of her past lives, although working through the theme of freedom and equality, did not have the same hardships that she had faced as Sugar. Her soul has lived both extremes, and she could now find balance with nonjudgment.

Following the session, Gabriella was ecstatic. She talked about the strong connection she has had to cotton plantations, which went beyond a passing interest. As a young girl living in the South in this current lifetime, her heart would cry out for the people on the plantations in the country near her home. But this time, she was born into a family of means who were able to give her a first-class education, nice clothes, and all the material comforts she didn't have in the life as Sugar. Gabriella loved beautiful clothing and jewelry but never judged those who couldn't afford them. Even as a child and in college, and certainly as a doctor, she had stood up for equality when she saw minorities being left out or treated unfairly.

Gabriella and her family (who were all part of the life as Sugar) have a special affinity for Williamsburg, Virginia, visiting regularly and even, in the case of Gabriella and her husband as well as her parents, becoming engaged there. Interestingly, her grandmother in this life, who was her mother in the life on the plantation, has always called her by the nickname "Sugar."

Gabriella's anxiety about taking tests is different now, because she knows that she's prepared and that the anxiety isn't coming from not knowing the material—it's coming from her lifetime as Sugar, when she had once before sat in a room of peers and been judged for the color of her skin. Knowing this has allowed her to "punctuate" the anxiety so that she can put peace around it, tremendously lessening the impact it once had in the past.

                                            ∽ *Bryn Blankinship*

We are all the same. We have been all races, all religions, all colors, both sexes, and many nationalities, because we have to learn from all sides. Leaving our bodies behind when we die means that we leave behind their skin colors, their genders, and their identifying features. We are souls, and souls do not possess such outer and transient characteristics. If everyone were to grasp this concept, racism would instantly disappear.

No soul is greater than another.

Unfortunately, even innocent children are not exempt from discrimination and prejudice. As a young girl, Sugar was prevented from attending school and playing with her friend. Donna, the author of the following story, remembered a past life as a child in the concentration camps. How many lifetimes will it take to learn the lessons of love?

. CHILDHOOD CONNECTIONS .

During a regression on your 2011 cruise, you led us back to a childhood memory. As you were telling us what you were going to do, I thought that I would go to a memory of when one of my little sisters was brought home from the hospital. However, I did not go there. Where I actually went was to a time when I was four years old, when Debra, another sister of mine, and I got our tonsils out. We were in the hospital and were put to sleep with gas. After a few days of eating ice cream and Jell-O, we were released. In order to leave, we needed to be wheeled out in a wheelchair. I cried and would not get in the wheelchair. My mother tried to get me in it by telling me I would be spanked when we got home. Sure enough, I was spanked.

You told us to move on to the lifetime that may help with the childhood memory. I felt gray—everything was gray. I couldn't see a thing. I felt enclosed and far away from anything. I was eight years old. We were asked to look at our feet and see what kind of shoes we had on. I had none; I was barefoot. I was being pushed in a wheelchair to my death in a gas chamber. When you asked us to see if there was anyone we recognized from this life, I didn't see any eyes, just the back of heads, and I cried.

I was a very active kid, so I always wondered why the wheelchair in my childhood scared me so much. Thank you for helping me to know what had happened. I enjoyed your seminars, and in each session I was able to regress. It has changed me. I understand more of my decisions and my path.

ᘓ *Donna Offterdinger*

We have all carried over fears, phobias, talents, affinities, and relationships from our past lives. In Donna's case, no rational reason existed for her panic attack and her reaction to the wheelchair when she was four years old. She had always wondered why she was so frightened. Her reaction did not fit. Once the past-life link to her gas-chamber wheelchair was understood, her behavior made sense. The phobia was extinguished—and it will never return.

Gail, who shared a somewhat similar past life as Donna, had severe symptoms of insomnia that completely resisted any kind of treatment. Once regressed, she found herself as a child in the concentration camps. Before being taken there, the Nazis, equipped with machine guns, had burst into her house while she was asleep. She awoke panicked and frightened, only to witness the Nazis shoot her parents. She had been killed at the children's camp as a young teenager. Gail had been serving her captors and "biting her tongue" because she had to, but when she went to her death she did so with dignity, showing no fear.

Shortly after remembering this traumatic lifetime, Gail's sleep difficulty disappeared, and it has not returned. Her insomnia was resolved because she knew that the sudden and terrifying awakening by the German soldiers was from her past life, not her present one. The initial or root cause of her issue was brought to consciousness; the past-life wound was healed. Gail can now speak her mind—her truth—without having to bite her tongue or hold back for fear of severe consequences. This also is of the past. Now she is free.

The author of the following story had to learn these lessons about holding back and standing up to those in power. She, too, once enslaved, is now free.

. OVERCOMING ENSLAVEMENT .

How could that be me? I asked myself. The woman that I was studying was someone whom I would never recognize as myself. Her body was deathly thin and wrinkled. She wore a burlap-type tunic that was held on her wraithlike frame with a rope at the waist. She looked eighty years old but was probably only in her forties. In contrast to her abject poverty, she wore a valuable gold ring with a deep blue, moon-shaped stone, about the size of a nickel. I had started this life as a young, beautiful, strawberry-blond girl. Only the harshest of lives and isolation could have caused this much change in one lifetime.

She loved to ride horses through the countryside and gardens. Because her mother was deceased and her father was unavailable to her, she rode freely—too freely. She was ignorant of the bands of men who roamed purposefully to conquer. The town dictator, a young man himself, had her kidnapped. Her horse was brutally killed. Her world changed permanently overnight.

David was the kidnapper, a man of influence in her town. After impregnating her, he had a wedding ceremony performed by the local clergy. Other men gathered around the couple to witness and guard them from onlookers who might interfere.

The baby was taken from her at birth. The woman was imprisoned until she became too unhealthy and undesirable to entice companionship, at which point she was threatened and beaten. Her life of enslavement to David was symbolized by her blue stone ring, which everyone who was connected to him was required to wear.

She became his deliverywoman. She transported valuable items, but she had become such an outcast in the community that no one would interfere with her deliveries. She might as well have been a leper. The townspeople always made a point to ridicule and mock her poverty and enslavement. She was glad to be left alone in her hut on the outskirts of David's property; it ensured a respite from the societal degradation and, worst of all, the constant threats of physical injury. Although her hut barely protected her fire pit from the extinguishing cold winds and mist, the fire was a greatly appreciated luxury to her starving body.

The most difficult of her tasks was going to retrieve from David the items she was to deliver. She had to pass by animal pens that housed small creatures who were used for torture. She saw them suffering from beatings and painful amputations. Worst of all was seeing the suffering but no longer having the feelings of empathy that would motivate her to release them. Her own suffering had dehumanized her to a state of dull existence.

Upon entry into the dictator's chambers, she showed her blue stone ring. She kneeled, expecting ridicule and abuse. It was common and inescapable. None of the abuse and horror affected her anymore. Her life was truly that of a victim. There were no choices or escapes unless she was to fight back, which would lead to death.

In the last moments of her life, I saw her squatting in front of a fire in her hut, the first one in many days. I could see and feel that her kidneys and other organs had begun to shut down due to starvation. She fell over next to the fire, and her heart stopped beating. It was a pathetic, unrewarding, invisible way to die.

As I left that body, I could see the mental enslavement that this body had contained. I had believed that it was better to do the work of evil than to fight back. I learned that fighting back and dying would have been better than living enslaved. Furthermore, complying with the dictator had caused him to become more entrenched in his power. I had nothing to lose by fighting back. I was going to die either way.

The familiar characters from that life and my present one were my mother, who died when I was nineteen and entering the adult world, and my father, who was emotionally unavailable and detached throughout most of my childhood. The dictator was my second husband, who was emotionally and physically abusive for the six months that my daughter and I lived with him.

The lessons I learned in that lifetime were that it was okay to be young and beautiful. Young people need support, guidance, and possibly protection as they face the adult world. I learned that it was better to fight back than to live in enslavement. Compliance is a slow death.

The things I brought to this lifetime are a deep love and empathy for animals and for those marginalized by society. I spent twenty-five years of my life working as an advocate for abused and disabled children. I brought a deep bond and protection for my daughter, my one and only child. I appreciate the choice to leave enslaving situations, and I exercise compassion for all, knowing that we are all shaped by our experiences—both past and present.

$\sim$ *Alice*

The debts accruing from Alice's past life will be an obligation to David and his cohorts. To abuse, torture, and humiliate or kill animals and humans creates karma that must be resolved. They will have to make it up to Alice and the others. Our lessons are of compassion and kindness, not hatred and violence. We are, in reality, spiritual beings.

It is never too late to reorient yourself to your spiritual or destined path and to learn these lessons afresh. Wherever you are now is simply a point in time, and the future is multifaceted, changing and growing as you do. No matter how we may have acted in the past, every moment presents another opportunity to treat one another with care and consideration. Even David, at the height of his tyrannical reign, could have decided to become a kinder person, to open his heart, to increase his understanding, to choose love. These are all things that we know so well yet don't always put into practice. A person who acts out of ego or strictly from intellect can wander very far from his path, but a person who acts from the heart cannot, for the heart will always pull him back. Listen to your intuition, for that is the open heart at work. Choose the loving path; it will never lead you astray.

The most difficult lifetimes often provide the opportunity for accelerated spiritual growth. Such lifetimes do not automatically imply negative karma from the past. Perhaps you chose the difficult life so that you could progress the most. Alice's existence as the deliverywoman was very hard and heavy, but she learned invaluable wisdom and, in her present incarnation, she is manifesting great empathy, compassion, and loving service. The most beautiful flowers often arise from seeds hidden and nurtured by the cold, wet mud.

During a recent five-day workshop, an attendee named Stacy told me that her breathing was becoming more labored, even though she had not yet experienced any past-life or childhood memories. She thought that pollens or other antigens might have been in the air, for grass, flowers, and trees were blooming in the early summer warmth of the New York Hudson Valley, where the intensive workshop was taking place. She also told me that she had a history of asthma. I suspected that other factors might have been at work, and so I chose to regress her in front of the group. I picked a volunteer to hold a microphone close to Stacy's mouth so that the group could hear any words that she spoke during the regression. Another group member, a surgeon from Alabama, was hunched forward in his seat as I began the hypnotic process. At the time, I did not know that my "randomly" chosen microphone holder, sitting right next to Stacy, was a speech therapist and an expert in respiratory conditions.

Stacy's first memory was of choking on a slice of apple when she was a young girl. She had panicked at the time, but her mother's response was to give her "bread balls" to help ease the apple down to her stomach. This failed to help and perhaps exacerbated the situation. The little girl couldn't breathe, and she became even more terrified. Finally, her mother held her upside down by the ankles and firmly whacked her on the back, dislodging the apple slice. I asked Stacy how she had felt just before the apple popped out from her throat.

"Frightened to death," she responded.

This phrase became the bridge that I used to uncover her past life. "When were you 'frightened to death' before?" I asked. Her answer quickly followed.

She had been an eleven-year-old boy who had fallen from a rowboat into a lake. The currents carried the boat away from him, and they carried him farther and farther from the shore. He finally became too fatigued to swim any longer. Nobody was around to hear his cries for help. He drowned, gasping and swallowing the lake's water.

Stacy's breathing was raspy and rapid, but when the boy's consciousness floated above his body and above the lake and the clouds, it completely changed. She could inhale so freely and deeply now, with no difficulty at all. As I awakened her, her breathing remained relaxed, and it continued to be so even as the audience asked her questions about her experiences as the choking girl and the drowning boy. She had a strong feeling that her respiratory problems would not resurface.

The microphone-holding speech therapist had also noticed the remarkable changes. Clavicular breathing, she had observed, had become diaphragmatic. The surgeon agreed.

Past-life outcomes shed light on present-day phobias and conditions. Once those are remembered, similar situations will never frighten you "to death" anymore.

Renata's story, below, provides more support of this concept.

. FROM FEAR TO FULFILLMENT .

I had memories of a previous life from a very early age, and I realized instinctively that it was not wise to discuss such experiences with anyone.

I was born in Italy in 1952, and I lived in a seaside town. My mother used to take me to a beach that was reached by passing through a strange concrete construction. We had to go up some narrow stairs, walk along an elevated large sort of corridor, and go down the other side onto the beach. The sides of this corridor had a parapet, above which was some barbed wire to prevent people from reaching more industrial constructions at a much lower level. I can't give a precise description of this place because I was too young. It was a sort of electric plant. Many years later, I asked my mother when it was demolished and she told me that it was in 1954, which means I was only two years old when I saw it.

Every time we passed there, I felt in a strange state. I was very uneasy, yet at the same time I was somehow eager to go as the feeling was so intense and mesmerizing. The heat was great in summer because the sun fell directly on the concrete. When I passed there, I had a kind of film playing in my mind: images of a woman and a man running in the direction of the beach, she in front, the man behind at a short distance. She was dressed in dark colors and had long, curled hair. I knew they were running toward the seashore, escaping something, and that they were in serious danger. Somehow, and I can't explain how a girl less than two years old could know this, I was that woman and the place was North Africa.

I also had recurring dreams or, rather, nightmares. One was of a gray sea and a wave that suddenly rose and submerged me. Sometimes I was on the beach, sometimes I was near the concrete pier, but the feeling was always of total panic, and I would wake up. The nightmares were still recurring when I was a teenager and, little by little, more details appeared: the landscape of a bleak beach, men in dark uniforms chasing us with guns, both me and my companion entering the water. I swam under to find protection from the bullets, but the waves became higher and pressed my head against the bottom of the pier until no space was left for me to breathe, and I drowned.

I had a curious problem with my clothes. My mother sewed many of my clothes, not only because she had studied dressmaking but also because I needed long zippers that no ready-made dresses had. If I wore a sweater, she had to help me by passing it over my head, keeping the collar far away from my face. Once, we went to a dressmaker, and my mother forgot to tell her of my problem. When the lady passed the dress over my head, I panicked and started crying and moving my arms frantically, unable to breathe.

I used to go to the seaside in summer, and although I had learned to swim, I was always wary when lying on the sand, because I had the illogical fear that a wave might suddenly come up and submerge me. For this reason, I never lay with my back to the sea. On one occasion, when I was approximately eighteen, I was lying closer to the sea than I normally did, and a much longer wave reached the towel of a friend. She laughed; I was frozen with terror.

At nineteen, I enrolled at the university. One day, during the lunch break, I was in the large faculty library. It was November and the weather was unusually mild, so the windows were open. The tables were very large, with a dark surface covered by a sheet of glass that reflected the images. Suddenly, while my mind was elsewhere and I was lulled by the gentle noise of the fans in the background, looking at my notes and books on the table, I glimpsed the reflection of my face—but it was not my face anymore, at least not the one I knew. It was me, but I was someone else. There was, again, this young woman in her late twenties or early thirties, with long, curled hair and dark eyes. The room was different, much smaller and with a large fan turning. There was a friendly French police officer speaking to me. He told us that we had to run away because the Gestapo had discovered our names. Then I had a more detailed flashback of the beach, our fear, and our death. This experience was strong and took me totally by surprise.

One early September after that, I went to visit a friend at the seaside. For some reason I didn't take my clothes off on that occasion, and we started to walk along the water line of the beach, chatting and laughing. The sea is shallow in that part of Italy, and the long beach is divided, from time to time, by tiny constructions of rocks, like minipiers. I was walking there, joking with my friend. I had just come back from some congresses where I had presented two papers and I was telling her how happy I was that they had been received so well. I felt light and enthusiastic. Suddenly, we reached one of these rocky constructions that, to be passed, required that we walk into the sea with the water reaching our ankles or shins. When I reached the farthest point of this construction, my body stopped working; I had no control over it, and my mind was filled with silent panic. I couldn't proceed; I was stuck and unable to speak. Later on, my friend told me that I was as white as a ghost. She came to me and took me slowly back to a rock nearby, where I sat down for a while. The first words I could say were, "So it's all true." Obviously, she didn't understand, and I had to explain.

For a few years, I had tried to cut off the idea of reincarnation and pretend that all that had happened to me in the past didn't have any specific meaning and was nothing. That experience hit me. I think that what triggered it was the fact that I was fully dressed and not in a swimsuit. The rocks, even if protruding for only a couple of meters into the water, were enough to recall a much bigger and more frightening pier. The experience was so intense and so unexpected, so out of the blue, that I went back to pick up all my old books on reincarnation, bought more, and started reading again.

These experiences have formed and directed my entire life in one way or another. I have dedicated my personal and academic research to the themes of reincarnation, symbolism, and the journeys to the other world. My Ph.D. itself was based on the study of a medieval journey to the other world, and I started to read books about hypnotic regressions and tried techniques with some like-minded friends. I qualified as a hypnotherapist and studied more advanced techniques that can be applied in past-life regressions, and for a few years now I have run a private practice of hypnotherapy in London. Although I deal with all sorts of problems that hypnotherapy can help to solve, I am happy to say that past-life regressions are among the most common techniques I use with my clients.

∾ Renata Bartoli

Renata's memories, which were so powerful and persistent, pushed her to dedicate her work and her life to helping others using past-life regressions. She knew that her experiences were real. She vividly felt the fear and paralysis that past-life traumas could cause in the present, and she is helping many people to overcome and release similar symptoms.

Of course, not all regressions are the result of using hypnotic techniques. Renata experienced flashbacks and glimpses when she was near or in the water, through recurring dreams, and even in the faculty library, where she observed her face from her prior lifetime. Her subconscious mind was giving her the information and tools to heal her in the present and, additionally, to steer her toward her soul's work. Renata had the wisdom and the courage to respond to her mind's urgings.

I too had to overcome old belief systems, skepticism, and left-brain conditioning to dedicate my work and my life to help people in the very same way as Renata. I have been so fortunate and so blessed to find this path.

Judith, in the final story of this chapter, was also a self-described "left-brained and skeptical person." Even with her doubts she remained accepting and curious, and she was able to have a wonderfully healing and intuitive experience at a workshop. This incident helped her achieve not only the elimination of a physical symptom that had long troubled her but also a greater emotional understanding that has forever changed her life.

. THERE IS NO NEED TO JUDGE .

I consider myself to be primarily a left-brained and skeptical person. I've been trained as a scientist and veterinarian and had been in practice for over eleven years when I attended my first Brian Weiss seminar. A friend of mine and I had read *Many Lives, Many Masters,* and we were so excited that he was coming to Fort Lauderdale that we got our tickets nine months in advance and counted down the days. We were both impressed that a well-respected and well-trained doctor had made such an incredible discovery, and we knew that he had faced ridicule and scorn from his fellow scientists and physicians by coming forward with this "mystical" technique to rapidly solve unexplained pains, complicated phobias, and hang-ups.

I had ordered Dr. Weiss's CDs soon after reading several of his books. While listening to *Through Time into Healing* one night, I had a completely unexpected and vivid vision of a woman looking into a gilt-framed mirror. Her face was long and thin, white and European in appearance, and I had the impression of late 1700s-style clothing and headdress. Her curly, reddish-brown hair framed her face. In the next flash of vision, "my" hand was trailing along a curved wall, like a tower, and I just knew that I was in a formal garden. I came out of the trance, completely amazed that I, who don't even remember my dreams, could have had such an experience.

The day of Brian Weiss's seminar finally arrived, and my friend and her husband met me early at the convention center. We were excited to see Dr. Weiss in person, and we had great seats in the second row. We were amused by the number of people who had brought blankets, pillows, and yoga mats (turns out, they were the smart ones). During the first morning regression, an incredible thing happened. At first, I saw nothing significant during the lifetime. When asked about the death scene, I felt the blade of the guillotine and observed a head rolling into a hateful crowd. The head came to a stop, and I experienced in first person (as if I were the head) a thirty-something, dark-haired woman leaning over the head, jeering and yelling insults at it. Quite separate from my thoughts, as I was engaged in the scene, I heard a message: "You know what it's like to be judged." I awoke out of the trance, and the chronic neck pain that I had suffered for over four long years was instantly gone. Afraid to believe it, I kept rolling my neck and bending it every way—no more pain.

After the break, we chose a person we did not know personally and exchanged personal items. I chose a woman in a seat close to me. She held my cell phone; I held her ring. During this exercise, Dr. Weiss instructed us not to filter the images that we might receive. My only distinct vision was that of the triangular window of a small speedboat, the type that is on the side of the windshield. I had a bare impression of a lake, with mountains and forest in the background. We came out of the trance, and I told her what I had experienced. She listened and said that it really didn't apply to her, but her aunt (who was visiting from up north and who was about four seats away from us) lived on a lake surrounded by mountains and forests, and she had a small speedboat.

My partner then told me that almost the instant she was into the trance, she had an almost overpowering scent of facial soap—not unpleasant, but very strong. She said that she kept seeing this white bird soaring around. Her aunt overheard her and said that she had had the exact same experience: an overwhelming scent of soap, so strong that she was sniffing the people around her during the exercise, trying to figure out where it came from. She too kept seeing a white bird floating and soaring around, and she heard the message, "There is no need to judge."

Excited about these incredible things that had never happened to a studious and often unimaginative person like myself, I took the opportunity to stand up and address the people in the audience as I told them about this experience. I also told them what it meant, which I will reveal in a minute. After I sat down, the two women in front of us turned around and said that they had both smelled the powerful scent of soap, and that they kept hearing the message, "Let go, let go." The smell that I had always associated with my paternal grandmother, who had died several years previously, was her Dove facial soap.

A week before the seminar, I had been thinking a lot about my life and the things I wanted to change. One of my many flaws is judging others too harshly, without considering facts and on very limited information. I suspect it's rooted in my loving but judgmental midwestern family, which would teach us children about life around the dinner table by speaking of the kids in other families who had turned to drugs or had gotten pregnant. They would always say, "We're so glad you would never do anything like that. We've got great kids." Of course, they meant to teach about staying away from drugs and premarital sex, but it had the unintended consequence of making us more judgmental, because there was little discussion of compassion for the actual person who turned to drugs or of the circumstances that may have led them down that path.

I had also been thinking of my beautiful and loving paternal grandmother, Sally, who was alone in the last years of her life after caring for my grandfather, who eventually died of Alzheimer's disease. She lived alone in a big house and did not get many visitors. I would come once a year to do genealogy research in the tiny town of Mount Olive, Illinois, which had been founded by my father's family and which had a rich history in old newspaper clippings. Each morning, I would rush out of the house to get in as much research as possible before the library closed. I remembered, quite clearly, an incident in which my grandmother, shy and sad, had said to me, "Of course you wouldn't want to spend the morning with an old lady like me." I had hugged her and told her that it was my last day there that the library would be open, so I had to go, but that I would see her that night. I have always regretted that choice. I could have learned just as much about our family history by listening to my grandma, and I worried that she thought I didn't love her. I know that Grandma used this seminar to tell me to let it go, and that someone was giving me a very good lesson about not judging others.

My life has changed dramatically since the seminar. I have a terrific story to relate to others, but more important, it stimulates interest in a subject of which most people are not even aware. Past-life therapy changed the way I think about others, made me a more loving person, stopped my terrible neck pain, and gave me the tools to help and teach others that the most important lesson that we can learn on this earth is how to love each other unconditionally.

Judith Oliver

Judging others and judging ourselves are negative and even harmful actions, often leading to great pain and discomfort. Judith eventually learned the ultimate lesson, that of unconditional love. We keep incarnating to learn this great truth in all its manifestations.

We see so much in Judith's story. A person can be scientifically trained, logical, and skeptical, and still have rich, life-transforming experiences. Just keep an open mind to the possibilities.

Consciousness does not end with the death of the physical body. Judith was not in her severed head in the guillotine scene; her consciousness was hovering above and around it, observing the people near her and the actions of the dark-haired woman. She received spiritual instruction even as she experienced the mob and its hatred. The lesson about judging others and allowing yourself to be judged transcended lifetimes. As a bonus, remembering the guillotine trauma instantly healed Judith's chronic neck pain in her present life.

Throughout time, we will meet with our loved ones again and again, either on the other side or back here in the physical state. Judith's grandmother seemed to be present, her soapy scent perceived by many people at the workshop, reminding Judith of her love and of the lesson to let go of judgment and of guilt. In the end, only love is real.

· 5 ·

Healing Physical Symptoms and Illnesses

Having past-life experiences often allows people to discard more than their fears. Physical symptoms or disease can disappear as well. Such events point again toward the validation of the concept of past lives, because imagination and fantasy do not cure chronic illnesses.

Physical healings can be dramatic and rapid, permitting the patients to throw open the jail doors of disabilities and leave behind the constricting conditions that have been robbing their lives of joy. They are healthy again, mobile again, free again. And a healthier body allows more energy, more time, and more opportunity to accomplish the tasks that we were sent here to do.

The body and the mind are interconnected. What heals one often heals the other. Stress can bring about physical disease as well as emotional illness. Remembering the past-life trauma or event that has resulted in a current-life physical symptom is often enough the cure. A deeper spiritual awareness inevitably accompanies the physical healing. If a wound to a past-life body has resulted in a similar symptom in the present-life body, the connecting consciousness, or soul, must be the bridge between the two. And we are that connecting consciousness, reaching across the years to manifest once again in physical form.

The soul itself is never harmed, because its nature is spiritual and eternal. But the pain and disability of physical illness can cause great suffering and can hamper the soul's progress during the incarnation. Past-life regression therapy can help people get rid of pain, breathe normally again, regain impaired or lost physical function and energy, and heal their hearts and other organs.

Here are some fascinating cases of people who were able to regain their health by remembering the past-life causes, and other origins, of their current-life symptoms.

. BADGE OF HONOR .

The very first regression that I ever conducted proved to be quite meaningful. It took place at Omega in the summer of 2006. The client was an attractive woman in her early thirties, with long blond hair and blue eyes. She had sought me out, saying that she would appreciate it if I practiced performing a regression on her. After issuing a caveat of "no promises," I agreed to do it that afternoon. She lay down on some pillows, and the regression took place on the floor in the big meeting room. Many others were in the room, practicing, performing, and receiving regressions. It was, to say the least, very loud in there.

The woman was single but had a long-standing relationship with her boyfriend. She had read *Many Lives, Many Masters,* although she did not know what to expect as far as the regression was concerned. I didn't know what to expect either. Her life in New York City seemed to be going pretty well. She did have one physical complaint: a back pain that she had had for most of her life. An accurate diagnosis of the cause of the pain had never been made. I wrote that down, making a mental note that it might be significant for the regression.

Though I had not met or studied with Brian and Carole previously, I did have an essential grasp of how they conducted regressions. I had read all of Brian's books to that time and had listened to a number of his regression CDs. I still needed to read from the script with which I was provided in the class, in order to stay on track, direct, and respond appropriately. Yet I was not nervous. Perhaps this was because I had been a psychotherapist for a long time by then. I guess you could say I took to regression like a duck to water; it came quite naturally to me, and I enjoyed the process.

As I started to deepen the client for the third time, I began to see signs that she was very deep already. All of the muscles in her face were relaxed, and the muscles in her body seemed to be as well. Soon, she had a beautiful remembrance of a birthday that she had as a young girl. She remembered her party, her friends who had come, and all of the gifts that she received. She couldn't get over how young and attractive her parents were. I let her linger there, drink it all in, as it were, and then began to take her back in time to another life and to an important memory that was waiting for her.

Her eyes began to dart from side to side rapidly beneath their lids. I knew that was a sign that she was beginning to see things. She found herself in a wooded area, a deep forest. Looking down, she saw that she was wearing moccasins and carrying a bow. A quiver of arrows hung on her back, and she wore a deerskin breechcloth. She was a handsome young Native American male, and he was hunting. She began to mix expressions of how beautiful the woods were with statements of concern about being there. She was nervous, for it wasn't safe. I asked why, and she replied that there were two tribes fighting for the rights to the hunting ground, and that braves from both tribes had been killed in those woods because of this ongoing battle.

She had spotted a deer and was about to draw her arrow when she suddenly felt another arrow strike her hard in the back. She fell to the ground. An Indian brave from the other tribe had shot her. Petrified with fear and in excruciating pain, she was on the ground, anticipating his approach. Her level of distress and perceived pain were palpable and so great that I performed my first-ever float-above technique. It worked. As she began to float above and observe the scene, she became significantly calmer, and she began to describe what was happening below.

The Indian who had shot her was now approaching with a tomahawk to kill her. Though she was now feeling no pain and reflecting a sense of detachment from what she was seeing, her breathing was still somewhat shallow and rapid, and her face began to show tremendous fear as he came closer.

"He's going to finish me off with the tomahawk," she cried. To her amazement, as the other man lifted it to strike her, he changed his mind and slipped the weapon in its sheath. He bent down, lifted her up, and threw her over his shoulder. "He's taking me back to his village, maybe to torture me or kill me there. Perhaps he wants to mock me, or make some kind of example of me, or hold me hostage," she said.

The attacker carried the wounded brave into his village, described as a circle of about twenty tepees with a large common area in the middle. He brought her to the tribe's medicine man. As the village healer began to carefully remove the arrow and apply some kind of herb poultice on the wound, the chief of the tribe approached. He was not pleased.

"Why have you brought this brave to our village? He should have been left dead in the woods as an example to the others who would steal our hunting ground," the chief said in anger.

The young brave replied that these same Indians had long been at peace with their tribe, and that they should not be killing their brothers over hunting ground. He said he would not kill them, and that they should kill them no more.

The chief was furious, and he asked the medicine man to finish off the wounded brave. "I don't kill my brothers, I heal them," the medicine man answered as he began to wrap and cover the wound. "This brave is right. We should not kill our brothers, but make peace."

I moved the client forward to the next important event.

"It has been a few days, and I am well enough to walk. Several braves are walking with me to my village, on the bank of the river," she said. Their party was well received as the wounded brave explained what had happened and why they were there together: to make peace between the tribes.

The chief of that tribe was visibly moved and thankful for the safe return of this brave. "Yes, this is good," he said. "For too long, too many of our braves have died for this hunting ground. In the past, we have shared this ground. We will share it again. We will smoke the peace pipe and make war no more with our brothers."

The treaty was agreed upon, the killing stopped, and the land was shared. The wounded brave made a complete recovery and lived a long life, during which he was somewhat revered as the instrument of peace that he had become. His passing was a calm one, surrounded by his family and friends.

I asked the woman to identify the lessons of that lifetime.

She seemed to be crying tears of joy. "We had long lived as brothers in this place, helping each other and sharing our lives in many ways. Killing our brothers was wrong. The way of love is the only way. I was an instrument of peace in that life. What a beautiful lesson I lived to tell. I believe that I have been wearing my wounded back like a badge of honor in this life. Somewhere deep inside, I remembered this life and this honor, and I became confused."

"How were you confused?" I wondered aloud.

"The place where my back hurts in this life is the same place where I was struck with that arrow so long ago. I became proud of that wound and would not let it go. I wore it like a badge of courage and honor, as it brought life and peace to both tribes," she said. Big tears were rolling down her cheeks.

I asked if she had learned that lesson, if she could be proud of what she had helped the tribes achieve but now set down this pain, as it no longer served her in this life. Yes, she said. She was ready now.

"Go ahead, then, find a place to set it down and walk away from it. You don't need it anymore," I directed her. "It was something to be very proud of, but it has served its purpose. Let it go. Lay the badge down."

Still crying, she described how she laid the badge down on a stump in the forest, near where she was shot, and walked away.

I then brought the client out of her trance state, gave her some time to readjust to the room, and asked her to tell me how she felt. She sighed heavily and said that she felt lighter, relieved, and very calm. Then, with a curious tone of awe, she added, "My back doesn't hurt anymore. Not at all. It feels like I really did lay down that badge of honor. I don't hurt anymore!"

I was equally amazed. "Yes, you didn't need it anymore. You realized where it came from and you let it go. Wonderful," I said, "wonderful." I would regress seven others that first week at Omega, but none were more significant or memorable than this first.

                                             ∾ *Michael Brown*

Michael is a talented and empathic therapist, and he did an excellent job with his first regression. I always stress the importance of the life review because it sets a perspective for the entire lifetime as well as identifies connections to the current life. In this case, the physical healing of the client's chronic back pain was immediate when the causal connection to the arrow wound was discovered. This pattern of healing pain, psychosomatic disorders, and other physical symptoms and illnesses is a classical one, and it is often encountered when doing past-life regressions.

The life lesson of choosing peace and compassion over war and violence is both common and important. We are here to learn about love, kindness, and cooperation. We must renounce hatred and prejudice and overcome our fears. I would not be surprised if, in a subsequent past-life memory or dream, Michael's client were to recognize the warrior who chose to spare her life in that ancient time as someone in her current life. The karmic bond between them is considerable. Such bonds help us to establish soul-mate connections.

Indigenous cultures often possessed great intuitive wisdom. They understood about balance and harmony, about moderation and simplicity, about caring for nature and the planet. They hunted for food and shelter, but they knew better than to eliminate species and to ruin living environments. They used only what they needed and did not accumulate obsessively or excessively. When we look at these cultures through the lens of past-life therapy—a kind of regression archaeology—these noble traits and values consistently emerge. It would benefit us to remember our roots.

In indigenous societies, shamans and other healers used natural substances to treat their people. As organized religions gained control, such healing practices became very dangerous for their practitioners. A thousand-year Inquisition transpired. Valarie's story, which follows, depicts this long and dark nightmare.

. INQUISITION ILLNESS .

A call from the soul generally comes in one of two ways. For some, it is a knowing that grows into a deep conviction and leads to action. For others, it feels more like a whap on the head or being shaken until your teeth rattle, which serves to wake you up. This is what happened for me when I first read *Many Lives, Many Masters*.

Fully engrossed in the wonderful stories, I came to the end of the book and flipped to the final page, where Brian's address jumped out at me. In that instant, I had a moment of déjà vu, when not only did I clearly see myself in America training with him but also experienced a deep knowing that I had found my soul's purpose in regression work. I suddenly felt sure that this was what I was here to do.

It was no small feat to pack up, leave a family, and venture off to the other side of the world on my own, but soul calls cannot be ignored. I can still remember the amazement of some of the other participants at his professional training in Rhinebeck, New York. "You've come from *Australia?*" they queried in disbelief. Although there were over a hundred professionals there from all parts of the world, I had traveled the farthest.

During this training, I was to experience a most powerful healing that took me completely by surprise. Brian was conducting stage regressions with selected audience members. How I longed to be one of them, but with so many of us eager to volunteer, he was only able to do a limited number of demonstrations before encouraging us to practice in small groups.

Visualize over one hundred people in a hall filled to capacity, with small group regressions going on everywhere, and you can imagine the noise level. I was feeling disappointed at not having a personal regression with Brian, and when it was my turn to be regressed, I clearly remember thinking as I lay down on the hard floor, *Yeah, like this is really going to work with all this racket going on*. I was acutely aware of all the background noise as one of the women in my group led me through the induction process.

My mind was wandering to different parts of the hall, hearing snatches of conversation here and there, when suddenly I felt my body jerking and my head turning to glance over my right side. I was to find out later that I had not moved my body at all at that point.

In some amazement, I found myself looking down at the wooden wheel of a cart as it was jolting along a cobbled street. At the same time that my subconscious mind was registering this, I was clearly aware of my conscious mind thinking, *Ah, that's why it's jolting, because it's carved out of one solid piece of wood; they couldn't get it perfectly round in those days.* It was most bizarre to be experiencing something on one level and understanding it on another, and yet in that moment it felt like the most natural thing in the world.

Shortly after, I became aware of an uncomfortable feeling of restriction in my legs, as if they were bound or tied in some way. Afterward, the women in my group told me that I was rubbing my two legs up and down against each other, as though I were trying to free them. Although I was unaware of this at the time, it later made perfect sense.

Apparently it was the Inquisition, and I was being taken on a wooden cart to be burned at the stake as a witch, simply for practicing my healing arts. Strangely enough, I wasn't scared, just angry. How dare they punish me (and many others like me) for trying to help people who needed healing! I was frustrated by their stupidity rather than the act of violence itself, and I was aware that this feeling was directed specifically at the men.

I have a vague recollection of flames and lots of jeering faces. Ten years later, the details are not as clear, but the experience itself is as vivid now as it was then.

The whole experience seemed to last a few minutes; I found out that it had taken almost an hour. The restriction in my legs was indeed because they were bound with rope. What was even more amazing to me was that I had suffered very badly from psoriasis for the last twenty years, particularly on my legs—at the exact place where I had felt the ropes rubbing. In fact, I was so embarrassed about it that I always wore long pants rather than skirts or dresses, because it looked so unsightly.

After the regression, my facilitator, a wonderful woman who was also there as a participant, told me that she felt intuitively that my anger with men was linked to the rash on my legs. Thankfully, someone had the presence of mind to suggest taking a photograph of my legs for future reference. I am thrilled to be able to enclose a recent photo, taken some ten years later, which show my legs almost completely healed. The healing process started immediately after the regression, and it continued until they cleared, about six months later.

Interestingly enough, I still experience a slight reoccurrence whenever I get stressed, which serves as a timely reminder to let go of any negative emotion surrounding my experience.

I am now a regression therapist working from Perth, Western Australia, and seeing many similar experiences in my own clients. Brian's belief that our experiences are held within our cellular memories makes perfect sense when I reflect upon the emotional and physical healing that I, and many of my clients, experience during regression work. Once the memory is released and made conscious, the healing seems to automatically follow in most cases.

I have even had a case of spontaneous healing from long-term pain in the breast, despite the fact that the woman I was regressing doubted that her experience was real. She later wrote to me to tell me that, to this day, her symptom has never returned.

෨ *Valarie Coventry*

This is a wonderful account of the power of past-life therapy. Valarie's summary is so simply and clearly stated: "Once the memory is released and made conscious, the healing seems to automatically follow in most cases." Psoriasis can be a very difficult condition to heal, but Valarie was able to accomplish such a feat just by remembering. In her case, she did not need medication, light therapy, or any other treatment. When using past-life regression therapy to treat illnesses or symptoms more severe than psoriasis, conventional treatments can be continued while the client is experiencing the regressions. This is the essence of complementary medicine—the use of simultaneous therapeutic modalities. It does not matter which technique is the more effective one, as long as the cure is achieved.

Valarie's regression demonstrates other features of a classical and real past-life experience, in addition to the remission of symptoms. Her sense of time distortion (an hour seemed like a few minutes) is a sign of reaching a deep level of relaxation and concentration. At this level, fears can be dissolved, and physical and/or emotional healing can be obtained. Ambient noise did not interfere, for her subconscious mind recognized the opportunity for healing and disregarded distractions. You do not need a sensory deprivation chamber to reach this deep, altered state. Also, her conscious mind was observing and commenting at the same time that she was experiencing the past-life scenes. She understood about the wooden wheel, yet she stayed in the highly focused state. Valarie's case is a good one to reread and contemplate because it genuinely reveals the nuances and essence of past-life regression therapy.

. ANCIENT ALLERGIES .

It all began when I was enjoying a bowl of homemade taco soup at a nice local restaurant and began experiencing immediate rhinitis and eye-itching. Thinking that I had come into contact with an allergen, I took a Benadryl and left the restaurant.

Once I arrived home, my allergic reaction had turned into full anaphylaxis, and I had difficulty breathing. My face was red and swollen, my throat was closing quickly, and I began to panic. An emergency room trip was necessary, and by the time I arrived I was in deep anaphylactic shock and could not breathe. The nurse triaged me into the trauma room, not even stopping to ask me my name, started two IVs, called the respiratory technicians to give me breathing treatments, and administered epinephrine. I had all sorts of doctors and nurses at my bedside. Once I received the treatment, I became well fairly quickly. This was so frightening because I did not know what had caused the near-death reaction but, as a nurse, I knew that due to the timing it had to have been something that I ingested.

The next day, I returned to the restaurant and spoke directly with the chef, who was very helpful. He handed me individual baggies of the spices that he used in the taco soup, which I took to the allergist for skin testing. I had such a violent reaction to the cumin during the test that the allergist had to administer epinephrine in his office. He stated that he had never seen such a reaction to a spice.

The allergist sent me to a research center in the hopes that they could figure out the severe reaction to cumin. After a week's worth of all sorts of poking and prodding, they could not determine what exactly was causing the reaction. They too had never seen anything like it.

Over the next six years, I had some five anaphylactic reactions in different cities and from eating different foods that the waiters or chefs promised did not have cumin but that actually ended up containing it in the flour or as one of the spices. This was verified after I had to be admitted to the emergency room. Truly, this was life-threatening, and even more troubling was the fact that cumin can be hidden in any prepared food or any type of spice. As a result, I began living on salad and ice cream. Meanwhile, I was so determined to do something to help myself that I contacted nutrition experts and allergists and e-mailed anyone and everyone that I could. I even thought that my anaphylaxis might be due to my breast implants, and I read volumes on the immune response to silicone. I had the implants removed, thinking it would be worth the chance if it helped. Unfortunately, shortly after I underwent surgery to have them removed, I experienced another anaphylactic reaction to food that, unbeknownst to the chef, contained cumin.

Desperate for any type of alternative treatment, I turned on the television one day and saw Dr. Weiss as a guest speaker on *The Oprah Winfrey Show*. As he talked, for some strange reason my ears perked up and I listened. Something just spoke to me, and I looked up past-life regression on the Internet. I purchased two of Dr. Weiss's books and read more about this phenomenon. Another year or two went by, and I located a seminar in Chicago at which Dr. Weiss was going to speak. My daughter and I flew to Chicago, but after attending three past-life regression sessions with Dr. Weiss, nothing happened.

The last session at this seminar was "Channeling with O'Brien." At the time, I did not even know what the word *channeling* meant, but as we had two hours before our plane left to fly home, we went to this session. My daughter was chosen to pose a question to O'Brien. When she inquired about my anaphylactic reactions to cumin, he replied, "Oh, I know, and she is also allergic to two other spices." My daughter asked how we could treat it, and O'Brien replied that I would need past-life regression because I had been killed by this spice, unintentionally, in two past lives. I was shocked.

I was able to locate a woman in Houston, Texas, who could help me work through a past-life experience. In one former life, I was about five months pregnant and feeling very nauseated. My neighbor tried to help with my symptoms, offering me some spice and water. I remember that my dress was white, the bed was made of wood, and the house was a log cabin with dirt floors. It was probably sometime in the nineteenth century. I was in my early twenties, and we were the only two who were home at the time. The woman made a mistake and put too much cumin in the water to try to settle my stomach, and it resulted in my death. I felt so guilty that I had killed my baby inside me that I cried. The past-life regressionist asked me to locate the baby's soul, but I could not. I realized then that I was not really pregnant, as I had thought. It was a tumor, but back in those days there were no tests to determine this, and because my abdomen was getting bigger I had assumed I was pregnant. Once I knew that I was not responsible for ending the life of my baby and that indeed it was a tumor, I felt fine.

I went back to the allergist for a follow-up skin test with cumin, and this time it was negative. Every single previous skin test had been positive. In fact, he had me get some Mexican food with cumin and eat it in his office while his nurse was personally assigned to observe me. There was no reaction. This was amazing; I felt like I had a life again. Indeed, discovering my past life gave me my present life back.

ᴄᴏ *Sandy*

Not being too familiar with cumin myself, I did some research after reading Sandy's story and learned that it is one of the oldest and most widespread spices. Although commonly used in chili powder and curry, it is, as Sandy knows all too well, found in a number of unexpected places: cheese, bread, liquor, medicine, and perfume.

In South Asia, the tea made from cumin seeds is a traditional remedy for gastrointestinal problems and indigestion—and morning sickness. Sandy in the nineteenth century, who believed herself to be pregnant and who suffered from stomach pain, was given cumin tea for exactly these reasons, but Sandy from the twenty-first century had no idea such practices even existed.

Trust the process. Sandy did indeed need to remember a specific past life in order to cure her severe cumin allergy. She flew to Chicago, but the therapist who would eventually orchestrate the healing was in Houston, Texas. To get there, she had to turn on her television and find me on *The Oprah Winfrey Show*. Then she had to fly to Chicago, try three group regressions, "coincidentally" drop into the channeling session later that weekend, and have her daughter picked to ask a question, which confirmed the past-life causation. She went to Houston and learned the specific details; the life-threatening allergy disappeared, even to a direct challenge in the doctor's office.

There is a wise, loving, and infinitely compassionate intelligence guiding all our lives, all the time. Our deep intuitive wisdom can access this process, can discern the direction, and can be in contact with the divine.

In a past-life memory that took place in Norway several hundred years ago, Margaret fell off a plow. She had never been there in her present life, but she knew it was Norway. She fell backward onto her upper shoulders and neck, at the place where they meet at the back of the head. Her shoulder and neck pain in this life, which was severe and disabling, had disappeared by the next day.

Natalia remembered a past life as a child in Europe centuries ago, one in which she had to hide her psychic abilities, healing skills, and knowledge of herbs. Her family members were also forced to conceal their talents, for they would be killed if the authorities discovered them. Years later as a young woman in that same life, she spoke out and was burned at the stake, confirming the dangers of going public at that time. In a connected past life, she was killed on the rack for being a "witch," merely for healing with herbs. In her present life, Natalia's significant joint pain improved after these two memories.

I received a message from an Australian woman telling me that she had been afflicted with severe arthritis in her hands for over a decade. She was resigned to living with the pain. After attending my workshop in Brisbane in 2011, she had no pain in her hands—nothing. The healing, she said, had been powerful and intense.

Another person who had also attended the very same event in Brisbane wrote in with her own story of healing. As a Hindu, she had learned about reincarnation early on; however, she had never known that meditation and past-life regression could actually heal. This woman had suffered from asthma since childhood and daily relied on her inhaler. A month after the workshop, she had recovered from this ongoing illness. Quieting the mind and opening the doors to the past can literally help us to breathe easier.

People who remember past-life memories or have spiritual experiences are often able to heal or to greatly ameliorate acute and chronic physical ailments, including arthritis, migraines, asthma, uncontrolled bleeding, severe pain, joint problems, and even ocular stroke. The people who have written the following four stories come from incredibly divergent backgrounds and cultures, yet their stories are strikingly similar.

. HEALING MIND AND BODY .

I have read all of your books, and they changed my life. Around 2003, I was on a faith breakdown because of many things that happened. One day, my mother's coworker gave her your first book, saying that she might find it life-changing, and he was right. We both read it, and I believe that she and I grew in every respect.

I had an accident in 1998 that almost killed me. I was close to losing my left leg. For a long time, I asked myself why it happened. I saw myself in a past life in which I died very young because of an accident that severed my left leg. I lived in a beautiful hacienda-style house. I knew the people around me: my mom was my older sister, and my cousin was the middle sister. Also, my grandmother was our mom; I believe that is why we are so close and loving to each other. I saw how I died; I saw all the preparations that were made for the funeral. Later, I found out that what I had seen was traditional for wealthy families in Spain around the year 1800. After my meditations, I realized that having deep scars from the accident in this lifetime was not the worst thing that could happen. It has helped me deal with the pain to a point that it does not bother me anymore.

On another occasion, I saw myself as a young lady in a big, castle-like house. I had a sister that I recognize as my oldest cousin. I knew my dad; he is my father in this life. He was a powerful person. I had a fixed marriage with the man who is now my husband. I felt as happy as I am now. At first, I couldn't make any sense of it; later, I was told that it was a response to a question I had had for a long time. It was true: I always asked myself if I had made a good decision getting married. Since then, I don't feel that insecurity.

I went to your Orlando workshop in 2010 with my mom and cousin, who flew from another country to be there. That day, I had the occasion to permanently get rid of a pain in my left hip that had been bothering me for months. Since then, I have practiced the meditations every time I can, and they have helped me with the arthritis in my left knee.

∾ *Jessica*

Jessica's "faith breakdown" has been reversed because of her courage, her motivation to help herself, and the therapeutic power of her regressions. She has not only been healing her left leg and hip but also uncovering past-life connections to many family members. Her private questions were being answered; her doubts and insecurities were being resolved.

Physical issues were repaired through regressions in the case of Maria's client as well.

. MIGRAINE MEMORIES .

I am a social worker who has been doing hypnotherapy and past-life regressions in my private practice work since I attended one of the weeklong Omega trainings in 2001. I am passionate about opening people to the existence of the afterlife and to their immortal souls. In addition to individual sessions, I do workshops and local TV and radio shows to let people know about our work. I always use this story as an example of healing through past lives.

David was a thirty-five-year-old man who came to see me as a last resort. He had been suffering with severe migraines since the age of twenty-two, when he joined the navy. He had tried conventional medical treatments, to no avail. The migraines affected his schooling, his jobs (as he lost time at work and would ultimately lose the job), and his career. We uncovered three past lives in which he died from a blow to the head.

In the most significant one, he was in the navy during the Spanish-American War. He had served on a ship in the Caribbean, shoveling coal. When he was twenty-two years old, his coworker accidentally hit him in the head with the shovel, leaving him paralyzed and in a wheelchair. He was discharged and lived another year in excruciating pain and depression, until his death.

David's migraines improved significantly after the regression, and they have become more manageable. Each area of the head where his migraines occurred in this life corresponded to one of the three blows that he had suffered in past lives.

Maria Castillo

Migraine headaches have plagued mankind for millennia. Although effective new medicines have been developed, all medications cause side effects. Remembering past lives is noninvasive and has no side effects. It allows migraines to be alleviated while spiritual insights and wisdom are being achieved. David has greatly benefited from this approach.

Dr. K. C. Vyas, who shares his story with us next, did not perform past-life regressions on his patients, as Maria did. Instead, he used all the tools in his arsenal as a surgeon here in the physical plane to help heal them and then asked the heavenly realms for a consultation. There is so much more to these miracles than modern medicine can even begin to explain.

· GUARDIAN ANGELS ·

My daughter is a clinical psychologist from India who has trained in the United States. She has read your books, as have I. Once, she told me about guardian angels. In case of difficult situations, we in India call on God and others, such as Hanuman ji, Bheru ji, and Ganesh ji, to come and rescue us. I would like to share one experience that I had with these angels.

I was operating on a gallbladder case. After I removed it, there was torrential bleeding from the liver bed, where the gallbladder is attached. Within a minute, the patient lost five hundred milliliters of blood. I packed the bed. Only one unit of blood was available. I could not know the source of the bleeding, so I packed and prayed. I invited the guardian angels to help and rescue the patient. She was moved to the ICU, where her situation was managed.

After seventy-two hours, I took the patient for a relaparotomy to remove the pack. With all precautions, I reopened the abdomen and took the pack out, and the bleeding occurred once more. I repacked and prayed for the angels, calling to them for assistance.

To my surprise, the bleeding stopped. The area became absolutely dry, as if no bleeding had ever occurred. To this day, I do not know the source of the bleeding. The patient survived, thanks to the guardian angels.

I had another case in which I operated on an elderly male for a bleeding duodenal ulcer, performing a laparotomy and duodenotomy to ligate the bleeding vessel. On the fifth day, it leaked; this would normally lead to a duodenal fistula with high-output fluid loss and death. In the night and on the next morning, I prayed to Almighty and asked him to come and seal it or else put his thumb there. It was done. There was no leak, and the patient was later discharged. He is alive today.

Prayers are heard. The whole universe conspires for the well-being of the patient.

∽ K. C. Vyas

Grace is the intervention, the reaching down from heaven to earth, by a wise and loving divine force in order to help us in some way. Is this force what we call God? Perhaps all energies and manifestations—people, animals, plants, rocks, anything in physical form—come from one supreme source, whether you call this source "God," "a higher power," or any other name. And so we are all born from the divine, for the divine is in every atom of our being. Can angels reach down too? Perhaps all higher beings are intermediaries from God to earth and are all manifestations of the source energy. If angels are the children of God, then we are the grandchildren. To approach everybody and everything with compassion and caring concern is to recognize the common divinity that we all share.

Another remarkable case of a physical healing is presented by Miriam.

. PERFECT VISION .

I had an ocular stroke in my left eye approximately four years ago. I was, at that time, driving back and forth between my home in Stuart, Florida, and my daughter's home in Port St. Lucie. My daughter is a full-time attorney who had just given birth to her first child, and Grandma Miriam was the caretaker. We would meet at the courthouse at eight in the morning; she would give me her baby, and I would care for him all day. It was an ongoing ritual, one that I treasured. However, the stress involved with driving on I-95 so often evidently took a toll on my left eye, which had previously been injured. The prior injury had occurred about thirty years ago, when

I was teaching at a high school. I was crossing through the large gymnasium when a basketball hit me in the face. During this same time period, I was involved in a car accident, which also could have added trauma to this eye.

I have had quite a bit of trouble driving on I-95, as the ocular stroke affected my vision so that I saw only large, wavy, gray, horizontal lines going across the left eye. I could not see out of it. When I asked the doctors about my vision, they said there was nothing that could be done.

I attended your workshop at the Tampa Convention Center. You had us do an exercise that involved relaxing and getting rid of pain. I returned from Tampa to my home in Stuart that Sunday evening and discovered that I could see out of my left eye. I no longer have the wavy strokes. This eye certainly does not see as well as the right eye; however, driving home from Tampa was a breeze, and I wondered why. Now I know!

∾ Miriam

In my workshops, I repeatedly help people reach deep levels of peace and focused concentration. At these depths, fear and illnesses can be dissolved. Body and mind become incredibly relaxed. Healing through past-life recall, or by enhanced perspective and understanding, or in other ways, frequently occurs. Sometimes the removal of symptoms is so subtle that the person is not aware until hours later. Miriam had suffered from a constant lack of vision in her left eye for several years until one afternoon at a workshop in Tampa, when she could see again.

The eyes are said to be the windows of the soul. A person's eyes may be bursting with wonder and enthusiasm, looking upon each experience as an adventure, seeing everything afresh. This may be one of their first go-rounds here on the earth, and they delight in its spectacles. The eyes of an old soul have seen it all before, and they are vast libraries of time immemorial. You might look into the eyes of an infant, born mere minutes ago, to find that she is a thousand years old. Their limitless warmth and wisdom belie her true age. And, with a sudden electric jolt, the eyes are often quick to inform us that that stranger is a soul mate, whereas the mind is slower to recognize this truth. "Eye contact" is actually soul contact.

Imagine how much our eyes have seen throughout our incarnations: the horrors, the beauty, the bliss. They have watched as time is traveled, transmuted, transcended. They have surveyed the terrain of every country on every continent, of the slopes of the moon, of the face of God. They have glimpsed enlightenment and perhaps, with each successive lifetime, held its gaze longer and longer. For eternities, they have looked down at our bodies—first this one, now that one, and then another one entirely— knowing that this is not who we are. As we enter the hypnotic state during a regression, we close the eyes, and that is when we begin to see.

With all that we have rested our eyes upon in our many returns to human life, it is no wonder that afflictions from a past life can manifest in them. Miriam's sight was restored after participating in an exercise at my workshop, as was my daughter Amy's, whose story concludes this chapter.

. SIGHT UNSEEN .

As the daughter of Brian Weiss, I have been asked many times about my own regressions and if I have discovered all my past lives. The truth is, although I have been to hundreds of my father's workshops, I rarely have any experiences. Perhaps it's because, to me, that's just Dad up there. Or perhaps it's because I have memories of being six or seven years old, sitting at my brother's baseball games while my father attempted to hypnotize me into clucking like a chicken. In any case, I've come to expect that when participating in one of his group regressions, I will not relive a past life but will probably have a most relaxing nap.

Several years ago, I was working at a hospital in Philadelphia that was devoted to the holistic treatment of breast-cancer patients. Many of the staff, some of whom were Reiki practitioners, had come to work at the hospital because of its dedication to complementary medicine. Needless to say, if they were not already familiar with my father's work, they were certainly the type of people to be open to it. So on a visit to see my brother and me, my father was kind enough to hold an intimate in-service at the hospital for all its employees.

The one workshop where I would be least likely to have any kind of regression experience would be one in a professional setting where I was quite conscious of being surrounded by my coworkers and particularly my bosses. So, of course, that's where it happened. Before I go any further, let me back up and give you a little medical history.

When I was twenty-five years old, I went in for a routine eye exam because I wanted a new pair of glasses and my prescription tends to need tweaking every few years. I was mystified when the technician told me that I had a cataract. I'd always associated those with people who were—I'll try to be tactful here—well over the age of twenty-five. She recommended that I have it looked into immediately. I can remember sitting in the parking lot afterward, calling my parents on my cell phone and saying, "I have cataracts?"

I saw several ophthalmologists, had numerous tests done, and even had state-of-the-art photographs taken of my eyes. All were in agreement: I had cataracts, a few actually, and they were congenital, meaning that I had been born with them. That was puzzling to me: for a completely different concern, I had had extensive testing of my eyes done as a child, and no cataracts had been found then. Surely if I had been born with them, they would have been discovered at that time or at least at some point prior? In any event, over the next few years it seemed that every time I would have my eyes examined, more and more cataracts as well as a variety of other eye issues would pop up; I was told that some of the more severe ones could even result in the permanent loss of my sight. No one was really sure why I had these conditions, and they would gently tease me about being their youngest patient. By that point, I had become a little anxious. What was going to happen to my eyes? Why was it happening so quickly? And why did I seem to suddenly have the eyes of an old man?

When my father was conducting the group regression at the hospital that day, he asked the attendees to think about a particular physical illness or symptom and to go back to a past life that would explain it. We had recently been discussing my situation, so I caught his eye and he smiled; that instruction, while certainly relevant for most everyone in the room, had been intended for me. Still, I hardly expected to go back to a past life or see more than a glimpse of one, as I had never done so before despite many years of trying.

Much to my surprise, I immediately saw myself as an old man living in the Middle Ages, perhaps in the fourteenth or fifteenth century. I knew that I was in the forests of Germany or France; it was difficult to tell, not because I couldn't see it clearly, but because I lived so deep within the woodlands that man-made boundaries were irrelevant. My name was "Althrimus" or "Althrymus," although I've never been able to verify that a name like that existed. I was around fifty or sixty years old, with a long, worn face and white hair. The small, stone hut in which I lived was circular, with a thatched roof: there was only one room, and it was exceptionally simple yet cozy. (In my present life, I've always felt at home in little cottages or rooms that others might find confining.) I could see myself venturing out into the woods every day, collecting stones and leaves and herbs and then examining them or placing them around my house. The neighboring townspeople called me a "wizard," although I was far from intelligent and hardly in possession of any special powers. In truth, I was developmentally disabled. They simply saw me spending so much time with natural objects and assumed that I must have been using them for magic. They didn't understand; I could not have cared less about people, much less influencing their behavior. I was no more a wizard than a little boy out in the dirt, picking up worms. A more accurate term would have been *naturalist*.

I never went into the town. I lived alone and rarely communicated with other people. My home was the forest, and I was content there. I was a simple man, and nothing pleased me more than being by myself, puttering around in the woods and in my house. This made me smile during the regression, for I recognized that some of these characteristics, although not to such an extreme, had carried over into my present lifetime. But the townspeople, believing that I was up to no good, formed a mob and came storming with their torches into the forest, burning down everything inside and around my house: not just my possessions, although they consisted of little more than my collections of rocks and jars with oddities inside them, but all the forest around me, those beautiful trees, those friends of mine. I had been inside my hut at the time and had been forced to flee from them, running away and leaving my home and my life as I knew it forever. However, before I escaped, the fire had permanently blinded me. I could see the man standing before me and pulling down his lower lids to show me his eyes, which had been covered over in a milky-white film.

Oh Althrimus, I said inside my mind, overcome with compassion for this man who was so deeply sad and grieving. He was I, of course, but I was seeing him from the twenty-first-century perspective of our soul. The man that I was then was consumed by his psychological pain. He could not understand why other people would purposely cause him such devastation, he who never had contact with them and wanted nothing more than to be left alone. He literally would not hurt a fly; I know this, for he spent his days seeking them out and befriending them. Perhaps he couldn't wrap his mind around it because of his intel-lectual disabilities, or perhaps because it's simply impossible for a mind to wrap around senseless brutality. As "stupid" as I may have been then, the villagers were the ones who acted out of ignorance. It wasn't the loss of my home or my sight that so strongly overwhelmed me: it was the knowledge that these townspeople were willing to destroy my life over some ill-conceived witch hunt, some mistaken impression that I was performing sorcery or evil, concepts that I could not even fathom. Even though far worse things happen to people all the time— even now, in this day and age—I was bitterly angry and self-pitying, and clearly not averse to playing the victim.

Althrimus never overcame his feelings of sheer despair. Like quicksand, they engulfed and swallowed him. My heart linked into his and I felt his pain as though it were my own, which, of course, it was, although at the same time it was not. I sat there in the chair in front of all my coworkers, tears streaming down my face as I cried in compassion.

It was then that my father asked the group if there were any messages to be learned from the life that we were experiencing. In response, Althrimus kept pointing at his useless white eyes. "Sadness clouds the eyes," he told me.

The message's double meaning instantly struck me. A cataract is, of course, a clouding of the lens of the eye. Althrimus's eyes had physically clouded over as a result of having been burned; my eyes had physically clouded over as a result of having been Althrimus. He had never let go of that heavy sorrow, not even after he died, not even after he reincarnated into the body that I now inhabit. As a result, I too have allowed it to cloud my vision of what Earth is like, of whether people are good, of whether I am safe, of whether life is painful. Certainly in this lifetime I have had my own share of sadness, as has everyone, which sometimes felt like it would never dissipate. Maybe I had been letting that dark, intractable cloud continue to hang over my head, to obscure my vision, in this life. Maybe my eyes were indeed broken, although not in the way that I'd understood them to be.

As meaningful as this connection was at the time, I basically forgot about it. Then, a few years later, I was fortunate enough to get an appointment at Bascom Palmer, a nationally recognized center for ophthalmology. The doctor, a renowned specialist in the field, was able to examine my cataract. This time, however, the description was very different.

"There's only one cataract," she told me, "and it's not congenital at all. It was the result of trauma." She drew a picture of my lens for me on paper, showing me how some unknown traumatic event had damaged my eye. I didn't have to worry; it wouldn't grow anymore because it was a "once-in-a-lifetime event," as she put it. She couldn't have had any idea that that lifetime was in the Middle Ages. It wasn't affecting my vision, she added—and it wasn't going to. (Sure enough, six and a half years after my initial diagnosis, when I went for another prescription-tweaking eye exam, I was told that I had no cataracts at all.) How funny that I had heard so many times that this was something I had been born with, but after remembering a past life in which I was blinded both literally and metaphorically, it had now become the opposite. It seems both impossible and yet perfectly possible that the past-life recall may have been responsible for this reversal.

Interestingly, when I was becoming certified in hypnosis some three years after the regression at the hospital, I learned how to hypnotize myself. One day, I became curious whether I could, in a self-induced trance, revisit Althrimus and talk to him. So I did. I met with him in his little burnt hut as we sat down and caught up on the past seven hundred years. I filled him in on everything that he and I had become. I told him how I played the harp, and his face lit up because he knew what a harp, that common medieval instrument, was. I told him how I liked to write. Althrimus was not intelligent or educated enough to ever know how to read, much less write. He was absolutely beaming, his face bursting with pride as he heard that his future self was literate. But perhaps the most fun and challenging part was telling him how I enjoyed photography as a hobby. It taxed my modern brain to try to explain to him what a camera was and how it worked. He was fascinated by the concept, his expression growing intense as he, this man from the Middle Ages, leaned forward in his chair to listen and to imagine what a photograph might possibly be. In this life, I like few things better than being alone out in nature, photographing the birds and flowers, and Al was delighted to know that his love of the woods had lived on and was now actually being recorded for posterity.

He and I are still learning how to see the world clearly. It has been a process that has spanned centuries and lifetimes, and it may take even longer. But I think we would both agree that we are ready for the clouds to be lifted from our eyes.

∾ *Amy Weiss*

From the time that she was a baby, Amy could light up a room. Her light was soft and soothing, an inner light, more like a paper lantern than a fiery torch. Her light was gentle compassion, and she always tended to animals and nature. As she gained knowledge, her physical eyes cleared. But the eyes of her heart were always clear and open and, like an eagle's penetrating gaze, could see through deception and hypocrisy to a person's inner core. Our hearts see what our eyes cannot.

Nearly eight hundred years ago, the Zen monk Dogen Zenji wrote: "Approach all things and all beings with a face of kindness." His words were wise and true then, and they remain so now. From the beginning of human history, kindness has been recognized as a supreme virtue. When our hearts open and overflow with benevolence, love, and compassion, mankind reaches its highest potential.

Althrimus, a simple man, was able to feel and express kindness to everything in his environment, to animals and to all of nature. He was not distracted by education and intellect. Like a child, he was able to maintain his native innocence until the violent mob robbed him of his joy as well as his sight.

To rob people of their happiness and joy is a terrible act. To nurture people and to help them achieve peace, happiness, and the fulfillment of their dreams is a divine one.

"Amy" is the spiritual essence, or soul, connecting her lifetimes. She is not a particular body or mind; rather, she is the continuing and eternal essence. She is immortal, as are we all. And so Althrimus, at the end of his lifetime, never really died. Only his body died, but he lived on, reincarnating as Amy later in the twentieth century. To recognize ourselves as the soul, not the body, changes how we perceive our deaths as well as the deaths of our loved ones, because we are always being reconnected, in spirit and on Earth. The next chapter depicts our immortality very clearly and shows how the awareness of eternity can loosen the suffocating grip of grief.

. 6 .

Letting Go of Grief

G rief can be so devastating and painful that it sucks all the joy out of life, making everyday functioning an unbearable burden. It literally takes your breath away. Ten years after the death of my first son, Adam, I learned, in my quiet office as Catherine began to remember her past lives, that we are souls and not just bodies, that we are all eternal and will be reunited with our loved ones. But I did not know these things when Adam died.

Adam's unexpected death in 1971, when he was twenty-three days old, turned out to be a guiding force in my work. I grieved after the death of my father also, but more so upon losing Adam, for the loss of a child is an aberration from the natural order of things. All one's hopes are dashed; the heart is torn. The pain is immeasurable and unspeakable. I know its depths firsthand, so I can empathize completely with others who are going through the process. Since that time I have learned about the continuity of consciousness after the death of the physical body. I have learned that our loved ones live on, that they are simply on the other side, and that we will meet them again and again. When the fear of loss and death is removed, grief ceases to be so suffocating.

These five stories demonstrate how acquiring spiritual wisdom can heal grief and restore peace and inner calm in our lives. They remind us that love is never lost. Past-life memories, prenatal and infancy memories, and mystical experiences are just a few of the ways in which this knowledge can be gained. Perhaps reading the words in this chapter is another.

Once the terrible burden of grief is lifted from our shoulders, we feel lighter and more alive again. I have lived this process, and I know the gratitude of being revived.

Let these stories breathe life into you, too.

. A VAST EXPLOSION OF LOVE .

My husband, Richard, and I had a stressful marriage and four great children. When he retired as an airline pilot, we moved to my home country, South Africa, to the small town of McGregor in the Cape wilderness. Here, surrounded by mountains and the beauty of the wild veldt, I was looking for something that I grandiosely called, to myself only, "the meaning of life." I found the five books that Dr. Weiss had written. With joy I read and reread them; there was an immediate resonance. This was truth; this was the all-loving, all-embracing meaning that I had sought. My husband said, "Lee, you are being weird."

For a few years afterward, we lived as we had before—not unhappily, but making the best we could of it. I went away for six weeks to visit our children and when I returned, Richard was different. He too had read Brian's books. With delight, we found that we could now talk openly together about anything, and the following months were the happiest that we had ever shared. We were able to say that we loved each other unconditionally for the first time, and we both began the changes that were necessary, but now possible, together.

In 2002, we went to France to look after the house of our oldest son, Will, when he and his wife were away. The joyous relationship continued and grew. We went to Andorra, and at dinner in that lovely country beneath the high Pyrenees, we talked of the utter joy that we both felt. Richard said to me, "If I die tonight, Lee, everything, everything is worth it for what we have now."

Richard died two days later of a massive heart attack. I was with him in the ICU at the hospital. His last words to me were "I love you forever" and a whispered "We *won*!"

Our two older sons flew in, and on that midsummer Sunday we held each other and roared our grief, rocking and saying nothing all day but Richard's name. That evening, Will went to walk his dog across the lane, and James, our second son, offered to accompany him. As they passed the gate, I heard Will say, "Dad built these gateposts for me last year," and James clung to one and stayed there.

Alone on the patio, I rocked and cried, took a small, shuffling step, and stepped into total peace. I held my breath so as not to break it, but I had to breathe again. The peace remained. Gasping, I whispered to myself, "Oh, Richard, if you were here and I told you about this, I know what you would say. You'd say, 'Lee, you are being weird again.'"

At that moment, Richard's arms came around me, and he held me tightly. In only my right ear I heard his voice. He said, "Weird? Lee, you don't know the half of it. It's so . . . wonderful!"

I turned into a block of ice. Dimly, I felt my sons return; I felt them turn me and sit me in a chair at the patio table. I kept my eyes closed and wished that I could tell them what had happened, but they were both skeptics, and they did not need a mad mother just then. So I simply held their hands.

Suddenly, James tore his hand from mine, and as I looked up his face was red and he was shouting. James said, "It's no good! I have to tell you. I'm mad, I'm mad, but when I stood by the gatepost, I felt the loveliest peacefulness. As I started to feel so guilty, Dad put his arms around me, and he said, only into my right ear, 'James, James, it's all right. Everything is exactly as it is meant to be.'"

Before I could say anything, Will flung both arms over his head and said, "Oh, thank you, God. Thank you, James! I thought I was mad too, and I'd have to give up my job because you can't have mad pilots. It was the same for me. I stood at that fence there and felt such blessed relief and total peace. Then, as I started to feel guilty, Dad's arms held me, a real Dad hug, and he said into my right ear, 'Will, oh Will, everything is as it is meant to be.' He told me to open my eyes and look, and I could see through everything, and it was all one, and all love!"

Then did I tell them what had been my contact. We spent the rest of the night silently, except for Will and James saying once to each other, "Certainty!"

The peace held all three of us through the next days, when my youngest son flew back to McGregor with me and helped me establish a routine. Richard spoke then to me, saying, "This is necessary," and "It will not be for long," but I was back in anguish. My grief was so great that I found myself only able to go on if I carried one of Dr. Weiss's books with me wherever I went, even if it was only to go shopping. I told my sister of what had happened with my sons on the night Richard died. She, who belonged to a fundamentalist religion, told me that I was "raising spirits" and called me the "Witch of Endor," and from then on would no longer speak to me or answer my messages.

Nevertheless, I was determined to continue to change, to become the person I was meant to be. Crying most of the time, I began to embrace total honesty and openness, learning not just to be loving but to be love. I walked the veldt alone a lot.

On one Sunday morning, I took my four dogs for one of our long walks into places where there were no other people at all. These were the times when I started to have strong memories of another, long-ago life, which I thought of as "interruptions." I tried pushing these thoughts away until one showed me myself sitting at a candlelit dinner, with rose petals on the table. It was during the Middle Ages. I sat beside a much older, very learned man, whom I could not look at for shyness. I was sixteen and in love with him. Looking down at the table, I saw his right hand, a gray sleeve falling from his arm as his fingers played with a walnut, rolling it exactly as Richard had always done with coins and other small objects. My heartbeat raced. Whoever this man was, he was Richard. I snapped out of it and steadied myself. All four dogs, still on their leashes, suddenly rushed forward up an incline where Richard had often waited for me when we walked together there. The dogs sat down in a semicircle and wagged their tails, and I felt sure that I would find the peace of Richard's presence as I stepped into that space.

And I did, for a moment. But totally clearly, I heard Richard say beside me, "You were born in the year 1100." I freaked out and turned back, dragging my poor dogs, and with every footstep I yelled aloud, "Prove it! Prove it!" as I ran all the way home.

I could not stop this reaction, so I immediately drove to see a friend who, although he did not then accept reincarnation, had been very good to me and had known Richard well. This friend, Manie, did not believe at the time that dreams mattered either. I found Manie lying on his bed, one leg bent and the ankle of the other on that knee. He was looking outside to a jacaranda tree in full, gorgeous flower. He gave me no word of greeting as I approached but said only, "Lee. I have had the most amazing dream."

Still looking out the window, he went on. "I dreamed that I was in the most beautiful garden. Green lawns of deep grass, and the flowers—oh, the scent of the flowers. I walked along the grass and then I saw Richard coming toward me. We met. We hugged. He asked me if I would do something for him. 'Of course,' I said. 'Anything, Richard.'

" 'Lee will be here later,' Richard had said. 'Will you give her a message from me?' "

Then Manie sat up on his bed and apologized. "Lee, the message is just gibberish. Gibberish. But I did promise Richard." He looked so sadly at me. "He said, 'Tell Lee that nine hundred years ago, I am a big, big dolphin.' "

Thirty years before as a fighter pilot, Richard had flown in the RAF with the Nineteenth Squadron, whose emblem, he had been delighted to find, was a dolphin. Upon seeing dolphins for the first time, he had fallen in love with them. Showing me his huge English Electric Lightning with his name on the side, he had pointed out the dolphin on its tail and proudly said, "I am now a dolphin!" He later left the RAF to join British Airways, and in the darkness one night I asked him if he missed being a dolphin. We talked then about the threat of nuclear war, and Richard had said that if he survived he would get a message to me, but I must never believe a message came from him unless he used the words *I am a dolphin* in it.

Until Manie said these words to me again thirty years later, I had completely forgotten this message. For the only time in my life, I fainted. When I came to, I told Manie everything. And, wonderfully, Manie soon enough experienced his own regressions and came to embrace the concept of reincarnation.

I accepted it all, but I was still in some sort of anguish. My children asked me what I'd do if I could do anything, and I immediately said, "I would like to spend one hour with Dr. Brian Weiss." Half an hour later, they had arranged for me to have a cabin on the ship where Brian was having a workshop, sailing from New York. It was in the first session with Brian, shining with love and light on the stage, that I found that hypnosis was exactly like planning a conscious dream, and with Brian's gentle, loving voice, I went back to that earlier life in medieval Paris. It had started with that tremendous love affair with the older Richard. That had ended when, at the age of eighteen, I was forced to become a nun. Richard became a monk, and I was desolately unhappy for the rest of the life. I saw him in a monk's cell, beating his forehead and arms against a stone wall until they bled, yelling my name out loud. If only I, in that life, had known that little fact, my many years of agony as a nun would have found healing.

But that life was the opposite of the life I now live. In the Middle Ages, I had no freedom at all; in my present life, I am incredibly free. I was jubilant to experience this regression. To me, this was the colossal change that I needed. It healed the grief that had felt to me like churning glass inside my stomach and heart ever since Richard died. I was blessed beyond anything I could have dreamed. Additionally, I received a short letter from my sister, who had not spoken to me for several years. She was responding to the experience that I had told her about with my sons upon Richard's death. My sister wrote, "This morning in my quiet time with the Lord, He told me that you and your family were given a vast explosion of love, and that I must keep right out of it." She signed it "with love." As the years pass now, my life is so very, beautifully, gently, wonderfully different, ever since the first moment I picked up those books.

$\curlyvee$ *Lee Leach*

This story is so touching and so beautiful that I can only urge you to read it again, and to hear and feel Richard's messages as if you were Lee or James or Will. The messages are so true. I say, "Trust the process," and Richard says, "Everything is exactly as it is meant to be," but these are the same concepts. While I write that we never die, that our souls or consciousness continue on after the death of our physical bodies, Richard actually comes forward to show us this and to add, "You don't know the half of it. It's so . . . wonderful!" Lee's regression to nine hundred years ago was merely the final validation, and she was now able to understand completely and to feel perfect peace. Her grief was healed.

In the 1980s, when I was chairman of the department of psychiatry at Mount Sinai Medical Center in Miami Beach, I often meditated prior to driving home in the evening after work. One time, as I began the trip home on a beautiful early winter night, I observed a perfect sliver of moon hanging low in the western sky. A softly scented sea breeze blew in through the car's open windows. A feeling of deep peacefulness filled my awareness. At that moment, a shift in my perceptions occurred abruptly, like a combination lock suddenly opening when all the tumblers are aligned. Solid objects had a golden light around them and no longer seemed so solid. I could almost see through their newly acquired transparency. The feeling of peacefulness expanded. I knew that everything was perfect, there were no accidents, and there was no need to ever worry or fear. A gentle voice then whispered to me: "Everything is as it is meant to be. Everything is perfect as it is."

I understand how far from perfect things seem to be on the physical level. Violence, accidents, illnesses, and other traumas seem to happen haphazardly, unpredictably, and constantly. Lives can appear ruined in an instant. It is only at the cosmic level that everything is perfect and as it is meant to be.

Physical life is like a stage play where unforeseen script changes occur all the time, and chaos reigns on the stage. When the actors go behind the curtain, the commotion of the play ends. The actors take off their masks. They resume their permanent identities and lives, no longer the characters that they are temporarily portraying. Our current bodies are the stage characters, our souls the enduring actors. While onstage during the play, the characters can experience terrible misfortune—even death. But the actors are never harmed.

In the context of our own immortality, in the eternity that transcends all time, everything *is* exactly as it is meant to be.

. A MOTHER'S EMBRACE .

A few years ago, I was in one of your seminars on a cruise to Alaska. In one session, you led a group regression in which you had us go back and relive our birth. I went back, felt myself in the womb and being delivered, and then the most amazing thing happened. I reexperienced being placed in my mother's arms for the first time.

You see, my parents died five months apart from each other, when I was eight years old. Because of the trauma of that, I have no memories of my mother. That day during the regression, you gave me back a very special memory.

As you were talking the group through, I recall the thought, *Boy! That doctor is kind of cute,* and then I was in my mother's arms and she was looking down at me, smiling. At that point you led the group on to a past life, but I thought, *There is no way I am leaving her. I have not been with my mother for forty-three years, and I am going to stay right here and enjoy this.* And that is exactly what I did until you brought the group out of the regression.

Before that experience I was a (fairly) well-functioning adult, but since then I have carried an extra glow in my heart that has translated into a calmness and confidence that wasn't there before. It is along the same lines of a small child, doubtful of her ability, who blossoms after the mother gives assurance of her love and support.

Yesterday was my mother's birthday; she would have been eighty-four. While I wasn't able to call her on the phone, I did communicate with her through a dream, and I give credit for that to the regression as well. The connection I made that day has left a little porthole open to the other side that I can access whenever I need my mom, and I am in gratitude forever for this amazing gift.

℘ *Patricia Kuptz*

I am so blessed to be able to help people have these experiences. Prenatal and early infant memories have been validated over and over again by parents and others. These are real and accurate recollections.

It is not difficult to retrieve these very early memories. I first help the person reach a deep level of concentration and relaxation. Then we go backward in time, back through adolescence, through childhood, and all the way to infancy and in utero states. I count in reverse from five to one as an image, a scene, a smell, or an event comes into focus in the person's mind. At first, the image may seem more like a snapshot or photo, although sometimes it may appear more like a movie. Sometimes there is no image but rather a feeling, a knowing. As I deepen the level even more, the scene, often accompanied by sensations, feelings, and emotions, becomes even clearer. We have arrived, and the wonderful reunions and memories remind us that love never ends, that our loved ones are alive in our pasts yet also in our futures.

On those cold Alaskan waters a miracle was unfolding, even though I did not know it at the time. Patricia's life was forever changed. The grief that she had been carrying for forty-three years was dissolving. A portal to the other side was opening. Reaching through that portal the first time was healing for Patricia and, even more wonderfully, it has now become second nature for her.

Our loved ones reach back through that portal too, although we may not always be aware of it. They visit us, daily if need be, to express their love, to soothe our pain, and even, as Jessica discovered in the next story, to hold us in their arms and dance with us one last time.

. DANCING IN THE FIELDS .

Jessica, a schoolteacher in her thirties with blond hair, blue eyes, and a soft-spoken voice, drove hours from central Florida to see me in my office. She had had two children who were delivered via cesarean section when she became pregnant with her third child, a healthy boy. She had opted to deliver Elliot naturally in her home, but during the process her uterus ruptured, the placenta detached, and the baby suffered from a fatal lack of oxygen as he was rushed to the hospital. He was immediately put on life support, but it was too late. He died only ten days later.

As Jessica told me her history, my heart sank. No one deserves to experience the loss of a child, surely, but the woman sitting in front of me was so gentle and kind that I couldn't imagine why such a devastating thing would have to happen to her. Neither could I imagine the death of my child, much less feeling the tremendous guilt that a decision I had made might have contributed to that outcome. Jessica had read my father's books and found solace in them. She was seeing another therapist who was helping her with the bereavement process. I was in awe of how well she was coping: I'd have considered it a success to simply get out of bed in the morning, put one foot in front of the other, and survive the day. It was evident that strength of steel lay under Jessica's sweet exterior. Nonetheless, it was as if she wore the pain on the outside of her body. I could see it; I could almost reach out and touch it. Its bottomless depth frightened me: I was a fairly new therapist, certainly new to hypnosis, and I feared that the trip down to my office might have been a complete waste of her time. What on earth could I say or do that could possibly alleviate Jessica's suffering? And what could even make a dent in that kind of pain?

Jessica described the difficulties she'd had with her physicians when she had delivered her first two children. Her soft voice grew an edge as she spoke of her mistrust of them, of how medical errors had been made and of how, understandably, these errors had led her to choose a different method for bringing Elliot into the world. She had scrupulously researched the benefits and risks of a vaginal birth after cesareans. She could not have made a more informed decision, and from her history with her first two deliveries, it was clear why she had chosen as she did. The more we discussed Elliot, the more I tried to detach from her trauma, but I felt that I was right there with her, as if, while our bodies sat there talking, our souls were hovering on the ground together, staring at each other with sad, disbelieving eyes. *Can life really get this painful? And how do you survive when it invariably does?* As Jessica brought up the hypothetical scenario of having another child, her anger dissolved into sheer panic. What would be the right thing to do then? How could she trust the doctors again? What if whatever decision she made turned out to be the wrong one? She had given her past and her future much thought, and it was clear that questions about both caused her great distress.

As I hypnotized Jessica and brought her to a past life, she first saw only vague colors, appearing as waves and dots. "It's all just lights?" she said, and for the next ten minutes it was all, indeed, just lights. *Oh no*, I thought, literally turning my hands into prayer and staring up at the ceiling, thankful that my client's eyes were closed. *Angels, God, whoever is up there, you have to do better than that.* I prayed before each client for help and healing energy, but that day it was no gentle request.

Suddenly, in the midst of these pulsating light forms, the image of an apron appeared in Jessica's mind. *Thank you*, I said to the sky, breathing a sigh of relief. Jessica saw herself as a young woman on a big wooden porch, like something out of *Little House on the Prairie*. She was leaning on a post, sweating from the summer sun and from physical exertion. The work was hard and stressful, a huge burden. Jessica could feel the tension in her neck and shoulders, not just from the manual labor but also from a crushing loneliness. She sensed that she wanted children and a family but did not have any. "It's all too heavy," she sighed.

We moved ahead in time to that night, where the woman was lying in bed, contemplating reaching out for the Bible on her nightstand but too tired to make even that little comforting gesture. Jessica saw the woman sobbing, feeling sad and frustrated and restless all at once. She had a large house but overseeing it was an overwhelming task for her, and the rural area in which she lived was isolated, offering no friendships. The townspeople considered her to be so fortunate; she owned a big house, that great front porch, a cow. But she felt no happiness in any of these assets. Although she was only in her twenties, she felt, it seemed, too tired and sad to live.

We moved ahead in time again, but it was more of the same: the woman, toiling away in the front yard, working so hard simply to survive this joyless existence. And then Jessica saw a little girl, dancing and twirling around the woman in the dirt. "The woman doesn't see her," she said, confused, "but the girl is just dancing, dancing away." Jessica saw a man, too: the woman's husband, standing off to the side of the porch. He and the girl were so close to the woman, loving her as she worked, loving her as she sat on the porch and cried, but she never knew they were there. Drowning in her pain, she was aware of nothing but loneliness.

Where had these spirits come from? To find out, we moved back in time. There was an accident, a buggy that crashed when a horse slipped on some wet rocks. The cart, carrying the child and the husband, fell off, killing them instantly. The woman had not been inside; she had wanted to go with them, had planned on it, but for some reason at the last minute she hadn't. She had loved them so much and felt terribly guilty and responsible for their deaths. "But it wasn't your fault. It wasn't even the horse's fault. Sometimes accidents just happen," I said, thinking also of Elliot. Jessica nodded, tears in her eyes, but she didn't seem to believe it. "It sounds like you wish you'd been in there with them," I said in a soft voice, and she moaned, "Oh yes."

The woman lived many long, lonely years. Throughout her days, she worked by the front porch where her husband watched her with nothing but love in his eyes, and her daughter, spinning into oblivion, danced right next to her every day of her life.

As Jessica floated beyond her old body, she started shaking her head, as if in disbelief of how she had lived. "We are not supposed to be miserable!" she said. "There was so much good she could have done." The woman had been so inextricably bogged down in grief and loss that she had never recovered. Thinking of Jessica as she was today, I asked, "But how could she have recovered from that kind of loss?"

"So easily," Jessica answered, smiling, "if she just could have seen them dancing around her." The little girl and the husband, faithfully showing up every day in the front yard, were trying to tell her that they were fine, that they loved her, and that they had never left her, but she could not see it. "She hurt—but she didn't have to. They were so, so happy," Jessica said. "It was love, pure love, pouring out of them and stopping right there in front of her! And she just didn't get it."

This was an extraordinary lesson to help relieve Jessica of some of her current feelings of grief. As unbelievable as it seemed given the trauma that she had recently experienced with her son, her suffering was optional, unnecessary. If she just could have seen the little girl dancing so close to her. If she only knew that Elliot was, most likely, still loving her from no farther than the air she breathed, she would never have cause to feel that unbearable pain again.

The following day, in our session together, Jessica slipped in and out of numerous past lives. In one, she was the daughter of a kind of hermetic medicine man, a soul so wise and advanced beyond his years; she eventually had her own family but died young, leaving behind a small child whom she loved. Jessica felt that Elliot was the young child in that lifetime. "It feels like he and I switched places this time. I left him early in that life, he left me early in this one. Oh," she said, realization dawning on her, "in this life, he wasn't punishing me at all. He was just showing me what it feels like to be the one left behind, rather than the one leaving early. But love doesn't go away. We do—but love never does." She sensed that Elliot was also her beloved father in the regression. "He seemed to have it all figured out," she said. "He was so loving. Nothing bothered him. Everything he did was in gentleness and kindness, for the betterment of humanity."

Jessica's lifetimes with Elliot were ancient, innumerable, arising throughout the years as their souls braided together again and again to teach, to learn, to love. It was no accident that he had appeared in her present life; he was intrinsically linked to her, a part of her, but the form, the relationship, the circumstances always varied. As she sat in front of me, Jessica's face completely changed. There were no lines of sadness, no weary eyes; only love, joy, even excitement. As odd as it sounds, she didn't even seem human anymore; with her fair coloring and her beatific expression, she truly looked like an angel, a blissful spirit, glowing with a peace beyond words. She was beaming, and the light transformed every part of her.

It was the end of our time together. I didn't think Jessica could get any happier, which seemed almost perverse considering the reason why she had come to see me. It was incredible to witness. *You do good work,* I said to the sky. I closed the session by bringing Jessica to a peaceful wildflower field in her mind and having her visualize her guide joining her to give her guidance about how she could continue to heal even after she left the office. Jessica's guide, her wise and loving teacher, was, of course, Elliot. She imagined holding his little baby body, from which a bright light started shooting. Elliot opened his eyes. (After the session, Jessica marveled at this fact. "He was born brain-dead," she said. "I never got to see his eyes.") In her mind, Elliot bopped her on the nose and winked at her, as if he were saying, "Gotcha!," as if this whole thing, this whole tumble throughout lifetimes together, this endless bubbling up of deaths upon births upon deaths, was nothing more than a cosmic joke. Here Jessica, as anyone would, suffered from the loss of a healthy baby suddenly dead in both brain and body, yet Elliot himself couldn't take it seriously; all he had to say about the matter was something like, "My turn. Tag, you're it!" To Jessica, Elliot the baby, who was now chucking her on the chin and winking at her, was clearly the adult and she the child; his was a soul so old and loving, very much an advanced teacher.

As Jessica held him in her arms, his body started to disappear, dissolving into the bright light that grew stronger and stronger, larger and larger until he was so big, big way beyond bodies, and his light filled up the entire field. The wildflowers, the grass, and the enormous blue sky shone with his light. He was larger than she was, larger than anything she could even imagine. I had Jessica reflect back on her feelings of responsibility, knowing that a soul so vast it could encompass the entire world could never be snuffed out by a single decision, a single accident. She just laughed, as if the very question that she had not once stopped asking herself no longer made sense. "Whose fault was his death? Mine, the doctors', no one's. It doesn't matter. It just doesn't matter."

Jessica then saw herself pregnant, and soon with the healthy baby in her arms in a hospital room. Elliot was not this child, but he was very much there with her, his light exploding. "He is radiating the whole room," she breathed. "It's as if every wall has light beams all over it. It is all him, all over." As Jessica held the new baby, Elliot held Jessica. He kissed the baby's head again and again. There was no sadness, no pain, only the purest love as Elliot protectively watched over them. Although Jessica was unsure if she and her husband even wanted more children, I recalled how she pored over every detail of birth plans, deliveries, and doctors as she thought about what might happen, what could happen, what did happen. I thought it would help her to know how the birth turned out, but she smiled as she brushed the question off as utterly irrelevant. "It doesn't matter. Those are human details. To answer your question, I had a C-section, but it doesn't matter. I'm just nursing." She looked down at the baby in her arms, knowing full well how present Elliot was in the room and in their lives. "I'm just nursing."

Jessica had tears of joy in her eyes; I did too. I was in awe of Elliot's infinite soul and of his love. Nothing could hurt him, which meant that nothing could hurt any of us, either. What room is there for grief in love? What does the death of anyone even mean when we can be with them again in our minds, when we can hold their bodies again and they can hold us again, when we can finally look into eyes that we could never clearly see here on the earth? Our own eyes remain closed to all the love around us and we suffer as we imagine ourselves to be alone or left behind, when all we ever have to do is just open them to find our loved ones dancing, dancing, dancing with us there in the fields until the end of time.

∾ Amy Weiss

Amy has said it all and said it so well. If only we could see our departed loved ones dancing around us, continuing to love us, to protect us, to wait for us. Then our grief would be so much less.

In my book *Many Lives, Many Masters,* I changed the name of the physician who had helped Catherine so much, and who had referred her to me. He is the one who unknowingly started this entire process, this discovery of past lives. I changed his name to Edward, for reasons of confidentiality. His real name was Elliot.

Once, in a deeply hypnotized state, Catherine's head began to move from side to side. "A spirit . . . is looking," she told me.

"At you?"

"Yes."

"Do you recognize the spirit?"

"I'm not sure . . . I think it might be Edward." Edward had died during the previous year. Edward was truly ubiquitous. He seemed to be always around her.

"What did the spirit look like?"

"Just a . . . just white . . . like lights. He had no face, not like we know it, but I know it's he."

"Was he communicating at all with you?"

"No, he was just watching."

"Was he listening to what I was saying?"

"Yes," she whispered. "But he's gone now. He just wanted to be sure I'm all right." I thought about the popular mythology of the guardian angel. Certainly Edward [Elliot], in the role of the hovering, loving spirit watching over her to make sure she was all right, approached such an angelic role.

Every one of us has an Elliot or two or three in our lives.

. HARDSHIP AND HOPE .

Clop, clop, clop. The horse held a steady and cautious pace as it exited the wooded area and entered the town. The woman on the horse rode through the main street of shops and businesses, waving at familiar faces. She wore a dark wool riding skirt and jacket, and her long braids were fastened closely to her head. With her unusually small frame, she looked like a doll mounted on the thoroughbred stallion. The townspeople gestured their respect for her as she passed. She was a skilled courier who delivered items from town to town, often through empty and dangerous territories of the southwestern United States in the 1800s.

She thrived on the speed and skill of riding the stallion. The woman was a small rider by any standard, and her dearly loved horse towered over her. She managed him with great speed and dexterity throughout the dry, dusty land. People did not judge her for taking an unorthodox role, because her job was so appreciated and her skill so highly respected. Likewise, her focus was on her work, the love of her horse, and management of the danger that she faced.

On one of her routes, she sped across a dusty southwestern stretch, up a rounded hill, and through a set of mesa tables and steeples. This required her to ride slowly, anticipating every step of the stallion's hoof. Her slow pace made her a target for the warring Apache natives, who were known to attack.

She rode the pass many times, but on her last ride a group of five native men hid in the mesa steeples and overtook her. She was forced to watch as her horse was furiously and senselessly murdered. The woman was raped repeatedly by the leader of the group, a giant in comparison to her small, childlike frame. His face paint and feathered headdress sickened her. She was disgusted and traumatized by his senseless murder of the valuable horse but not terrified, as he had intended.

The band of warring natives left her to die within the steeple pass, but she was able to walk back to her family's ranch. When she arrived and returned to health, she put away her wool suit, cut her hair, and sat in the armchair that looked out to the hills she rode. The rest of her life was spent mourning the horse and her life as a courier.

In the backdrop of her life was a stable hand who secretly loved and admired her. He spent the rest of his life watching over her, even though she was inattentive to his presence and love for her. She never moved on past the loss of her youth.

I, of course, was that woman. I carried into this lifetime a love for horses and some riding skill, and I practice ever-present compassion and respect for animals. I brought stamina for hardship into this lifetime and can move on with hope, something that I could not do as the horse courier. And, most important, as I observed the sad courier sitting in her armchair, I learned that we must move on after tragedy. There are always gifts, like the loving stable worker, on the other side of difficulty.

∾ *Alice*

Time is not measured in minutes or hours or years. Time is measured in lessons learned. Alice has mastered this wisdom. She has learned to overcome grief's power to immobilize, to freeze time, and she is now able to move on. There are always gifts—there is always love—on the other side.

Human beings create such misery in the world, with their penchant for violence and for killing. Spiritual beings, aware of higher dimensions, multiple lifetimes, and cosmic karma, repair the world by nurturing and protecting all life.

As we fully evolve from human beings into spiritual beings, we will comfort and heal each other's pain rather than cause it.

Alice easily let go of the sorrow that she had experienced in her prior lifetime as the courier. Michelle, the author of the next story, was able to accomplish a similar feat. It does not matter whether the loss is fresh or ancient; with the awareness of the endurance of our bonds and of our souls, its burden can lighten and disappear in mere moments.

. RELEASING GRIEF .

As I stared out at the sea of expectant-looking faces in front of me, my heart began to beat wildly in my chest. I hadn't realized how many people were in the audience until I'd reached the front of the room, where I now sat perched on a chair next to Dr. Brian Weiss. I resisted the urge to look in the direction of my husband, for I could feel him frowning at me. My face felt red and hot as I realized what I had just committed myself to. I was about to be hypnotized in front of several hundred people who were going to watch the whole thing.

What if I can't remember a past life? What if I make a total fool of myself? As I had these thoughts, the faces of the former selves that I had seen during the group regressions over the past couple of days began to drift into my mind's eye in a colorful parade. Feeling somewhat reassured, I then looked around the room at the faces of the audience in front of me. They looked friendly and supportive, some even smiling warmly when my eyes brushed past theirs.

Dr. Weiss, who had been addressing the audience while I became acclimated to the stage, turned and spoke directly to me. I focused on his instructions, the soothing sound of his voice calming me instantly.

This is going to be okay, I reassured myself. He smiled and nodded at me, as if he had heard my thoughts and was giving his reply. I relaxed a bit in my chair, ready to give myself over to whatever was about to happen.

I could hear Dr. Weiss's voice, which seemed quite far away, telling me that I would see a door in front of me. He then informed me that on the other side of that door I would encounter a memory from my childhood. I could hear him counting backward from three, and in my mind the door began to swing open, just as he had said that it would. I eagerly walked through it in my mind, anxious to discover what I would find on the other side.

Stepping into the brilliant light that lay behind the door, I felt as if I needed to blink from the brightness, even though my eyes were firmly shut. I looked down at the floor and saw linoleum with a yellow-and-white print. There were countertops, cupboards, and a sink with a window above it that was covered with pleasant yellow curtains. The light that streamed in through this window had a sunny, midmorning quality to it. There was a large olive-green refrigerator next to the sink, from which a low humming sound emanated. Dr. Weiss began to question me about what I was experiencing, and when I spoke to answer him, I was surprised to hear that I was using a voice much softer and lower than my usual speech.

"I'm in my kitchen," I said, although the room was completely unfamiliar to me. It was not any kitchen that I could remember, and it suddenly dawned on me that it was from the house that we had moved out of when I had been only three years old.

Upon that realization, I looked down at my own body and saw that I was a baby, sitting up in a high chair. I saw my pudgy legs below me, and I could feel the sticky vinyl seat on my skin. This was clearly from a time well before my earliest memory, which had been around the age of four. I had never remembered anything at all from the few years that we had lived in the house where I was born.

"What is it that you are doing?" Dr. Weiss asked.

"Eating applesauce in my high chair." My automatic response surprised me. I could almost taste the bland baby food in my mouth.

Then I saw her. She was sitting in a wooden chair in front of me, holding a small spoon in her hand. Her broad smile made her high cheekbones look like two rosy apples, and her beautiful green eyes crinkled at the corners. *Momma,* I thought, as the tears started to run down my cheeks.

"My mother is with me," I whispered. The moment the words left my lips, I felt an overwhelming sense of love. *Was that really my mother?* I did not think that I could remember her, but there she was, sitting in front of me. My heart was so full of emotion that I felt as if it would burst as I sat there looking at her. She had died so long ago, this woman who gave me life and who left me with no working memories of her whatsoever. Yet here she was in front of me, cooing and smiling. It almost felt as if I were truly in that kitchen and that I had been transported back in time. She was real, and I was there with her.

I sat with my eyes closed, savoring the feeling of being cared for by her. She was there with me, she who did not live to watch me grow into the woman that I had become, she who had left a large gaping hole inside me. I had missed her every day, despite the fact that I could never even picture what her face had looked like. My joy in the moment that I beheld her was indescribable.

Gazing at her smiling face, I could feel how much she loved me, how much she had loved being a mother, and how much she enjoyed spending time with me. I could hear her speaking in a soft, soothing voice, and the sound of my name escaping her lips was the most beautiful noise that I had ever heard. The tears continued to fall as there was nothing save that moment of pure bliss. But I was fully aware that it was only a memory. Oh, how I longed for her!

I could then again hear the kind voice of Dr. Weiss, telling me that it was time to leave this scene behind. My heart ached at the thought, but I was willing to do as he asked. His words were gentle, prodding me onward and promising me that I would remember this scene. This memory had been brought to the surface after having been buried deep in my subconscious for so long. I knew, without a doubt, that the image of my mother's face would never fade from me again.

He instructed me to move back through the door that I had constructed in my mind, and as I did, the scene in the yellow kitchen instantly disappeared. Feeling strangely effervescent, almost as if I had been charged with electric energy, I had never been so completely alert or alive, though my body was a limp and nearly useless object on the chair.

Suddenly, a second door appeared in front of me and opened. The moment I went through it, I was hit by a strong smell that was instantly recognizable as the salty scent of sea air. *I am near the ocean,* I thought, although I was aware of the fact that, physically, I was indoors inside a conference room.

Upon being instructed to look down, I saw a pair of dirty, bare feet. My clothes consisted of a burlap sack that had been crafted into a makeshift pair of pants, which were tied onto me with a rope at my waist. I could feel the coarse material against my legs. I could hardly believe what I saw when I looked at my hands. My fingers were fat, and my hands were massive, filthy, and calloused. They belonged to a man, one who used them to do very hard work. *Whose hands are these?* The answer came with complete assurance from deep within me, and it spread over my entire being. *These were my hands.*

I looked around me, and right away I could see the ships. I was on a wooden dock surrounding a seaport of some kind, and I was unloading heavy barrels from the ships, which had just arrived from the New World. The year *1689* popped into my head, firmly appearing as if from nowhere, as did the name of the port city: *Barcelona.* Rum was being imported from the New World inside these heavy barrels under which I struggled. The work was difficult and physically taxing, but I didn't mind it too much or feel the need to complain. I was not very intelligent, and perhaps I did not know any kind of work other than this backbreaking labor.

As Dr. Weiss moved me on from this scene, I saw myself inside a small, wooden, shack-like structure with a dirt floor—my home. The house was only one room, and I could tell that we were extremely poor. At one end there was a stone fireplace, in which a large, black metal pot hung over a fire. Something pungent was cooking in the pot. Several mattresses stuffed with straw were on the floor in one corner, and a few rough blankets lay on top of them. I immediately sensed several presences in the house with me. Turning, I saw three small children standing there, all dressed in dirty rags. The connection that I felt to them was so palpable that it nearly choked me. I could not see their eyes, as their faces were fuzzy and out of focus. Their familiarity, however, was undeniable, and I knew beyond any doubt that these were my children. I loved these three little souls, whom I had never met, with all my heart.

I looked again toward the fireplace and saw a pleasant-looking woman in a long dress. She had a white cap on her head, and she was busily stirring something in the pot over the fire. She was my wife. A lump formed in my throat from love and longing as I gazed at her. She turned around, and I was momentarily startled to see that, unlike the children, the details of her face were very clear. I looked deep into this woman's eyes, and the recognition instantly washed over me.

It was my mother.

Nearly in disbelief, I sat there and watched her in my mind's eye. She had the same eyes and even the same distinct apple-like cheekbones that she had in this life. But even more powerful than her appearance, I could feel her energetically. This beloved wife of mine was the same woman who had given birth to me in this life. I knew it in the core of my being. As I gazed at her, I could feel how much we loved each other. I started to see scenes of our life together, moving in rapid succession as they painted a beautiful picture of a relationship based on mutual adoration. She greeted me each evening with a warm smile and an embrace after my long day of difficult labor. Although we were impoverished and it was an endless struggle to survive, we were so happy together. She accepted our simple life with all of its difficulties. *This is what real love is.* A flicker of a thought entered my mind, a sudden realization that my current marriage seemed quite second-rate in comparison. *This is what I want,* I said to myself as I basked in the perfect, balanced, and spiritual love that I had with this woman.

Finding real love is the most important thing we can do in life. And then when we find it, we must give it in return. The thought floated into my mind on a current that felt like a song. *Did I just think that?* I wondered, as it had been a much wiser message than I thought I knew how to deliver.

Moving ahead a few years in time, I saw myself in that same house. I stood on that dirt floor as a choking sadness hit me like a dull knife. My wife was lying in the corner on one of the straw mattresses, covered by a rough blanket. She was very ill. Her skin looked gray, and her cough kept startling me out of what I could feel was a downward spiral of grief and anguish. I had tried everything that I could to help her, but our extreme poverty prevented any real medical care. She was about to die. As I acknowledged this, my ever-extending grief spiral darkened as I realized how angry I was. I was being pulled down into a sheer misery that was unlike anything I had ever known. My rage mixed with unimaginable sadness and then flowed out of me, leaving behind a numb emptiness.

I was sitting in a chair, staring into space, fully wrapped up inside my dark emotions. My three children were there, huddled together in the corner. I could feel their fear as they held on to each other and watched their dying mother. Not working to comfort my still-young children in any way or nurture them through what was undeniably a painful and frightening experience, I remained seated at my table.

Watching myself sit there and ignore my children, I started to get upset at the way that I had dealt with this. *Why aren't I holding them?* I wondered, remembering how much I loved them. *This is wrong; they need me.* Shame filled me as I looked at their faces. Turning back to the corner where my wife was, I saw that she had died. Her eyes stared out lifelessly from her gray body. I did not move from my chair toward her or comfort my children, who were now wailing. Instead, I just sat and stared into space as if it were my body that was now lifeless, not my beloved wife's.

Images began floating into my mind, showing me the years directly after her death. I became withdrawn and bitter, spending my time alone and miserable. I lost my spark and my love for life, and I never regained that part of myself. My work, which I hadn't minded before, now seemed like drudgery. My evenings were spent sitting in my chair, staring into space. I could feel my incredible loneliness, despite the fact that I still had three children who needed me more than ever to care for them. *How selfish of me,* I thought, as a feeling of remorse washed over me. I loved them. Why was I neglecting them?

I moved ahead to the last day of that lifetime and immediately felt a crushing pressure on my chest. The sensation was so intense that I had to remind myself where I was, that it was impossible that something could actually be crushing me. It felt so real, and I fought the panic that began to creep in. It was hard to breathe, and my chest rose and fell with great effort. The air smelled of the sea once more; I was back on the docks where I worked. There was confusion as to what was happening. And then, instantly, I was lighter. As I drew a breath, the oxygen filled my lungs with much more ease. The sensation that had made my chest seem so heavy was gone, and I could then see what was happening, as it was no longer dark around me. I was floating above the body of this man that I had been. He was lying lifeless on the ground, a few of those heavy barrels on top of his body. They had fallen down from the ship above and had accidentally landed on top of him, completely crushing his chest.

I felt light as air as I hovered above this terrible scene of my death. The contrast between the heaviness I had felt in this body and the complete weightlessness I was now experiencing stunned me. It was as if I were made of nothing, yet I knew that I was still very much who it is that I am. My broken body lay useless and abandoned, but I still existed. I began to move upward, feeling beautiful and free, experiencing an elation unlike any I had ever known.

A bright light appeared in the distance; it was in front of me but higher, in clouds that began to thin into mist. The colors inside these misty clouds were of every imaginable hue and so vivid I knew they could not be perceived by any human eyes. I could feel myself being gently drawn toward this incredibly brilliant light, and a tremendous, peaceful feeling washed over me as I gazed at it. A strange humming sound increased in intensity the closer I came to the light, vibrating through my whole being. This electric vibration consumed me, and it felt like I was being recharged. There did not seem to be an edge where the light began; it just gradually enveloped me until the light and I had merged. It was as if I were the light, even though I still had a sense of myself and where my own boundaries lay. I was home once again, back where I belonged, feeling completely at peace.

And then I saw her. She was standing there, looking expectantly at me with her warm smile and her rosy apple cheeks. My mother, who had been my wife, was waiting for me. Upon seeing her, I felt an overwhelming love unlike anything I knew I was capable of outside this light. She did not say a word but just embraced me fully, as my nothingness fell completely into hers. We had no human form to prevent our complete connection, and our pure love passed directly into each other. I was filled with her, and she with me.

In this state of complete bliss, I heard Dr. Weiss ask a question. "What is the lesson that you learned from this life that is important for you to know in your current life?"

I didn't even have to think of the answer, as a wave of remorse returned for my actions as that man. "People die, it is a part of life," I said. "You cannot let your loss keep you from living your life to its fullest. My children needed me, yet I could not escape my own grief to be there for them. It's important to grieve our losses, but then we must accept them and move on."

After I finished the last sentence, the connection to my current life became clear. I had lost my mother to Hodgkin's lymphoma in 1977 and had spent the better part of my formative years grieving her. It had been especially difficult the last few years after having become a mother myself. The loss of her felt constant and inescapable.

At that moment, I was ready to put my grief aside and move on with my life. I knew beyond any doubt that I would see her again and that our love for each other would never die. Feeling a heaviness lift from my heart, I acknowledged that I would always miss her but that it was time to release her. I had never felt so free as the tears flowed down my cheeks. My deep sorrow had been replaced with a warm comfort. I had experienced firsthand that she continues to exist—and always will.

As I emerged from the hypnotic state, I took a very deep breath and then slowly opened my eyes. Blinking to bring the room in which I was physically present back into focus, I immediately noticed that something was different. In front of me were the hundreds of faces I had seen earlier that had witnessed this incredible experience; only now, they each appeared to have a soft and ethereal glow emanating from them. These glows appeared in various shades and colors, the perimeter stretching farther away from some than others. Scanning the audience, I tingled from head to toe as I beheld this glorious and otherworldly vision. *Auras.* I had never seen anything so beautiful as these people, and still feeling light and energized, I absorbed each one with awe.

ᕫ Michelle Brock

In her beautiful and comprehensive description of the cycles of life and death and life again, Michelle confirms and validates Alice's lesson and the very same wisdom perceived by Amy's client, Jessica. Jessica said, "We are not supposed to be miserable! There was so much good she could have done." Alice said, "We must move on after tragedy. There are always gifts . . . on the other side of difficulty." Michelle knew deeply that it was "important to grieve our losses, but then we must accept them and move on." Each saw and felt the paralysis that grief could cause; each saw and felt the pain and the waste that this paralysis could cause.

Michelle believed that she had no memories of her mother. Yet within minutes and even in the potentially uncomfortable position of being on-stage in front of many observers, she was vividly recalling detailed scenes. Her remembrances were not only visual. She could feel the vinyl seat, she could taste the bland applesauce, she could hear her mother's soft voice, and she became overwhelmed with emotion. The decades-long separation from her mother was bridged in an instant, and her loneliness and grief would never again be so severe.

We can remember everything. Just like Michelle, we harbor a wealth of memories in the locked treasure chest of our subconscious mind. They have been forgotten—but not lost. They can always be reclaimed. To unlock the chest and to recapture the scenes and images of our loved ones when they were young and healthy, we only need the key. The key is this regression technique, so safe and so simple. And then we too can once again see their smiling faces, feel their arms around us, smell their perfume, and bask in their love.

Furthermore, we can access a particular past life as often as we wish and as often as we need, just as we can with any conscious memory. Perhaps not all lessons and understandings from the lifetime experienced during a regression can be extracted the first time. We can go back to recover more details or to explore the life at deeper levels. There is no expiration date on a memory.

But our dear ones are not just memories. Their souls survive the death of the physical body. Michelle was twice reunited with her mother's soul, in addition to the wonderful reunion on the other side, her mother waiting for her in the light. We never lose our loved ones.

I am reminded of what I have heard and experienced so many times with my patients. Whether the message is heard in a dream in which the departed loved one appears, in a meditation, during a regression, or just being whispered into your ear, as Richard whispered into the ears of Lee and the boys, it is remarkably clear and consistent: "Do not grieve so much for me. I am still here, I am always with you, and I will love you forever."

· 7 ·

Intuition and Other
Psychic Abilities

We have so many more intuitive abilities than we know or use. The knowledge and wisdom that can be gained from these untapped talents are extraordinary, and they mirror the incredible insights that can be accessed through past-life memories.

In my book *Messages from the Masters*, I describe an exercise that I have been including in my workshops for years. This exercise is called *psychometry*, and it has led to many amazing and wonderful moments, a number of which are described in this chapter.

In this experiential exercise, which I usually conduct in groups of two, the participants exchange small objects belonging to them. The object may be a ring, a watch, a bracelet, keys, lockets, and so on. The item chosen should be one that is touched and handled primarily by its owner.

I begin the experience by doing a brief relaxation exercise, which helps the participants to focus and to quiet their minds. With their eyes closed as they remain in a relaxed state, the two people hold their partner's object gently in their hands. The participants are instructed to become aware of any thoughts, feelings, impressions, or sensations that come into their awareness.

The impressions may be psychological (feelings, moods, or emotions), physical (bodily sensations), psychic (visions, messages, thoughts, childhood or past-life scenes), or spiritual (messages or images from other dimensions).

After about five minutes have elapsed, I instruct the group to share every aspect of the experience with their partner. It is very important to share every sensation, thought, and impression, even if it seems silly or weird, because these are often the most accurate and powerful "hits." Frequently the validation of one of these strange impressions is immediate and most meaningful.

Whether it is the energy of the object being held that facilitates the intuitive transfer of information or the relaxed focusing of the mind, the net result is an awakening and a validation of the intuitive ability we all possess.

This exercise is safe, simple, instructive, and a lot of fun.

Information about our past lives and the spiritual dimensions can also be gleaned from other intuitive insights as well as from dreams, through meditation, or even spontaneously, as in déjà vu experiences. The quality and detail of these psychic perceptions are similar to those found in past-life regressions. For example, the following account of a psychometry encounter evokes many of the same feelings and messages that Lee experienced after Richard's death in that marvelous story from the previous chapter. Both stories share the powerful and immediate presence of a loved one who had recently died and who brings comfort from the other side. Whether the avenue to that other side is established through past-life regressions, or through psychometry, or spontaneously through other intuitive channels does not matter. All these roads lead to the same place, the same awareness. We are always loved. We are never alone.

. THE LAKE HOUSE .

They say that it is best to begin at the beginning. My very first experience with the fact that "we are all connected," as Brian says, took place on the first day of a weeklong training in the summer of 2006. Brian was explaining the process of psychometry to the entire class of approximately 130 people. I had no previous exposure to it, and frankly I did not think that I could do it. I listened to Brian say that images might begin to come to our minds as we held a personal object from a neighbor in the class. Our task, he said, was simply to allow this, to notice what the images were, and to refrain from judging them. And then, of course, to share them.

The person next to me was an attractive, casually dressed woman in her fifties. We exchanged comments regarding how interesting yet strange this felt, and each of us professed our hope that the other wouldn't be too disappointed, for we had never done this before. We gave each other our watches as the house lights were dimmed and the exercise began. I truly did not expect to "pass" this little test of my psychic abilities, but I remembered what Brian had said about noticing what we experienced without any questioning or judgments.

As I held the woman's watch, the first image that I saw was of a lovely house on the edge of a lake, surrounded by tall pine trees. The roof and sides of the house were covered with beautiful cedar shakes. At the water's edge was a nice green canoe, with a paddle resting inside. Next to that, pulled up on the bank in the same fashion, was an old rowboat with two oars. On the porch of the camp was a ten-speed bike, and to the side was a fire pit made of large rocks. A big, beautiful fire burned inside it. I saw an elevated, fast-moving train in a major city, and then the camp again, with a light blue Frisbee on the porch and the same wonderful log fire in the pit. I felt an immense sense of peace, love, and happiness enter me, though I did not know why or from where. The lights came on, and Brian asked us to share everything, however seemingly meaningless, with our partner.

As I disclosed the images that had come to me, my partner began to weep. I started to stop, but she insisted that I continue. When I finished, I asked what this meant to her. Still crying, she began to reveal the following.

She and her partner of many years had shared a profound, spiritual love. He was her best friend. He had recently died of a fast and aggressive form of cancer. He had learned of it in January and crossed over a few short months later. She was still deeply grieving. They owned a camp on a lake in the Northeast. They loved to go there together whenever they could, to relax, rejuvenate, and recuperate from their stressful, hectic jobs. A nice little place in a beautiful setting, it had cedar shakes on the roof and the sides. At the water's edge were an often-used green canoe and a rowboat. They liked to hang out and toss a light blue Frisbee. The ten-speed bike on the porch was his, and it was always there. He loved to ride whenever he could, there in the country and also in the city, where he lived and worked. Every day when he went to work, he almost always took the elevated train. Outside, next to the lake house, was a large, beautiful fireplace. They often sat out under the stars, gazing at the fire and talking.

His funeral plans had been left to her; he simply requested immediate cremation. His passing had devastated and immobilized his partner. She had now finally begun to summon the strength to have a proper memorial service for this man whom she so loved. She had just sent out over a hundred invitations to the service, as he had friends and family all over the world. On the front of the invitation was a large photograph of a beautiful log fire burning in their fire pit.

Now *I* was overwhelmed and amazed. I explained the feeling of peace, love, and happiness that had entered and enveloped me while holding her watch. Still crying, she said that she had no doubt that these images and feelings were given to me by her partner. She could sense him there in the room with us, and she now knew that he was with her still, that he loved her, and that he was at peace and happy. She also felt a message that he wanted her to feel that same love, peace, and happiness. Now, finally, she had felt it, and she could begin to finish her grieving process and move forward with her life. She and I, two completely random strangers, were sitting together at a conference. Moments later, a deeply personal, touching, and spiritually cleansing experience had taken place between us.

ᡝ *Michael Brown*

Michael is a wonderful therapist, not a famous psychic or a medium. In fact, he had very little confidence in his psychic abilities and, as he explained, hoped that his partner would not be disappointed.

We actually are all psychics and mediums. We all possess incredible extrasensory talents that our ego and logical mind keep hidden from us. With my permission to let his intuitive gift emerge from the shadow of his left brain, Michael was, within seconds, describing this very detailed visual and emotional vista. He even saw how many oars were present, the green canoe, and the old rowboat.

His intuitive visions brought great relief to his partner on that warm summer afternoon. Michael is humble and will minimize his contribution, but he changed his partner's life that day. He helped her move past her despair and into her healing, allowing her to feel the love, peace, and happiness that her lover so wanted to share with her.

Jacqueline, the author of the next story, also participated in a psychometry exercise with a stranger, and she too was able to relay and receive messages that helped to lessen grief.

. THE THREE LITTLE PIGS .

Several years ago, I attended one of your workshops at the Omega Institute. You asked us to exchange a personal item with a stranger, and I did so with the woman who sat in front of me. She gave me the necklace that she wore, and I gave her my ring. As we sat with our eyes closed, you guided us in a meditation and told us not to discount any images that appeared in our minds, no matter how nonsensical they appeared.

The woman in front of me spoke first. I had been wearing my daughter-in-law's wedding band, and that was the ring I passed on to this stranger. My daughter-in-law had been murdered three years prior; she was eight months pregnant at the time. The stranger accurately described her blond hair and saw her standing in a red kitchen that overlooked a body of water as she watched a couple playing on the dock. She had a loving message for my son, her childhood sweetheart, who, along with his new wife, had just purchased a lake house that had a red kitchen.

To say I was flabbergasted is too mild an expression. And, needless to say, after receiving such a vivid vision from a stranger, I was embarrassed to tell her what I had seen. Apologetically, I confessed to her that the only image flashing through my mind was that of the three little pigs tap-dancing across my field of vision. I tried to banish them, but every time I did they danced right across my brain, refusing to be dismissed. As if that weren't bad enough, they were performing their dance right next to a swimming pool.

My stranger started to cry. She had handed me a locket containing a lock of hair from her father, who had recently passed away. She had spent many hours at his house over the years, hanging out by the pool that he loved. Unbelievably, in his garden by the pool, he had a statue of the three little pigs in a dance pose, wearing top hats and canes.

Both she and I were in shock. Had you not told us to share any image, no matter how strange, I would never have confessed the silly pigs. We both agreed: this could not be coincidence but true communication. Although we did not understand it, we could not help but believe.

Jacqueline

The exact confirming details of the scenes and images shared by Jacqueline and her partner, a complete stranger to her, stagger the mind. How could the information that was received from the other, perhaps aided by the held object, be so clear and so accurate? It defies logic, and yet I have witnessed similar results a thousand times.

We are capable of using channels far beyond the usual five senses. We are designed to connect with each other at levels much deeper and more detailed than we can begin to imagine. Even their choice of a partner was not really coincidental. This is all part of the process that impels us along our spiritual paths.

Every one of us can connect to and be comforted by loving presences from the other side, the heavenly dimensions. A stranger describes Jacqueline's murdered daughter-in-law, standing there in a lake house that she had not known when she was alive. Her daughter-in-law is not vengeful, not tortured, not even jealous. She has loving messages for the childhood friend whom she had later married. She seems to be around Jacqueline, letting her know that she is fine and that she is transmitting love.

In more than twenty-three years of conducting this psychometry exercise, I have had no one other than Jacqueline mention seeing the three little pigs from the famous fairy tale. She described them to her partner, who perhaps needed to hear this more than any other person on the planet. Her father had placed a statute of the three little pigs in his garden by the pool. Who else has ever done this? And he had just recently died. What better message to convey through a complete stranger to his grieving daughter?

We never lose our loved ones. They are always with us, always around us. They are not in physical bodies, and we miss them terribly, but they are still here, hugging us with arms of loving energy.

Shirley's husband let her know that he was around her by sending her not only messages but also extraordinary gifts from the other side. Her story follows.

. FLOWER ARRANGEMENT .

There were so many extraordinary experiences for me on the cruises that I attended with psychiatrist Dr. Brian Weiss and a well-known medium, but perhaps the most unusual was the time that I received flowers from the other side.

We were in Tahiti. It was the first week of October in 1999, and the seminars were coming to a close. In the afternoon seminar with Dr. Weiss, we were invited to choose a partner, someone whom we had not met, and temporarily exchange a personal item. Although little happened to me, my partner became excited and began to describe my husband, who was recently deceased. She became quite articulate in describing an unusual tweed coat for which he was celebrated in northern Ontario. This was a first for me and the realization put me into shock, so I begged her not to call attention to us. This was a mistake, as such events are most interesting to everyone.

The next day, the last in Bora Bora, I took a small boat to seek a flower for my hair. There were few shops on the island, but I saw a lovely hibiscus flower in a window and attempted to buy it. The elderly salesperson spoke neither English nor French, yet she began to fill the openings in a large straw hat with flowers of a similar pink color. I tried to stop her, insisting on one flower only, but I was ignored.

A younger Polynesian woman entered, and I explained the difficulty. She replied, "It is you who are mistaken. This hat is a gift." The last boat was about to leave, and I could but give them each a hug and run toward it. Others told me afterward that the hat looked illuminated.

The last seminar was about to begin. In a meditative mood, I quickly became alert when the medium called my name and said that a man in top hat and tails wanted to dance with me. I knew that it had to be my husband. When first married, we would dance to records in the library. He went on with messages of gratitude for answering all the meaningful letters of bereavement and commented on the way that I'd reframed his picture and on its new setting. All was true. Then he said that I loved flowers and that he was sending me some, with love.

Someone in the group said, "And there they are, beside you, on your hat. They're magnificent!" How on earth (or maybe it wasn't on earth) did the Polynesian woman get the message?

One week later, I was invited with a small group of ladies to attend a party at Neiman-Marcus to introduce a new line of crystal. We were each given a brick of clay with utensils to free an enclosed gift in crystal. My gift was a small, pink, crystal hibiscus bloom.

ᘯ *Shirley*

Shirley's late husband was persistent in letting her know of his gratitude and his love. His tweed coat preceded several gifts of flowers, both real and crystal. The real ones appeared to be illuminated. Love can do that.

Spiritual messages can transcend the usual senses and be received in many ways. They do not require words or language. The older Polynesian woman spoke neither English nor French, yet she perceived the impulse and transformed it into the flowery gift. This might be normal in Bora Bora, but it seems like a small miracle to us.

As the author of the next story reminds us, "Anything is possible."

. HEALING AND HAPPINESS .

Recently, I went to see you at a seminar in Boston. It was the first time that I had ever been to anything like that before. I had read all your books and am interested in the subject of past lives and regression therapy. I have only been regressed once, at this seminar, and although it was just a short experience, it was nonetheless truly amazing.

We, the audience, were told to exchange something of personal property with the person sitting next to us in the auditorium. I gave to my neighbor the necklace that I wore. We were then told to close our eyes and to follow your instructions in order to try and "see something" into our neighbor's life. After the process was over, I told my neighbor what I had seen and envisioned while holding her item and listening to you. It so happens that I was very accurate in the telling of things that were going on in her life at the time, causing her to rethink some things that she had decided upon.

It was then my neighbor's turn to share what she had seen about my life. She began to tell me about a young blond-haired boy she saw that was playing and doing "boy things" across a river. The boy looked happy; he smiled at her. He was also waving a white flower. She gently touched my arm and said, "I have to tell you this. I wasn't sure if I should or not because it doesn't seem to make sense, but I feel like I need to. The young boy told me to tell you he's okay. He's happy. Do not be sad about him." I started to shed a few tears but tried to hold them back in front of this woman I did not know. I simply thanked her and left.

The reason for my crying is that when I was young, I had an abortion. I did not want to have one, but I felt pressured by my parents and boyfriend. I strongly believed at the time, and still do, that the baby had been a boy. I have felt guilty for this act since it happened. I often thought about the baby boy that I should have had.

This experience has helped me see that the baby is happy, playing and doing "boy things," which reassures me that I can be happy myself. Why else would this stranger feel the pressing need to tell me what the boy had told her? Why, out of all the people in the seminar, did I sit next to her? Obviously, there is no way that she could have known about this; very few people do. I believe, after this, that anything is possible. I finally feel much better about things that I cannot change.

$\sim$ *T. H.*

We carry so much unnecessary pain and grief on our shoulders, and we can let go of this burden through understanding. T.'s partner, a stranger to her, was not imagining the boy; she saw him clearly and felt a pressure, an urging, to deliver his message.

The river separates our physical world from the other side. It is an ancient symbol, prominent in Greek mythology and in many other cultures and religions. The concept of the other shore is found in the Buddhist Heart Sutra and numerous spiritual texts from the world over. Her partner did not see the river by accident.

The soul can never be harmed—not by death, not by abortion. The soul is evolving and growing on the other side. So T.'s son came to Boston to tell her not to grieve anymore because he is happy, he is okay. He is speaking to us all, because we all have lost or will lose loved ones. And when they visit us after they have died, whether in our dreams, reveries, meditations, through strangers, or in any other manner, their message will be so similar to the one given to T.: "Don't be so sad. I am fine. I am happy. We will always be together."

. *BRAIN* .

Landing at Iceland's International Airport on my way home to Tel Aviv was the perfect end to a wonderful vacation. I had been a participant in your workshop onboard a luxurious cruise ship from Fort Lauderdale to the Caribbean Islands.

As I wandered about the airport, I saw a shop exhibiting small figurines shaped like human heads. They were made of brilliantly colored transparent glass. When I approached them, I lifted one that was completely transparent, but I placed it back immediately as it looked so much like a skull of the dead. Instead, I chose another statuette that was made of a bright green color with a silvery mask. It was the work of a Swedish sculptor, an artist from Stockholm. I jumped at the unexpected opportunity to buy it. On the back side of the head was a blue shadow that looked like a human brain. It turned out that the artist himself called it *Brain,* recommending that people use it in everyday life as an object to reduce stress.

A year later, I participated again in another of your workshops on a cruise vessel, this time sailing from Puerto Rico. During one meditation session, I heard the sound of a drill behind my head, but I did not know then what it meant.

I went back home, and two months later I had an unexpected operation to remove a brain tumor.

After a long sick leave, I retired from my judicial status, and I even stopped working as a lawyer. Now I do things that I like to do: seeing my granddaughters, writing short stories, and painting. And I have never stopped thinking about this mystical, profound experience that I had with my brain and with *Brain.*

∽ *Aviva Shalem*

What we think of as accidents, coincidences, and random happenings are really not so at all. Aviva began receiving subconscious alerts, signs, or premonitions about her brain tumor more than a year before the diagnosis and surgery. At first she picked up the wrong figurine, but her intuition, perhaps enhanced by the workshop experiences and certainly the psychometry exercise, quickly led her to reject that one and to choose *Brain.* The drilling sound during her meditation the following year was another sign. Everything turned out to be fine, and her postsurgical life is much more peaceful and less stressful, just as the Swedish sculptor intended.

By selecting the object, holding it in her hands, and picking up on its unique energy and messages, Aviva was performing her own personal psychometry exercise. We all can do this at any time with the millions of objects around us—and then with the people whom we meet. Imagine how our world would expand if we allowed ourselves to become conscious of the beautiful energy that comprises every single thing. We would finally understand the magnitude of love and wisdom that surrounds us at all times.

Even strangers whom we have never met can provide us with incredible personal messages and insight, as Lori, the author of the following story, discovered one day during a workshop.

. CALL YOUR MOTHER! .

While attending your weekend seminar at the Omega Institute, I noticed a woman who seemed to be, shall we say, very uninterested in the topic of reincarnation. From her uncanny ability to sleep through most of the lecture that day, I assumed that she was every bit as disinterested in all that Omega had to offer.

About halfway through the day, you had everyone choose a partner who was not someone we knew and meditate while holding an item from him or her. Our task was to remember every image and thought that came to us while holding this item, and then share what came to us with each other.

As the crowd began to choose partners, it was apparent that others had also noticed this woman's disinterest. They seemed to be avoiding teaming up with her. I decided to ask her to be my partner, half to save her from being left alone and half to wow her with my intuition and thus prove to her that this was a worthwhile event.

I held her item, concentrated oh-so-very hard, and received plenty of images: a little white dog, a pool surrounded by a fence, an awning over the back porch leading to the pool, the feeling that it was very hot, and what seemed to be a message from the dog that all was okay.

We completed the meditation, and I was so excited that I simply had to go first. As I rattled off the list of visuals, all this woman kept saying was, "Hmm. No. Um . . . a pool, no. I live in the Bronx. Hot, no. Lived there my whole life. Dog, white, no."

A little let down by my partner's failure to connect with any of my seemingly astute details, I sat back to hear what she had received from my item. I was truly not expecting too much, due to the fact she had slept through most of the lecture. Boy, was I wrong!

In her very strong New York accent, she proceeded to tell me my entire life. "Cwall yur mutha" was how she started, and she went on to tell me about two homes with which my mother was having trouble deciding what to do, a miscarriage that my mother had had that involved a little boy spirit that had stayed with me (this was the second time I had been told this), and much more. All turned out to be true—I know this because the first thing I did afterward was, naturally, call my mother.

I was so excited after talking with her that I could not wait to tell everyone what had transpired. When you called on me to tell of my experience, I was floored again. What I had picked up on seemed to be for an audience member in the front row from a pet that had recently passed on. Every detail seemed to fit her life, and others had also picked up on the message from her beloved dog.

This wonderful experience taught me so much about how connected we truly are, and that we need not worry about the future or dwell in the past but rather live each and every moment to the fullest. And while we are doing so, we must always remember to "Cwall our muthas!"

ᐁ Lori Bogedin

This is why we are told not to judge a book by its cover; more so, not to judge at all. Lori was kind to choose her partner, and she was rewarded by a spot-on series of important messages, culminating with the little boy spirit.

Projection is the act of attributing your thoughts, feelings, or judgments onto others, and this act frequently creates distortion in reality. Things may not be as they seem or as you assume. For example, perhaps Lori's partner had been sleeping because she was tired, not because of disinterest. Maybe this was the second or third time that she was taking the course and already knew the lecture part, but was really returning for the experiential exercises.

We are connected to many more people than those in our immediate proximity, in this case Lori's partner. Lori accurately received information from a person in a different part of the room, a person who had just lost a little white dog. The same after-death message was there again: everything was okay. Animals have souls too.

Lori felt the deep peace, the flow, the unerring wisdom that all is as it is meant to be. Knowing this, she could live in the present moment, which is where happiness resides, instead of living in the future or the past. We must all do as Lori did and stay mindful. In my book *Only Love Is Real*, I elaborate on this concept.

> The Vietnamese Buddhist monk and philosopher Thich Nhat Hanh writes about enjoying a good cup of tea. You must be completely awake in the present to enjoy the tea. Only in the awareness of the present can your hands feel the pleasant warmth of the cup. Only in the present can you savor the aroma, taste the sweetness, appreciate the delicacy. If you are ruminating about the past or worrying about the future, you will completely miss the experience of enjoying the cup of tea. You will look down at the cup, and the tea will be gone.
>
> Life is like that. If you are not fully present, you will look around and it will be gone. You will have missed the feel, the aroma, the delicacy and beauty of life. It will seem to be speeding past you.
>
> The past is finished. Learn from it and let it go. The future is not even here yet. Plan for it, but do not waste your time worrying about it. Worrying is worthless. When you stop ruminating about what has already happened, when you stop worrying about what might never happen, then you will be in the present moment. Then you will begin to experience joy in life.

We must take the time to enjoy our tea—and our lives. It is so simple, and yet it is not easy. Let go of the worry and the fear. Fear is a toxic and debilitating emotion that robs us of joy, replacing it with anxiety, stress, and dread. Instead, be mindful of the sweetness that each day brings. Life is so full of exquisite beauty. Drink it all in.

Like Lori, I too have found that being at Omega Institute, or at any longer workshop of several days, leaves me in an altered state, one in which I can truly live in the present moment and feel the interconnectedness between all beings. I know that my consciousness is not in its normal mode; it moves from the everyday to the "other" perspective. Some characteristics of this perspective are a sense of loving detachment, of timelessness, of being nonjudgmental and more observing, and of a deep inner peace and calm.

The mystic and philosopher Krishnamurti, a wonderfully wise man, once wrote that you can set the table for this altered awareness but you cannot make the guest appear. In other words, you can create the conditions for it, yet you may have to wait for it to happen. Frequently, in teaching at Omega, my wife, Carole, and I leave the week or weekend with this extremely sublime feeling. We both know that it won't last, but we're always watching to see how long it will. Often, we will get from Rhinebeck, where Omega is located, to the airports in New York, and then something will happen there—rudeness, people shouting—that shifts us back to the ordinary consciousness. The transition is very abrupt and although we're quite aware of it, it is nonetheless difficult to return. The last time we were up there, however, it happened even more quickly.

Carole and I were driving away from Omega, and after about thirty minutes we stopped at a convenience store in a heavy rainstorm. She went into the store as I parked nearby, with many spots in front of and in back of my car. Inadvertently, even though there was nobody around me when I parked the car, I must have taken a spot that another person wanted. In this pouring rain, as Carole was inside the store while I waited in the car with the windows up, a man around my age, wearing just an undershirt, started circling around my car and yelling at me. I had no idea why, until I could hear him saying, "You took my spot. I want this spot."

It seemed so out of place to me. I was still feeling detached and filled with peacefulness, although it was now starting to ebb. As he stood outside my window, I noticed that he was wearing a medallion of the Virgin Mary around his neck. It struck me as extremely odd—and even inappropriate— that a man who wore a Mary medallion was yelling, screaming, and acting somewhat violently. The Virgin Mary is a symbol of loving-kindness, of reaching out to help people with arms of grace. This man wore her right next to his heart yet acted in a completely contradictory manner.

I knew that he could damage the car or break a window; he was capable of anything, ranting that way. And, at that moment, the shift happened.

Perhaps anxiety, alarm, or fear kicked in and required me to return to regular consciousness. I said something to him like, "I'm sorry. I didn't realize you were there. My wife is in the store, and I'm waiting for her. She knows that I'm here, but if I move, perhaps it will be difficult to find me. I apologize." With that, he left. I don't know exactly what was on his mind, but he disappeared.

Carole came out and we drove off. I explained the story to her, and that brought her out too.

It has occurred to us that people who meditate regularly or who reach transcendence have to deal with this issue. How do you relate to mundane concerns while in that beautiful space? How do you retain a state of peace, of love, and of compassion, yet not have people manipulate or take advantage of you? This is a very difficult task. Meditation, contemplation, introspection, and even reading a spiritual book will help. What I have found over the years is that some reminder of the state also helps to assist in returning to it. You just have to remind yourself of what it felt like. What was your breathing like? What was in your perceptual field? What physiological changes did you notice at the time?

I also find myself feeling similarly when I'm awakening from a particularly striking dream. I know not to eat or read the newspaper right away but just to stay with that state, because in that perceptual mode I'm aware of so much more. It's at once a feeling of being intuitive, of knowing things at a deeper level, of understanding. However, when going off to work, contemplating traffic, or engaging in some similar action, it is often necessary to return to that normal waking consciousness.

It is important to remind yourself that every step is sacred, every breath is holy. Stay in that mindful mentality and there will occur in you a shift in consciousness. You will have a feeling of complete peace. It is healthy for you—healthy for your body, healthy for your mind—to do this. You are a spiritual being, and this is your natural condition. Think of the "other" as your normal state, and think of the "everyday" as a temporary mode to help you get by in the physical world.

The exact manner in which a held object can facilitate the transmission of private facts and details in the psychometry exercise is not really known. It is possible that there is a transfer of energy, for many people describe the object as feeling warm or becoming hot as they hold it in their hand. Several ancient cultures have described a life force that empowers all beings and all of reality, one that contains a wisdom and intelligence beyond words. It has been called *chi* (or *ki*, or *qi*), *prana*, the Tao, the source, and numerous other names. The art of feng shui has attempted to describe its flow. Maybe this indescribable ocean of energy underlies the entirety of existence and is responsible for the transfer of intuitional insight and knowledge.

I have often wondered about the nature of the unknowable energy field. For example, how does it possess wisdom and other humanlike qualities? How do physical objects relate to the field? How do we appear from it and eventually return to it? How are its vibrations or frequencies modulated?

Perhaps this indefinable, omniscient, ethereal energy vibrates at the highest possible rate, and as its frequency is dampened it begins to manifest form: at first like a gas, wispy and spiritlike. As it condenses, the delicate gas becomes a sleek and smoothly flowing liquid, not yet with rigid boundaries. The solid or physical form, which takes shape as the liquid condenses even further, does have such boundaries and is relatively restricted compared to the other forms. The objects that we hand to our partners during the psychometry exercise are examples of this. And so, too, are we. Yet the basic energy is the same, all derived from the etheric. At the end, we simply return to that divine, idyllic form that is our source. There is no birth and no death—only transformation.

Earlier in my career, I sometimes wondered why I did not encounter the phenomenon of ghosts, or attached entities, or negative spirits in my practice. Others had written entire books about doing de-possessions or clearings of the clearly unfortunate host. And although I recognized, clinically, that most "cases" were actually projections of unwanted or uncomfortable impulses by the patients, perhaps not all of them were purely psychological. Yet I never actually came across any cases of malevolent spirits. Two subsequent meetings, one with several Tibetan rinpoches and the other with a Taoist master, helped me to understand why.

In 1994, I had the opportunity to sit down with some Tibetan rinpoches at the University of Michigan. During a lively discussion about reincarnation,

I was able to ask them why I had never once had a patient with an attached malevolent spirit.

The rinpoches immediately began laughing. Perhaps my question was too simplistic?

"No," one lama explained through an interpreter. "Your energy does not permit that in such close proximity." They laughed again. The question was not simplistic, I understood; I just had never thought of it in terms of energy fields. There was some kind of repelling force that kept those kinds of spirits from interacting with me.

By the spring of 2010, I still had never personally come upon such a case with any of my patients. At that time, I was traveling in China and had an audience with a leading Taoist master in the gentle green foothills outside Xi'an. Several Taoist scholars from nearby universities also attended. We spoke for an hour and covered many topics. Eventually, I asked the same question that I had posed to the Tibetan rinpoches sixteen years earlier. Once again, it was met with laughter. Once again, the answer was the same. This time, two interpreters were needed, one for the regional dialect into Mandarin and the other to translate from Mandarin to English, yet I am sure that there was little to no distortion.

"That energy would be too uncomfortable in your energy. That energy could not flow there. It could not happen."

There is nothing unique about my energy field. I meditate often, and this may raise one's vibration. Yet this practice is free, universal, and available to all. The answer of the lamas and the Taoist master was not specific to me; it applies to each of us. "Evil" spirits or manifestations can be equally as uncomfortable in your energy field as in mine. The important point is that by mastering our spiritual lessons, we become incompatible with that kind of energy. This is how you can cast out your own demons.

In addition to meditation, another way to raise our vibration is to fill our hearts and our minds with loving-kindness, with tranquility, and with peace. These qualities, I suspect, are very important in the process of re-fining the energy field. If incorporating these practices and principles into your daily life rids you of affliction, in whatever form, what a blessing you will receive.

The comments of the monks and scholars reflect the acceptance of the idea of negative spirits, but my impression from the discussion with them is that *ignorance* would be a more appropriate word than *evil* or *malevolent*. There is no real evil. Ignorant spirits might appear to be dark, but they are simply at an unenlightened (literally, "in the dark") level. They are like first-grade boys in a school yard, a bit wild and mischievous, perhaps pulling the girls' hair—but not evil. First graders are qualitatively the same as graduate students. The only difference is their level of knowledge and maturity. The boys are young and ignorant, but eventually they will become the graduate students.

. 8 .

One of a Kind

Some stories defy easy categorization because they touch on new or rare concepts, on modern physics or parallel universes, on future lives, or even on psychically turning babies who are in the breech position prior to birth. The cases in this chapter fall into this category, and they offer fascinating insights into our deeper natures and the characteristics of the soul. We are eternal and multidimensional beings, in these physical bodies for a brief time to learn important spiritual lessons. As the Jesuit mystic Teilhard de Chardin stated: "We are not human beings having a spiritual experience. We are spiritual beings having a human experience."

Spiritual beings are not constrained by the usual limits of time, space, or the physical body. This seems an extraordinary freedom—and yet it is our natural state. It is who we are; we merely forget this.

Allow the stories in this chapter to remind you.

. PROGRESSION TO THE FUTURE .

My experience was a personally moving one that occurred whilst taking the course you provided at Omega in 2007. It took place in a revelatory practice session that turned out to be a progression, rather than the intended regression.

My reason for attending your past-life regression therapy training was to expand my therapeutic arsenal. I have a private complementary practice that offers interventions based on techniques drawn from the field of energy psychology. Along with my academic studies in the general field of psychology, I have also spent the last twenty years studying much of the metaphysical literature on healing and well-being, in particular *The Seth Material,* authored by Jane Roberts. You informed me that you were reminded of this work by a question I had asked about the possibility of "recall" of a concurrent lifetime. Back in 2006, it was my study of such material in relation to a percentage of clients who were failing to respond to a variety of approaches I offer that led me to believe that other lives of such individuals may be involved.

The practice session began with the class being paired off with someone unfamiliar to us. I was paired with an American woman for the purposes of practicing the rapid induction technique. I went first as practitioner, and she appeared to respond well to the induction. I proceeded to guide her through a past-life recall of some detail as a pioneer in the exploration of the American West.

When we reversed roles, I too was receptive to rapid induction, and she proceeded by guiding my mind to a series of doors leading to past lives. I passed through a door made of frame-to-floor lengths of beading, which were popular as space-saving entrances to kitchens and such over the years. On the other side of this entrance, I was greeted by two beings that were physically intertwined: their heads were cheek-to-cheek, foreheads higher and broader than usual, with crystal blue eyes also somewhat larger than the human norm but not as large as the alien-face depictions commonly seen in science-fiction illustrations. Their bodies appeared to meld together into a plaited form, where limbs were barely discernible and legs disappeared into a tapering wisp of material.

I sensed a benevolent and loving energy emanating from their being toward me. I knew that they were my guides. More than this, though, afterward I was drawn to the term oft used in recent years—"guardian angels"—although I don't adhere to the religious overtones associated with this term. I had no idea as to where they may have been guiding me as they each put out a hand to grasp mine before flying out into space, leaving Earth behind us.

After a seemingly brief trip through the stars, we eventually began approaching another world, a planet with an atmosphere, a blue-and-white globe similar to the Earth that we had left behind. We began hovering above this strange world, high in the stratosphere. They still had hold of my hand, although I could sense that they were encouraging me to release my grip and drop through the clouded atmosphere below. I became apprehensive about doing so, but I also sensed that they were reassuring me that my fears would be readily dissipated if I would just trust in myself and them. What I needed to see was on the surface of the planet below.

I managed to let go of their hands and begin a slow, gliding descent through the clouds. Before long, the land below came into view: a green carpet of vegetation clearly of a temperate climate zone, and then signs of management of the landscape, with fields and hedgerows coming into view. Instantly, I found myself in a field, a pasture that seemed to be sloping very, very gently down toward a river, although the river was not visible to me. I was standing on the meadowland of the floodplain to the river. As I took in this beautiful setting and noticed the sun striking various patches of meadow as it broke through the clouds, I became aware of someone standing close to me. He was a tall, silver-haired individual, with an air of distinction about his countenance. He wore pastel-colored cotton robes that appeared light and appropriate for the warm ambient temperature.

It was me! An older me, but definitely me. I watched myself turn and look over my left shoulder, up the hill to a building about two hundred yards distant. It was a château, a three-story building of considerable size, nestled amongst the trees. I knew it to be a place of learning, a sanctuary or retreat. I knew that I was in France, that the year was 2037, and that the "me" that stood before me was on the faculty of the learning establishment up on the hill. This was a scene from my future, and I was a teacher, clearly at one with himself and his role.

Needless to say, my fellow student was quite amazed as I recounted my feelings about the experience and my certainty that I had progressed forward to an age of eighty-four. What had been shown to me by my "guardian angels" was something that I had never consciously contemplated before. I had never considered becoming a teacher; if anything, it was a profession that I had always dismissed as hard work with little reward.

The following year, through past-life regression work with clients and on myself, together with further study of contemporary metaphysical information sources, I came to realize my true intent and purpose for my life: to teach. I experienced an epiphany that my spiritual guides, a year or so before, had shown me a probable outcome if followed up. What was I to teach? This came very quickly to me: to teach others what I have learned about the nature of one's being from my diverse studies over the last twenty-five years of my life. To do for others what I had done for myself: integrate knowledge from science, metaphysics, philosophy, and spirituality into solid, practical guidance on the discovery of one's purpose in this current lifetime. I now know that this knowledge is the key to leading a life of value and fulfillment. It is knowledge that is implicit to the change in consciousness that mankind is currently experiencing.

∽ *Chris Johnson*

___

Regression therapy involves taking a patient back to some earlier point in time, whether in this lifetime or a prior one or somewhere in between. Progression therapy, on the other hand, moves the patient ahead in time and, as Chris's story illustrates, it can be equally therapeutic. It is a subject that I have written about and documented extensively in my previous book, *Same Soul, Many Bodies*.

There are many possible futures, both our personal ones as well as global ones. Our individual and collective decisions will help determine which are realized, although many or all may be concurrently progressing in alternate dimensions.

Yet there seems to be one that is most likely or probable to happen. Here Chris's spiritual guides (or the manifestation of his subconscious wisdom) are letting him glimpse the one in which he will feel happiest and most fulfilled. Having seen this "best" outcome, he can now knowingly connect the dots and reach this goal. His decisions in the present can actually take him to the future he most desires.

Interestingly, Chris appears to travel into space and "through the stars" to reach France in 2037. This prospective Earth seems to be not quite physically here. Perhaps it represents an alternate dimension or reality that is connected to Earth of the current time, yet not exactly the same. If we patiently wait for time to unfold, we will meet it. However, if we can travel out of body and through space, maybe we can meet it much sooner. We travel the fast route to tomorrow, we grab the blueprint of time, and then we return to the present with this precious map. Knowing the plan and the goal, we can consciously choose the journey to our optimal future.

Even if you are not able to see your own optimal future so clearly, you can nevertheless trust your intuitional wisdom to guide you there. Do not let fears or doubts cloud your vision and obscure your path. Listen to your heart.

The geographical locations of our next lives are not important. The quality is the critical factor. If we are progressing to lifetimes filled with kindness and understanding, we will inevitably wind up in the proper dimension.

In his story, Chris mentions the possibility of recalling a concurrent life, or one that is happening at the same time as your present one. What would a regression involving nearly simultaneous lifetimes look like? Read Donna's story, next, for one possible example.

. TRILOGY IN TIME .

One of my favorite and most compelling past-life memories is a trilogy. I was shown three consecutive lifetimes that were very poignant and that demonstrated how an individual grows from his or her experiences.

In the first scene, I see myself wearing the green uniform of a German SS soldier. Three of my buddies and I are standing next to our military vehicle, which is pulled over on the shoulder of an isolated country road in Germany. We are smoking cigarettes, talking, and laughing while writing a report of our completed assignment. It is cold out, and I can see the white mist coming from our mouths as our breath hits the cold air. On the right of us is open farmland, which is surrounded by wooden fencing, a few cows, charming farmhouses, and the Alps in the background. On the left, across the street from where we are standing, is a pine forest, pristine and untouched—except for the Jewish camp that we have just decimated with our rifles and machine guns. A farmer had spotted a campfire during the night and alerted the "authorities." We had been sent out to investigate the report, and we found a group of Jewish families, men and women of all ages and many children. We systematically wiped them all out and then proceeded to go through their belongings to see if there was anything of value that we might want.

In the next instant, the scene changes. Now I am a slightly heavyset, Jewish Polish woman standing inside a women's dormitory in a concentration camp. My little five-year-old son is standing in front of me. It's cold, and my son is wearing a too-large, coarsely woven sweater that is rolled up at his wrists and that hangs down to his knees. He has straight, blond hair falling into his eyes; it looks like it could use a shampooing. With surprise, I recognize him as my son in this lifetime. There is a loud bang behind us, and the dormitory doors fly open. Camp guards barge into the dorm, shouting *"Alle der kinder aus"* ("All the children out") and pushing the children along ahead of them with the butts of their rifles. The mothers are screaming; the children are crying and clinging to their mothers. Just as a guard approaches my son, the boy turns and grabs on to the wooden structures that serve as beds to hold on and keep from being swept away. My heart explodes with pain and horror as I watch him being shoved along with the other children, who are all taken away.

Then the scene changes again. This time, I am a German officer. My uniform is brown, and I am wearing heavy leather boots. I am in an empty office; I can hear my footsteps echo around me as I walk to a desk in the center of the room. The room has high ceilings and is dimly lit by a gray light filtering in from the only window. I search the desk drawers for a stamp with which to mark the documents that I am carrying in the inside pocket of my jacket. The documents are meant to assist in the escape of Jewish individuals. I keep looking over my shoulder to make sure that I am not discovered. I sense that later I am caught and executed by firing squad, but not before I have assisted in the escape of a large number of Jews.

∾ Donna West

Once you leave your physical body, you bring your knowledge, your wisdom, and the fruits of your Earth experience to the other side. You have to face the results of your thoughts and deeds from your temporary sojourn on this physical planet. Your good and kind actions are greeted with great joy, for you have been learning and mastering the lessons that you were sent here to accomplish. Your negative, violent, and unkind actions are met with dismay. You feel the pain of those you have harmed. You understand at a very deep level that this is not the spiritual path. In future lives, you must repay the people you have hurt with love and compassion. You make it up to them, you make them whole, and great healing occurs. This repayment is not a form of punishment on the other side—it is just learning that the consequences of our actions must be repaired.

In the first memory of this trilogy, Donna's behavior hurt others. As the mother in the concentration camp, she experienced what it felt like to be the victim of such behavior. The final lifetime of the three gifted her with the opportunity to again be a German soldier, but this time she reached out with love to save the lives of others—even at the expense of her own life. There were no more scenes after this; there was no need. Donna had not only learned about love and compassion but had embodied them beautifully. The lesson was complete.

Donna's recollection of three simultaneous lifetimes is not far-fetched. It probably reflects the shared memories of her soul group. The writer Jane Roberts, author of the Seth books that Chris references in the first story of this chapter, describes the ability of souls to split and to experience concurrent lives. Souls are not constrained by the limitations of the physical body. We are connected at the soul level and can share all experience. The concepts of the akashic records, a knowledge of all things, and the collective unconscious, a similar idea offered by the psychoanalyst Carl Jung, reflect this potentiality. Perhaps we are all emanations or sparks of the One. Perhaps we are descended from an all-encompassing, invisible energy. Or perhaps, as Catherine uttered so long ago and as I recorded in *Many Lives, Many Masters,* "there are many gods, for God is in each of us."

The conscious, left-brained mind can often get in the way of our experiences, interrupting a spiritual encounter with overly intellectual questions and speculations. It tells us that we are our bodies, that time is linear, that we exist in the physical dimension only. But when we fall asleep and dream, the grip of our conscious mind is relaxed and released and our subconscious is in control, just as it is during hypnosis. For that reason, dreams are often the settings where past-life memories and mystical insights reveal themselves, as the author of the next story discovered.

. NIGHT FLIGHT .

About six years ago, my friend and I attended one of your weekend workshops. I listened and participated in all of the lectures and hypnotherapy sessions and was amazed at what other attendees experienced, although I had no personal results. I was a bit frustrated, albeit fascinated.

We were staying nearby at a bed-and-breakfast, and on the last night, while sleeping, I had a lucid dream that I will never forget. With increasing vibrations, I flew out of the window of the room and found myself "flying" over a lush green valley with houses strewn around randomly. I knew it was an ancient village, although I do not know where it was. The roofs were thatched. I had a profound feeling that I was observing a place where I had once lived. I then came back to my bed, again through the window, and had the same experience all over again.

The memory stayed with me because of the intensity of the vibrations. The next morning, I realized that I had probably experienced a past-life episode, but that rather than during the sessions, it was on my own during sleep. Therefore, the hypnotherapy had "worked" for me, but I must have been resisting it during the active sessions.

I often wonder where that little village was, and I would love to go back.

                                        ∽ *Victoria*

Past-life memory fragments may emerge in dreams. These are actual memories, not Freudian symbols or metaphors. Victoria's experience was of this type, and it also incorporated elements of a flying or out-of-body dream and lucid dreaming. The daytime regressions, which were not particularly successful for her, may have helped set the stage for its occurrence. I have frequently observed this delayed effect, where the regression experience happens after the session, whether through a dream, or spontaneously in a déjà vu feeling, or in other ways. The mind has been made receptive, and so the memory follows. Patience and practice facilitate this process.

If I were regressing Victoria in my office, her dream would be the doorway that I would use to recall that lifetime with the thatched roofs.

It is the experience that is important, not the method used to reach it.

To illustrate these points, only a day after I conducted a one-day workshop in New York City I received similar and simultaneous messages from two people who had participated, although neither knew the other. One wrote that she had had no past-life recollections at the event and had in fact fallen asleep, just as she had during the previous workshops she had attended, and just as she had every time she listened to one of my regression CDs. The morning after, she decided to play the CDs consecutively and, once again, fell asleep. But this time, she awoke intermittently as they were playing and saw not one but many lifetimes. In the CD, I encourage listeners to visualize their past lives like a strand of pearls on a necklace. This woman had never successfully visualized anything during her many attempts at regression, but suddenly she could very clearly see her "child-made necklace with different beads." It was an amazing breakthrough, she wrote, and I must agree.

The other participant had also attended the workshop and had not had any past-life memories, but she too remained patient. That night, she had a series of dreams. "Upon awakening," she described, "I fully understood what I needed to do in my life. It was amazing to have the clarity. I suppose my avenue of communication is easiest in the dream state. Now I have the skills to interpret them." Engaging in the meditations during that day's workshops might have seemed fruitless at first, but that very night she had dreams that had elucidated her entire purpose in life. What a wonderful gift to be given!

In the next story, Horace presents another potential method to reach conceptual understanding. I encourage you to physically engage in the exercise he describes, if possible, for doing so provides an intuitive comprehension of how reincarnation can occur in the multidimensional universe.

. FLATLANDERS .

I am a theoretical physicist with a Ph.D. from Yale that I received in 1968. About the time that I read your book *Many Lives, Many Masters*, I was also reading a number of theoretical physics papers on large higher dimensions. Some physicists now are testing for the evidence of higher physical dimensions. For example, they could test for the existence of a fourth extraspatial dimension by seeing if gravitational forces at very small distances change to an inverse cube instead of an inverse square law. This is still speculative, but it is of possible relevance for your work in giving reincarnation a physically intuitive mechanism.

To explain what I mean, I take the ideas of the nineteenth-century author A. Abbott, who wrote the book *Flatland*. In that book, Abbott describes what it would be like to be a two-dimensional being, and how such a being would experience a strange extra third dimension. From this point of view, consider the model of a hand. Take your hand and place the fingertips on a flat surface (a large-enough flat surface would be a "Flatlanders universe"). Now, suppose the tips of your fingers represent the physical manifestation of a group of Flatlanders. Their interactions with one another would correspond to the tips of your fingers becoming near to one another on the Flatlanders world (the flat surface). I envision the soul of each Flatlander as the whole finger itself. For a Flatlander, the finger would be like a higher three-dimensional manifestation of his "physical" two-dimensional self.

What happens when the physical two-dimensional Flatlander dies? Lift your finger from the flat surface, leaving behind the two-dimensional manifestation of the three-dimensional soul. As time passes, that same finger (soul) arches back down toward the plane, and it plants itself at a different location. The soul (third dimension) becomes reincarnated into another two-dimensional Flatlander body. The many fingers of the three-dimensional hand become like the many souls that seem to be associated with one another from one two-dimensional life to the next.

I have found that this demonstration gives people a much clearer intuitive sense about how reincarnation may occur. It also gives a possible physical explanation of how ESP, mediumship, precognition, and the whole panoply of paranormal phenomena could work. Now all the physicist must do is find experimental evidence for this hypothesized "third spatial dimension" (or fourth spatial dimension for us, of course).

∽ *Horace Crater*

This is a very intriguing model of the possible mechanisms of the paranormal, and of how physics may one day be able to explain the mystery of reincarnation and the journey of the soul.

Physicists have become the mystics of our own age, bridging miracles and science. I remember the words of the great physicist Albert Einstein:

> A human being is part of the whole we call the universe, a part limited in time and space. He experiences himself in his thoughts and feelings as something separated from the rest . . . a kind of optical illusion of his consciousness. This illusion is a prison for us, restricting us to our personal desires and to affection for only the few people nearest us. Our task must be to free ourselves from this prison by widening our circle of compassion, to embrace all living beings and all of nature.

We can use scientific principles, such as those found in physics and chemistry, to grasp our divine nature, just as Horace eloquently does. For example, in my workshops I often use a metaphor of ice cubes to help explain human nature and the relationship of the body to the mind and to the soul.

Imagine if ice cubes floating in cold water had consciousness. There would be discussions about ice cubes from one particular tray to another: "Our edges are sharper than yours," or "We cubes are clearer and more symmetrical than you are." Eventually, these discussions would lead to arguments, and then to war, and we would have the equivalent of life here on Earth. But we know that if we heated the water, all the ice cubes would melt. Every ice cube, from every tray, would be the same: water.

Water has always been a metaphor for spirit. The ice cubes never truly had an independent existence. They originated from water, and they disappeared into it when they were heated. The essence of the ice cube was really the H_2O molecule, vibrating at a slower rate. As heat is added, the rate of vibration increases and the ice cubes melt. The entire time, their existence was an illusion. They were just the H_2O molecule, just water, all along.

What happens if you keep heating the water? Eventually, even this disappears. Everything is steam, invisible—but not empty. The H_2O molecule is still there, but now it's vibrating at a very rapid rate. It becomes steam merely through a transformation of the molecule. We know this because if you condense or cool the steam, it turns back into water. If you keep cooling the water and you put the ice cube trays back in the freezer, after some time you'll have the ice cubes once again. This is their cycle.

Now imagine that you keep heating this steam; in this case, once again, with heat energy. As the H_2O molecule splits, you get subatomic particles, quasars, quarks, and other elements of these types. So even beyond the steam are more states, and as you go further and further they become more and more indescribable by human thoughts or words.

And this reflects our own nature. Here in these earthly bodies, we are like the ice cubes: vibrating at our slowest rate, solid, heavy. What happens if you heat us? In our case, this is done not with the energy of heat but of love. This is what raises our vibration—the presence of unconditional love, and the capability to open our hearts; to live with empathy, compassion, kindness, and altruism; and to help others to reach their potential.

The equivalent of the ice cubes melting into water would be our transformation back into spirit. Our true nature is that of spiritual beings. As we continue to raise our vibration, what is the equivalent of the steam? Well, it would be whatever exists beyond spirit. Then there's whatever exists beyond that—and beyond that. So we are, in this sense, like the ice cubes. We have many dimensions, all of which are connected through the vibratory rate.

We may talk about the existence of God and the higher planes, but we do not have the words or the comprehension to understand it completely. This is one reason that it is very difficult to answer the questions, "Why did God even create the earth? What is the purpose?" We cannot know what is going on at these spheres that are equivalent to the subatomic particles in the ice analogy. What we do know is that we are here, and that we are the physical manifestation of this highest energy. Our energy is love—not the H_2O molecule, but love.

In this sense, we do not have to know all the answers. Frequently, I tell people, "I don't know," because I really don't know the answer to some of these most difficult questions. But what I do know is that we are spiritual beings whose basic essence is of love, empathy, kindness, compassion, and altruism. These are the actions and attitudes that elevate our vibration, raise our consciousness, and enable us to return to that home where everything is one and everything is connected.

Once, as I was explaining the metaphor of the ice cubes, the water, and the steam, I was talking to an audience while sitting in a chair on the podium. I realized, at that moment, that sitting in the chair was connected to the idea of those ice cubes. Here on Earth, the chair was solid to me. I trusted it to support my weight, I sat in it, I stood up, I sat in it again. But I was aware that, at another level, the chair was composed of molecules: ones that made up the fabric, others the wood, and so on. These molecules could also be separated into their component energies. So while the chair was solid and supporting my weight, it was also molecules, atoms, nuclei, subatomic particles, and even smaller particles—and eventually, of course, energy. How amazing that an object that I could touch and sit down in was actually pure energy. It could probably power the planet if completely and efficiently harnessed.

We are also like this chair: we are physical, but we are pure energy. So when we say that we are not human beings having a spiritual experience but spiritual beings having a human experience, these things are really happening at the same time. Only the smallest part of us is in the body; most of us is not. Consciousness is not limited by the brain or the body but surpasses them. Much like the ice cubes, water, steam, and beyond-steam state, we simultaneously exist in the material realm, the spiritual realm, the ones that lie beyond that, and then into the light realms and others that we cannot even fathom.

Think of all the solar systems, star systems, galaxies, and universes that cosmologists tell us are constantly being created. These are limitless and of a magnitude way beyond our grasp, yet they are just the beginning. There are also nonphysical dimensions, energetic ones, and ones that defy our imagination. It truly baffles the mind and brings us back to the concept that we are humans and yet that we are energy.

This is a glimpse into our nature and into the nature of God. When you think in these terms, there has to be something that existed before anything else: something that had no cause, that had no precedent. When we have a chair or an ice cube, we have a cause, a precedent. There was the water molecule, or the water that existed before we froze it. The chair existed as trees and as plants before it was made into a chair, and those trees and plants existed in their own precursor form, perhaps as seeds. But there is something that had no precursor, that has existed forever, that is incomprehensible to us, that was never formed, that never disappears. Everything else is simply different states of energy, like the chair or the ice cube—except for this.

In ancient cultures, some people call this the Tao. We say the same thing when we say, "Trust the process." That means following the Tao, or the way, or the flow. The words do not matter; it is a concept of a wise and loving intelligence that has existed before creation, that will always exist, and that from which emanates everything else: all the ice cubes, water, and steam; the chair; our bodies; our spiritual nature; and whatever lies beyond that. It is something wise, hidden, and completely and unconditionally loving that lies as a foundation of all created things.

In understanding this, we are able to let go of those things that are not important: fame, success, recognition, money, objects. We take none of these things with us. What we bring back are those lessons that we learned and mastered. We bring back the opening of our hearts. It does not matter if we do not understand these things completely at the present time. Our heart knows in its deepest recesses. And as we follow our hearts and our intuition, we are led back home.

The concept of reincarnation and of past-life regression relates to many branches of science, not only physics. Susie, in the next story, discusses how she has applied this work in the field of anatomy and physiology.

. HYPNOSIS AND PREGNANCY .

I am a reflexologist specializing in pre- and postpregnancy sessions, and part of the reason for my trip to the Omega Institute for your 2010 training was to find out more about the unborn child.

One of the most fascinating topics that we discussed was how we can be regressed to being inside our mother's womb. I have done this personally, and I've found it to be not only very interesting but also equally moving to actually feel the emotions of such a small person before setting foot on this earth plane.

Over the past few months, since the training ended, I have seen ten women with their babies in a breech position. All were around thirty-five to thirty-eight weeks and were desperate to try anything to turn their babies. Whilst working on their feet, I talked them through a visualization that I had created to help them connect with their unborn baby. It starts by having them, in their mind, tiptoe into the uterus, where they simply talk to the babies, reassure them that all is well, and, more important, tell them that Mummy loves them. The women tend to stay there for a few minutes and then I bring them back, finish the work on their feet, and awaken them if they've fallen asleep. To my amazement, all ten babies turned, and each was birthed in the normal position.

I know this is only a small section of women, but so far it has been 100 percent successful. The other interesting fact about this is that an overwhelming majority of the women had experienced a miscarriage before this pregnancy. If I had my spiritual hat on, I would say that the women had not fully dealt with the emotional trauma of the miscarriage, that there was still emotion locked in the body, and that, sadly, the baby was picking up on it.

∽ *Susie Gower*

Are these wondrous events, or is it that we do not yet understand the science and physiology underlying babies turning from the breech position? I do know that mother-and-baby communication is profound and real, even during the prenatal period. Susie is helping to validate these multilevel in utero bonds—these tiny miracles.

Even if our minds cannot fully comprehend the events described in the stories of this book, it is essential that we keep them open and inquisitive so that experience and learning can occur, as the next story demonstrates.

. SHIFTING FROM SKEPTICISM .

In April 2011, I attended your seminar in Sydney, catching the bus from Canberra the night before. I was of two minds about attending because I had started to have doubts about whether or not any of this "New Age" stuff was really true. I thought that I would just attend the morning session, see how it went, and then wander around Darling Harbour for the afternoon if I wasn't convinced of its worth.

While I was a little skeptical initially, my main hope was that I would be able to work on reducing or eliminating my phobia about wearing tight clothing and to get rid of that claustrophobic feeling of being constricted. These feelings result in panic attacks that affect my personal life and my work.

During the second exercise at the seminar, the person whom I was sitting beside took my wedding ring and had a feeling of a train struggling through a dark, smoggy, dirty city. As the train moved through a tunnel, it came out into a wonderful green landscape with beautiful views and pastures. More amazingly, she picked up on tightness around my chest and the difficulty breathing. This is exactly how I feel with my claustrophobic clothing.

While I can't say that I saw a huge difference straightaway, as I was wearing loose clothing, I felt extremely pleased that I hadn't left at lunchtime. I was on the bus on the way home, thinking about all of the exercises I had participated in at the seminar. That night, I had one of the best sleeps I have had for years. No waking up in the middle of the night with worries about work. No trouble falling to sleep.

∾ *Cherelle*

Shifts were occurring in Cherelle's psyche. She slept better than she had in years. For the insomniacs among us, this is hugely important. To have doubts is all right, as long as the doubts do not block you from opening your mind and allowing yourself to experience. Try not to get caught up in overly cerebral arguments about what you are discovering. Don't stop reading about it, don't stop learning, and don't stop growing just because you have an intellectual objection. Perhaps there is an answer to your question, even if you have not yet uncovered it. Do not let the unexamined opinions and judgments of others influence your heartfelt actions and compassionate nature.

Dr. Helen Wambach, a psychologist who was highly cynical of the idea of past lives, led a large-scale scientific investigation into the field in the 1960s. She began her series of experiments with the intention of disproving the theory of reincarnation, but her results had the opposite effect: she found that an overwhelming majority of details recalled during past-life regressions were consistent with historical data and records. After publishing her findings in books such as *Life Before Life* and *Reliving Past Lives*, the former skeptic concluded, "I don't believe in reincarnation—I know it."

Our past- and present-life ailments span an entire spectrum, ranging from mild symptoms like claustrophobia and insomnia to severe depression and thoughts of suicide. The next story illustrates a question that comes up frequently about one end of the spectrum: What are the consequences of taking your own life?

. UNDERSTANDING SUICIDE .

In many of my lifetimes, I committed suicide and in this lifetime, not surprisingly, as karma would have it, I lost a brother to suicide. I have also "talked down" a number of my friends from attempting it, well before I was a therapist, and I have worked with many suicidal clients.

                ∽ *Gregg Unterberger*

Although I do talk briefly about suicide in an earlier chapter, I have excerpted this portion of one of Gregg's stories because it makes several additional points. Gregg took his own life in a number of his incarnations. Eventually, he recognized that it did not benefit his education here in this earth school to keep cutting classes so early. He had learned one piece of his lesson. But to truly understand and feel how his decisions affected his loved ones during those lifetimes, he had to experience it firsthand with the death of his own brother. Now he was on the receiving end of the action. His brother's untimely death was not a karmic punishment for having taken his own life in the past and, although undoubtedly a difficult and painful event, it afforded Gregg a new perspective with which to understand the impact and effects of suicide. Having learned from both sides, Gregg was finally in a position to integrate his knowledge and put it to use by helping others.

You can never harm the soul. Your consciousness awakens on the other side after a successful suicide, only to learn that it is intact and must return to this earth plane to face and master the very same lessons from which it had tried to escape. "So that was not the solution," it realizes. "I should have stayed; I should have made other choices." It will oftentimes be faced with similar circumstances as those that may have precipitated the decision in the first place, and it will need to find another way of coping without harming the physical body, that great gift which provides our souls with so many opportunities to evolve and grow. The lessons must be learned, no matter how many lifetimes are required.

Gregg has learned them, and he has become a lifeguard to those in despair. He has acquired a special insight and empathy to help those contemplating suicide, and they would be wise to listen to him.

Some forms of suicide have less consequence than others. For a ninety-year-old person with intractable, permanent, and disabling pain to end his life, or for a person afflicted with severe mental illness to do so (as it may be the illness itself that is responsible for that decision) is not the same, karmically, as it is for a forty-year-old businessman who has been embroiled in some financial scandal. Yet I have found that there is a commonality among people who take their own lives—as well as among children who die young—in that their souls are returned to Earth more quickly, for there is still so much that needs to be learned.

I believe that we learn up to the last moments of our physical lives. For this reason, suicide is never part of our soul's plan. Our lives always have more to teach us. As students in this earth school, some of us may be in the first grade, the sixth grade, or high school, but eventually, with enough education, we will all graduate and leave this school behind. And then there are other schools, higher dimensions or levels where we continue our spiritual progression. But until we *all* graduate, none of us does, for we are all one. We may come back voluntarily to help other people, or animals, or sentient beings to evolve. Or we may help out from the other side even if we do not incarnate in physical bodies, and there we will continue to work to assist those other souls with whom we have been connected for eons of time.

Do not be concerned with how many millennia it takes you to complete your classes. If you are progressing to be a kinder, more loving, less selfish, less violent person, then you are moving in the right direction. The direction is more important than the speed. It makes no difference if this is your first lifetime or your last, or if you have many more to go. Only the end matters.

Of course, the act of harming or killing the body is not limited to the self. History is filled with examples of how we have perpetrated ignorance, hatred, and violence by hurting one another. But they provide an important legacy from which to learn and their lessons are invaluable, as the next story beautifully illustrates.

. THE EASTERN THEATER .

I first attended your workshop in the late nineties at the Jewish Book Fair, and again several years ago in St. Louis. Since childhood, I had been seeing "pictures" of what seemed to be history from different time periods. Whether reading or listening in history classes in school or watching movies, I would sometimes experience the events depicted very dramatically, as though I were actually there and seeing, hearing, smelling, and feeling those things around me. One past-life experience, in particular, ended tragically in World War II in the Eastern Theater and remained very disturbing for me up until several years ago.

I wish to preface this with the current-life fact that even though I was not raised Jewish, I was descended from European, Native American, and some Jewish lines. I knew little or nothing about Judaism. In the midnineties, I began being unavoidably drawn to Judaism, immersing myself in the Jewish community and attending a synagogue. I also began a two-year extension course in Jewish studies offered by Hebrew University and started studying Hebrew. At that time, I saw a therapist and asked to be hypnotized to find out more about what seemed to be memories.

From that point, I began to draw pictures of what I remembered. I was startled to notice that they seemed to be parts of a story that could be arranged in order because of how old I was in each memory. As difficult as it was, I allowed myself to recall more and more, and to write down the details of what I recalled. This is my story.

In that life, I was born in the late 1920s in Eastern Europe, near Prague, to an interesting family of good people. There was a brother nearly two years older than I, and a sister a little more than three years older. My mother was related to the Polish ruling family; my father was an agent for the Jewish resistance in what is now Israel. As they both were trying to report events to influence peace for Europe, it was a natural attraction. I suppose that you could say that they shouldn't have had an interfaith marriage in those times. But as my father told it, my Jewish grandfather smiled and sighed when he was told about his son's intentions with his future bride. Our general story, as we traveled over Europe, often in volatile cities where history's outcomes were being made, was that my father was a traveling salesman selling kitchenware. But I never saw any pots or pans, only a leather briefcase filled with papers with lots of typing.

Still in that lifetime, as a girl of about two years old, I visited a farmhouse in southern Poland, one with a view to the north across a valley. I awakened from napping on a rug on the floor and, hearing the muffled cry of a baby, went to the window and crawled up on a wood box. I saw my mother and a young cousin taking down the laundry from a weblike winding laundry line on a pole. I could hear tall aspen and pine tree leaves clattering at the near edge of the narrow clearing. It was very windy. I noticed the laundry basket with clothes piling up in it and was concerned that the baby might be in there. I tried to call out, but the wind took my breath away. As I looked out over the valley, there were ominous clouds coming from the wrong direction. There was a vague scent of fear deep in the air that wasn't good. I didn't know it then, but it was a hint of what was to come. (I think feelings such as joy, fear, anger, and so on are molecularly present in the air and are rather revealing to little tots, who are quite aware of feelings of danger or safety.)

In the early 1930s, when I was just a little girl visiting my Jewish grandparents near a city in central Europe, there was a particularly bad winter. I dearly loved my paternal grandfather. He was so wise and kind, and he spoke different languages. We were crossing an icy, snowy street, and I saw a fruit tree. I was about three, and as we went through the cold archway, I asked him if the tree would live. It seemed out of place there in the median in a high, cold city. He said, "If God wants it to." A sharp wind blew through the archway and caused fear in me.

Times were hard for my grandparents. My mother would take food to them whenever we visited; that is, whatever small goods she could carry, smoked from her sister's farm. Once, she "accidentally" left a pretty Russian fine-woven scarf there for Grandma. Grandma's name was Lisa, but once, while visiting, I overheard my grandfather call to her one night, "Leah, let down your hair," in a soft and loving way.

For a while, my mother would take us three children on the train to visit Father, who traveled with business to different cities in Europe. He was always glad to see her. But as things got rougher, she could only take me, perhaps somewhat for protection. We met one time in northwestern Europe—Berlin, perhaps—with a stout businessman. As we had no babysitter, I got to attend, as long as I was good. I was nearly always good, except when I teased my older brother. I loved my sister and him so much. I would deliberately mispronounce Peter's name as *Pater,* which means "father," because he was always trying to imitate our father. Except for mother, we all had different names, especially to hide Jewish heritage. I was Anna Shoshanna, which means Anna Rose. Sometimes, I would say, "Anna ssh-Anna," and I thought of it as an Anna-"gram" (a small measurement of me). I loved puns.

Some of my days were in a residential area near Prague, mostly near Mother's family. I remember the cars' backward-opening doors and smelly exhaust fumes. One time on the farm, as I looked up from colorful chickens scratching in the road, I watched the large, friendly family horse approaching with an elderly man who wore work clothes and was seated on the buckboard. It was a good time. It was a time of new and old, with horse-drawn carriages and new cars. Clothes were beautiful. People were beginning to recover from World War I.

However, in the evenings my relatives would all gather around and listen to the radio announcements. These were harried listenings; no one spoke. Some were seated, leaning forward, some standing with arms crossed. My favorite aunt wore a pretty flower-print dress. I remember some of the announcements, the beautiful music that was played at other times, and the *eeei*ng sounds as the dial was tuned to airwaves.

At some point during those years, I did attend school in Amsterdam, when I was about eight years old. But one day we hurriedly left Amsterdam, first edging along the canal using small inner tubes during a moonless night, and then on a boat with an engine. I went to sleep under a canvas and don't remember docking. At one place, Mother approached a young soldier and asked if she could travel with me on the road. The soldier said, "No, madam." She asked when it would be allowed; he responded, "About 4:30 this afternoon." I suppose that he wanted to seem important and knowledgeable. It was in this way that she got information to pass along about convoys, size, and timing. However, the wind blew his coat open and his pants had a swell in them, so she began to know that she could not travel without Dad, who agreed with this, especially because of other things he was hearing.

Sometimes, there was peaceful normalcy. Once, our family went to a reserve in northeastern Poland. There was a place where the tree line stopped, and grasses and lichens grew above the line. At that area was a small, round house built of gray granite boulders. There was a doorway, a little window, and a peephole. Dad said it was from the old days of the Norman invaders. The weather was good, and we slept in there. So much the better for some family work, getting poles and fir branches to form a roof for some protection from the night and morning dew. I woke up early one morning and went to the cold lake. There was an old wooden dock, and as I stepped onto it a spotted white owl became startled and hovered briefly in the air right in front of me. The owl reminded me of the way I had seen Adolf Hitler standing in his open motorcar, looking out at everyone. I was at that motorcar event, on the edge of the crowd but in an elevated position to see clearly. At another time, I was the little blond girl to whom Mr. Hitler gave a bouquet of roses as he stopped his motorcade. I wondered how he would have felt to find out that the little curly-headed blond girl was part Jewish.

There was an earlier event, when I was about four; at the last minute, my well-dressed parents were to go to a fine dinner restaurant that had dancing and an orchestra. There was no babysitter! So I got to go. We were seated in the restaurant, near the back of the raised floor and also near Mr. Hitler, who had his German dinner guests around him. He had an odd way of clapping, with the palms near his fingers and his fingers doing the clapping. He was sweating, drooling, and laughing, clearly enjoying a good time. I didn't like him. He seemed mean.

A dark indicator happened one peaceful morning, when a young man on a postman's bike brought a letter. My brother answered the doorbell, tipped a coin to the young man, and brought the letter to my mother, who was in a housecoat. She sat down at the table and opened the letter, but something just didn't feel right. It was from a friend of my Jewish grandfather. He wrote that when Grandfather didn't show up to play checkers, he had gone to inquire. He had already known that Grandfather was outspoken by word and writing against Hitler's annexation of Austria, and that my grandmother had been taken away in a truck for questioning when the Nazis arrived. He had discovered my grandfather's suicide by hanging; then, together with others in the apartment, he had cut him down. After my mother read that letter, she was never the same. Was it really a suicide, or it was made to look like a suicide? I don't know.

One of the next things I recall was that Dad got a job near an *altenhaus,* or roadside inn, in northern Poland. He was hired as a cook and waiter, and our family was to help serve meals. We were setting up for the officials to have dinner after their meeting. Father instructed me, "As someone's glass is emptying, or they want anything, you go get it." I was experiencing anger and sensing that these were bad, dangerous men; it became the only time that I ever had an outburst or that my father reprimanded me. I snapped, "They should get it themselves!" Father leaned over behind me and sharply whispered in my ear, "Do you want to get us all killed?" So I did serve the guests very well following that incident.

There was snow on the ground when I went down the back kitchen steps. I had heard some muffled noises from around the side of the building. I went to see what the noises were. Two young soldiers were viciously kicking my brother, who was down in the snow. A third young soldier leaned against the building, smoking the nub of a cigarette. The two were kicking him in the ribs and back and face. He was not defending himself. The snow darkened with blood; it was such a sharp contrast to the snow on the boughs of the pines, which stood as witnesses while I backed up in horror. I stumbled against the wooden steps and hurt my right shoulder. After that, my shoulder always hurt, my arm was somewhat impaired, and a cough showed up whenever I was tired because of the frequent pain.

We stopped working at the altenhaus. Father was trying to keep his family together, and both of our parents were trying to help with the war effort. But Germany took over Poland in spite of the counterefforts of many people. We went through a checkpoint town, staying in a temporary barracks-type house for frequent travelers. The commandant was a colonel, a kind man who didn't look at things too closely. He too was trapped in the rapidly unfolding events.

One night, we left, slipping into the countryside and moving hand-over-hand along the roots by the river's edge. The water was too cold for me. A man offered to carry me; while I was on his back for warmth and carrying, he held my child arms together at the wrists in front of him, edging carefully with his other hand. Some soldiers came along the roadway, so we were still, but we could easily hear the dogs barking and growling. However, the soldiers dismissed the dogs as reacting to a raccoon or other small river animal; they probably didn't want to go into the woods in the dark, so they moved on.

We traveled on when it was safe. Arriving in northeastern Poland or western Russia by an open-door cattle car that swayed to and fro with a monotonous *clack-clack* sound through mountains and tumbling fresh water streams, we were to work as a family at a place where a utility was being built along a river. The snow was starting to fall heavily as we got into a transport truck. Each truck caravanned forward in the tire marks made by the previous truck's tires. Always there was the loud engine's roar, which we hoped would keep roaring so that we would not get stuck in a northern winter.

When we arrived, the men and women were put in separate barracks. Ours had one stove at the end, with the potty bucket near the front door. One day, during spring thaw, my sister, about fifteen by then, came home all disheveled. She had been cleaning a trailer for an officer. My parents had always previously been in tune, but this time they openly argued about staying anywhere in Europe, or even fighting for their cause anymore at all. The conclusion was that we would try to leave by railroad, going south and then eastward to eastern Russia or

China. We all dressed up as well as possible in our best clothes, carrying only one small picnic case, and went to the train station, a building adjacent to the tracks. My brother wore a hat to cover the scar that had been left on his face from the beating he had gotten at the altenhaus. I felt so sorry for him and wished he hadn't been hurt. The five of us all looked our "Sunday best" for a holiday.

When I saw the corporal trainmaster, his lips were thin in a near smile, his eyes dark. I didn't trust him, but I knew that he was our last hope. We could only get transport in a cattle car, though it did have some soft straw. I remember seeing the familiar blue-green mountains again. The train's back-and-forth swaying, combined with the *clack-clack* noises, were soothing. I fell asleep toward evening and was vaguely aware of the train's starts and stops, of cars connecting and disconnecting. But something didn't feel right. When I awakened, there was a collection of other people on the train in the car with us. They were vacantly staring. The sun was coming through the wrong side of the slats on the side of the cattle car. We had been betrayed.

Instead of going south and then east, we had gone south, farther south, then north and west to a detainees' camp. When we deboarded, there were cattle chutes by the railroad tracks, which we had to walk along toward an officer. His hand occasionally motioned to some people, but it was mostly already determined who would go where. My sister went one way with other young girls into a chute that would load into a departing truck. My father and brother went another way into an open, grassless yard surrounded by barbed wire. My mother and I went yet another way. I never saw my father, sister, or brother again.

My mother and I were in a barracks with other women. We were dressed in civilian clothes. I do not recall anything like tattoos. I do recall that, one day, a tall, fat sergeant came in and motioned to the women, toward my mother. There, in front of all of us, she had to lie down on the floor while he mounted her. He didn't even take his coat off. I was nearing thirteen, and I could feel my face turning red as my anger increased to rage. My mother would never choose to lie with such a pig! I might have jumped on his back and begun beating him, but she motioned with her hand, raising it flat in a halting motion.

It gets harder for me to remember. I was left in a painted cellar room, without clothes. It was cold, but I was able to get used to it. I was not given food or water. Sometimes, a little window in the door would suddenly slide open; a woman would look at me and then slam it shut. The pipes were painted, all off-white or pale yellow. There was one bare lightbulb in the ceiling. I think I lost the ability to see color. I could see bars on the one high window that formed little crosses. I tried to remember everything, especially the family I loved. I thought of them again and again. I don't know how long I was there. I lost awareness.

Then, I was on something like a stainless-steel rolling table. I was being examined by people dressed in white lab coats. I was near death but weakly aware. There was pain, lots of pain. I think that they looked at my liver or other nearby organs and then sewed me back up.

The next thing I knew, I was back in the barracks with my mother. I was lying down with my head in her lap. I could not see well, but I was able to make out other women around her. One, a friend, stood nearby. Mother told me, "Don't be afraid to die." But I wanted to live. She withheld food and water from me to speed up my death. Her friend consoled her.

The next morning, a little after ten o'clock, I awakened on top of a pile of bodies. I had been revived a little by the morning dew, and I became aware of a dirty man groping me. I was conscious of two things then: one, spiritually traveling along beautiful clouds in the sky toward a loving light; and, in an earthbound way, being cremated and then shoveled with the ashes of others into a common grave in a trench. Following that, I was only aware of indescribable beauty and love.

After a while, I made two attempts to return to earthly life: one in which I did not come to full term, and another in which I was born deaf and died early in the crib. Finally, I remembered being born into this life, one in which I can remember so many details of that prior life. I think that after WWII there weren't enough Jewish homes for Jewish souls to be born into, so God sent us to the nearest possible home; for me, that was one in which I would have the incentive to remember other lives, especially the WWII past life, and gradually come to terms with those tragic events.

The reason I chose to reincarnate was to try to make a difference for good, and to fulfill the life I would have had. In this life, I garnered a governor's award and two community awards for social service work with the poor, and I have received numerous other recognitions, including in teaching. The disturbing feelings of the WWII memories stopped when, in this life, I chose to become part of the Jewish community, officially becoming Jewish. Only then did I feel right, because in the sequel of this life I had become who I was meant to be.

Looking at my past life, I marvel that I was able to witness key events of the drama of WWII. And, although I had searched in many places, I had wondered just why it was that I had been unable to find any pictures of my family, as we were very often right there in important photographed events as witnesses and participators. Then one day, I was watching the History Channel on television; the show was *Gideon's Spies*. It briefly flashed on a picture of WWII agents, which had been recently released by Mossad (Israel's special secret service). There in the background was the man who had been my father. He had been an agent and a spy. That was the reason why I couldn't, until then, find historical photographs—as spies, my parents didn't want to be photographed! They had mostly remained behind cameras. The television show said that Mossad only released pictures of their agents if all known family members were dead.

Finally hearing that all my family was dead, I was able to move on. There was yet another sense of freedom from the past. I reflected that for a long time in this life, I would see things through my past-life sister's eyes, as she had survived her challenges. After WWII, she had traveled in Europe and was sometimes based in Paris. Then, one year, the sense of her stopped. After seeing the Mossad picture, there was a second type of closure, because I realized that all of the people I had known and loved had died and moved on.

Now I continue to recall many other lives for many reasons—to know more about different kinds of things, to gain wisdom and understanding, but mostly to know about God and love. A person can survive the worst and heal if they are aware of loving and being loved. I keep the beauty, the loving-kindness, and the love. They last forever.

∽ *Kaaran Bowden*

Kaaran's beautiful and touching story depicts the horrors of hatred and the hopefulness of love. The process of bringing peace to this planet will require courage and patience. Overcoming ignorance is difficult. Yet this is the task of the enlightened soul, and we will receive lots of help toward this goal.

As I mentioned in a previous chapter, life in the physical dimension is filled with pain and suffering. We cannot avoid the fact that our bodies and those of our loved ones will one day meet their ends, whether through accidents, illness, or any other cause. But the additional pain caused by the ignorance and violent actions of some people is avoidable. As more and more people become aware of their higher nature and the true purpose of their lifetimes on Earth, crimes, wars, and other optional acts of cruelty will diminish and eventually disappear. We have reached a point in our souls' evolution where we can decide to end all prejudice, all hatred, all violence, and all wars. People like Kaaran are dedicating their lives to this purpose. And so must we all.

Spiritual beings will choose the compassionate path, not the violent one.

· 9 ·

Eternal Relationships

We come back over and over again with our loved ones, reuniting in countless lifetimes. Our bodies change from incarnation to incarnation, but our souls are the same. When we recognize the other as one of our own beloved soul mates, the gulf of separation between us vanishes. We are reassured and comforted. Loneliness and despair disappear.

We learn through our relationships, which present opportunities for giving and receiving love and for practicing patience, compassion, and charity. They are also tests, supplying us with feedback on whether or not we are learning these and other lessons. Are we patient and loving with each other, or are we fearful and frustrated? Our relationships provide the answers and point the way to spiritual growth.

The following stories illustrate the bountiful treasures contained in our relationships and show us how we can reap these treasures to accelerate our progress. As we do so, we not only heal ourselves and our loved ones, but all the souls on Earth.

To see and appreciate the soul of others with whom you are in a relationship is a higher state of awareness. To see only their outer characteristics provides a limited and incomplete perspective. Their current personality, just like their current physical body, is a temporary manifestation. They have had many bodies and many personalities but only one enduring soul, only one continuous spiritual essence. See this essence and you will see the real person.

You are in relationship with all other beings. The relationships may be brief, such as with the waiter in a restaurant, a sales clerk in a store, or another driver on the road. Each of these has had many lifetimes and therefore many personas. Each has had his or her own infancy, childhood, and adolescence in his or her current body. They have brought all these past-life and current-life elements into the present moment, the moment of relationship with you. If you can understand and appreciate the beauty and depth of their soul, all its history and spiritual experiences, your relationship with them will be much more meaningful and fulfilling. You will be in relationship with their soul.

. THE PATH OF THORNS .

A number of the regressions that I experienced at your weekend workshop in 2002 in Los Angeles led me to resolving a heartbreak that I had been dealing with for too long. I saw three different experiences, all with the same man, a man who had said to me in this life, "I have never felt for anyone what I feel for you. I have never been so comfortable or attracted to anyone else in my life. But you need to realize that just because we are soul mates does not mean that we will be getting married, because we will not."

I had replied, "That's fine, as long as you realize that I will not be coming back around for you again." At the time, I wasn't sure why I said it, but I knew that I meant it.

That special weekend, I had three regressions of our pasts together. In one, we were both the students of a Druid, and we handfasted. But when the Druid died, he ran from the marriage. In another, I was his younger brother. He had promised our parents, as we went off to war, that he would look after me. When we entered the city and were attacked by enemy soldiers, he ran off into the fray, leaving me alone by the gates, a very young and terrified boy. I was the first to die, an arrow through my throat and one to the chest. In the third life, I was once again a student of a Druid, and he a warrior. He went off to war with my father; I went to the grove to learn the secrets of the trees.

When I came back, the gate had been destroyed, the town was cinders, and my father's and lover's chariots were outside the walls. All my people were dead. I took the horses from the chariots and rode to the next town for safety.

Those were three lives in which I saw him repeat his pattern: he loved me dearly, but he always left me alone with a broken promise. This life has been no different, and I knew I had come back for him for the last time.

In the final regression, I sat in my garden on a bed, and I tried to get him to come take my hand. He looked at it and started to reach for it; he wanted to take it. But instead he screamed and ran off into the thornbushes, using a scythe to try to hack his way through as he gathered scratches and cuts.

I was sitting on the bed with my guide, a being from somewhere else, and I asked why he would try to break a path through thorns when I offered him a way out. I was told, "You can only make choices for yourself. You can offer to help others find their way, but it is their decision if they will accept your help. You cannot force them to accept, even if you are in the right. The choice to take the path set out for them must be theirs. If they are too afraid, then they will force a path as they will. You can do nothing about it but mourn their loss and yours."

Through my tears, I looked down and saw a spark inside me. "I'm pregnant?" I said, and my guide said, "Here only, not in your world." I didn't understand how that was possible, and so the guide explained. "What you see inside you is waiting to be born, but it isn't a child of you and a man; it is you as you can be if you do not turn from your path. That is *you* who is waiting to be born. The choice is yours to either embrace that child and watch it blossom and grow, or let it die as you too force your way through the brambles. Only you can make this choice, as only your beloved can make his."

I chose to let it blossom and grow. And even though the path that I have taken has seemed harder at times than cutting through brambles and thorns, I know I made the right choice. I still get lost, I still forget, and I still need a hand to help me up when I fall, but I would rather take those offered hands than walk off in armor, letting no one in.

Both Brian and Carole and many of the people I've met through the workshops and professional training groups I have attended have offered me helping hands, as I hope I have them. This has enriched my life, and hopefully I have, in some way, touched them as well. We all move through this life together.

∽ *Faith Susan*

Faith has picked the path of courage. Destiny leads us to the decision points, but then our free will selects which path to follow. Her lover has not chosen as courageously or as wisely as she.

Before you are born, your soul plans the trajectory of the life that lies ahead. Who will the significant people in that life be, and when will you meet? Whom will you choose to be your parents? Will you be a teacher, or an artist, or will you take on some other role? Destiny will place you in those particular circumstances; it will dictate that you encounter a certain person, at a certain time, and perhaps in a certain place. The people it arranges for you to meet are frequently the people with whom you have lived in a past life. There is karma together. They may even be your soul mates, pushing you on toward greater spiritual growth.

Once you meet them, you then exercise your free will: Do you stay? Do you leave? Do you cut your own path through the thorns and brambles, or do you take the outstretched hand reaching forth to help you? You may choose to love them, to befriend them, to work with them, to marry them. Or you might reject them, arguing that they do not look the way you want them to, or have a different religion than you, or live in the wrong part of the world. These are your choices, and this is how you learn. Everything is part of a master plan for the soul's growth.

The act of making such decisions sets off alternative futures: the future with those people, the future without them, and so on. This is where destiny and free will interact together, and this is where things become interesting.

Advanced souls can point the way and illuminate the path, but they cannot decide for us. Ultimately, the path is an inner journey that we must all make ourselves. Faith's final regression was a metaphor about choosing wisely. Her spiritual guide presented a compelling explanation of the process. Reading Faith's story, I was instantly reminded of the messages that the Masters provided me through Catherine, the patient I described in *Many Lives, Many Masters*. Even the Masters could not make such decisions for us. We must learn and climb the spiritual steps ourselves. We must have faith.

. PRISONER OF WAR .

"I know it's coming," he said breathlessly, a look of horror on his face. "It's getting closer now. I can hear the explosions." His jaw was rigid, his breathing rapid, his face constricted. "The problem is, I can't see anything. We can't see over the tops of the ditches." His voice tensed even more; he was clearly getting agitated, the terror building. I knew that I had to act quickly before the experience overwhelmed him.

"Let's go back to an earlier, happier time," I said in a gentle voice, "a time before these explosions started."

John took a deep breath and exhaled, his grim countenance fading as he settled into the chair. Although his body was in my psychotherapy office in the twenty-first century in Austin, Texas, his mind was deep in a nonordinary state of consciousness, and his awareness was somewhere in Bavaria nearly a hundred years ago, experiencing a prior lifetime.

Long before I was a therapist, I was fascinated by the concept of reincarnation. As a boy, I often wondered who I might have been in another life. As an adult, I discovered the work of Dr. Brian Weiss through his bestselling book *Many Lives, Many Masters*. In training directly under Dr. Weiss, I found him to be different from many other so-called spiritual teachers or workshop leaders. He refused to sensationalize the work and wasn't afraid to talk about the limits of regression therapy or to remind people that regressions themselves were not "proof," in a scientific sense, that reincarnation existed. He was, however, adamant that regression therapy could be profoundly healing.

Why would someone want a past-life regression? It is not enough for my clients to remember that they were a peasant in the Middle

Ages. For the regression to be healing involves not only understanding the roots of a negative pattern or recurrent issue, which often arches over many lifetimes, but also an emotional release so that the clarity can be fully internalized.

A successful scientist, John was curious about reincarnation, but he had come to me for a past-life regression specifically because he had a hard time connecting with others. He was in his sixties with thinning hair, a salt-and-pepper mustache, and piercing eyes. His wife told him that he could be cold and distant at times, and both his adult children were estranged from him. John's initial interaction with me had been respectful and courteous, but hardly warm.

This guy would never make it as a greeter at Wal-Mart, I thought to myself as John curtly announced that he doubted that he could be hypnotized. I have regressed thousands of people, both individually and in groups, many of whom had insisted the same thing. While I do believe that people cannot be hypnotized against their will, I have come to believe that the vast majority of people can be hypnotized, to some degree, given enough time with a skilled clinician. I would guess that over 90 percent of my regression clients go deep enough on their first attempt to experience some past-life memories.

Bearing this in mind, I took steps to induce hypnosis slowly and gently with John, always reminding him that he could safely come out of it at any time if he wished. He gradually went deeper and deeper, following my instructions. Some thirty minutes after inducing the trance state, I gave John the suggestion to go to the events that led to his chronic emotional aloofness. His subconscious led him to an experience in World War I, when he was a buck private in the German army, deep in the hell of trench warfare. I was concerned that this incident might be confusing or initially overwhelming, hence my instructions to go back to an even earlier time so that he might be able to put his battle experience in perspective.

Following my lead, John described himself earlier in that incarnation as a teenager, growing up with six siblings in a middle-class family on a verdant farm. He fell in love with an attractive village maiden named Helga, and he saw himself going to her farmhouse to court her. "Truth is, I barely know her. We've kissed each other once or twice as I walked her home from church." He had a broad smile. "But I think I am in love and want to marry her. She comes from a good family: hardworking, salt-of-the-earth kind of people, like me." John volunteered for the army, to "serve the Fatherland" and because it was his only chance to get enough money to marry Helga.

To my surprise, John told happy stories about life in boot camp. The comradeship of his fellow soldiers and his sergeant warmed his spirits. "Some of them are smart, some are stupid, but they are all good men. Many are farmers, just like me. And we get one hot meal every day," he added, grinning with amazement. Apparently, this was better treatment than he had expected.

John continued on with stories of endless marches. "It's tiring, but not so bad, really. You can rest on one foot and then the other," he said, making what was doubtless a common joke of the time with a forced cheerfulness. "The problem is, you can't ever lie down and rest. You have to keep marching. You have to, you *have* to . . ." He swallowed hard, fighting back his grief and weariness, ever the good soldier. With an abrupt chuckle, he shook off the intensity. "The men just kid about it and we keep going."

Under my direction, John moved ahead to his arrival at the trenches, where the intolerable waiting for the war began. "We know it's coming," he said ominously, "but we don't know when. We wait for days."

I asked him how he passed the time. "We laugh and joke," he replied with a halfhearted smile. "But we don't ever talk about our families or girls back home. It would just be too painful, too personal. I think we're afraid that if we thought about it too much, we really might desert."

At once, John became more animated. "It's here now," he said, his eyes darting beneath his closed eyelids. "It's here, and there's smoke and flashes, and I can't see anything." His breathing was rapid. "Oh God! Oh God, we are just firing into the darkness, we don't even know what we're doing, and . . . and . . ." He trailed off, his voice thick with emotion.

I reminded him that these were memories and that he couldn't be physically hurt by looking at them now in hypnosis. He was safe in my office.

"It's okay," he said. "It's over now. I never felt any pain." He paused for a long moment, his face enigmatic. "I'm looking down at the battlefield. I must have left my body behind. There are bodies everywhere. All I can see is my leg."

I suddenly realized what he meant by this statement. It wasn't that all he could see was his leg—all that was *left* was his leg. His brow knitted as the grief became palpable. "It's so sad. The guys were good guys, the sarge was good." John's face became tense, his breathing labored. A tear crept out of his eye. "But if everyone is so good, how could this happen?" His voice was breaking. "How could this happen?"

I sat in silence for several minutes, simply allowing him this cleansing emotional release. After a while, he heaved a sigh.

"There's a light in the distance, on the horizon." I watched John; it was as though his face were bathed by a gentle glow. "It's quiet there, no smoke, no explosions," he said wistfully. "I think it's the sun. No, wait." He seemed puzzled. "No, it's brighter than the sun. All the smoke is going away."

"See yourself going to the light," I whispered. John's expression softened, the horror of the carnage falling away as he found himself floating in a brilliant, sacred light. He was making contact with something eternal. A gentle, peaceful smile came over his face, his eyes moist with a different kind of tears.

I asked him what he had learned from that lifetime.

"I was loyal and hardworking in that life, and I still am in my current life. I saw the senselessness of war, but I also seemed to learn of its inevitability." This accounted for both several happy years in his current life spent doing community volunteer work to "make a difference," and also dropping out of college to enlist in the Vietnam War because, as he put it, "they were going to draft me anyway."

Most important, John saw how, in both lifetimes, he had repressed his feelings and avoided the feelings of others. "I learned not to feel, not to ask anything too personal about my comrades. In the trenches, it was rude and too painful to ask, it just hurt them," he said, the tears beginning again. "But not now. I *have* to ask my kids and my wife how they are doing!" His voice choked with regret. "They aren't soldiers— they are people and they want to tell me about their feelings, and I want to know . . . I *want* to know . . . *I want to know.*"

I gently placed a hand on his shoulder as he sobbed for a few minutes, and I realized that John was achieving a clarity in a single three-hour session that might have taken months in traditional therapy. He had recognized that his habitual way of dealing with uncomfortable feelings by not discussing them, while appropriate with his comrades in wartime, could not work for him with his family. Until his regression, John was unconsciously driven by the echo from a past life to avoid discussing his feelings.

As a therapist, I recognize that past-life regression therapy is not a magic bullet that dramatically resolves all life issues in a single session. Still, in regressing thousands of people in workshops across the country, I have discovered the enormous healing potential in past-life memories that run the gamut from traumatic to joyous. A woman remembers that her husband was her lover in another life and has been reunited with her now, and this awareness reinvigorates her marriage. A part-time artist commits her life to her craft when she remembers a lifetime in which she had great skill as a painter. A man with a thirty-year phobia of doctors is cured once he remembers its roots in a tribal lifetime when a medicine man failed to heal him. All are different experiences. All are healing.

∽ *Gregg Unterberger*

I am particularly pleased that Gregg allowed and encouraged John to review the past life and its lessons, and to understand the connections to his present life. John had been treating family and friends as if they were soldiers, although clearly, in this life, they were not. In this kind of life review, the therapist guides the patient to extract and to understand the important themes and lessons of the lifetime that has just been remembered. When the patient experiences the death of his body in that past-life memory, his consciousness becomes aware of floating above that body and entering a light-filled, serene, spiritual state. That is when the therapist begins to conduct the life review, asking questions like, "What were the lessons of the life that has just ended?" After these lessons have been identified, the therapist may ask, "And how do those lessons connect to the present life, to the present time?" Recognizing these connections is often a key component of the healing process; it is not merely the reliving of the past life that is healing, but understanding and relating that life to the current one.

A therapist will often conduct this kind of life review with the client during a past-life regression session. But another type of life review happens to all of us when we die and our consciousness leaves the physical body at the end of each lifetime. This time it is not done with a therapist, but rather with our spiritual guides or other wise beings; it is not a clinical life review but a karmic one. As we are replenished by the beautiful light, our awareness is directed to review the results of our actions while we were on the physical plane. We see the people we have harmed and we feel their emotional reactions, magnified greatly. Similarly, we feel the emotions, again enhanced, of those we have aided and loved. In this manner, we examine all our relationships, and we deeply experience all the anger, hurt, and despair that we have caused—but also all the gratitude, appreciation, love, and hope that we have elicited. This life review is not done in a spirit of punishment or guilt. By truly understanding the result of our behavior, we learn the importance of loving-kindness and compassion.

As the therapist, Gregg, in the story that you have just read, demonstrates the former type of life review. As the client, in the story that you are about to read, he demonstrates the latter. Our souls, whether here or on the other side, are blessed with infinite opportunities for learning and growth.

So many of us, like John, have died repeatedly in battle. We are born, die in another war, and reincarnate only to fight and die again. At some point, we will realize that we are here to learn and to love. Whenever we kill another person, we also kill a part of ourselves. To be violent, to hate, and to kill are wrong. We fail the lesson; we have to repeat the course. At a deeper level, we can never really be killed because we are consciousness, we are soul. But in this physical dimension we can die corporeally, and we must stop the violence. It is time to act like the spiritual beings that we truly are.

. AN EXPLORATION OF EMPATHY .

I trained with Brian in 1999 at Mount Madonna. I was a happy guinea pig onstage as he supervised a therapist who regressed me to a lifetime as a French monk in the 1600s. I had some mystic experiences during that lifetime, yet I sat on them for fear of what others might say. I had developed a relationship with a fellow monk (who was my first wife in my current incarnation) and spoke secretively of my experiences of God as someone who would never punish or condemn anyone. My fellow monk agreed but refused to "come out" with me. Still, I was bolstered by his friendship, and I angrily confronted Father Francesco, who ran the monastery. He slapped me for being blasphemous and kicked me out of the order, arranged for my excommunication, and threw me out of the church. The monk who had befriended me stayed mute, paralyzed, and with the church, watching me leave as the bells tolled mournfully. (This may account for, in part, why my ex-wife always was afraid that I would abandon her.) Devastated, I tearfully and hopelessly climbed a nearby peak, getting colder and colder, and died alone freezing to death in the snow, a de facto suicide.

In an interesting twist, I spontaneously had a partial life review at the end of that onstage session, in which I was shown alternative choices that I might have made, and how life would have gone had I made those choices. I could've approached Francesco more gently and caused, if not a revolution, an evolution in the monastery that focused more on God's mercy and love and less on hell and sin. This approach would have brought more people into the church and soothed many of the poor, who often believed their poverty was God's punishment for their sins.

In a later regression, I intentionally reviewed Father Francesco's life. I was curious as to whether, under hypnosis, I could be directed to relive someone *else's* experience, and a fellow student successfully directed me there. I first saw Francesco beaten bloody by his own father as a child, and then I experienced his emotional torment directly as he writhed and cried out. Literally, his father believed that he could beat "the hell" out of his son, driving the demons out of him through pain.

I was filled with compassion for my former enemy. Poor Francesco, understandably, grew up seeing himself as sinful and his heavenly Father as angry. He did unto others as was done unto him. Our spirits met, and I tearfully forgave Father Francesco as he apologized to me, saying he knew not what he did.

Father Francesco returned in my present incarnation as my counseling supervisor, Frank, to be a much healthier mentor to me as a therapist; I returned to him as his ardent student for many years in this lifetime. Before I had the past-life memory, one of the things that I confronted Frank about was that I felt he didn't offer me enough emotional support. He replied that I was unteachable. We were both right, and well before the memory I became more open to Frank's coaching as he became gentler and more compassionate with me. He literally changed my life. We actually did your training together.

∾ *Gregg Unterberger*

There are so many lessons to learn in this earth school—too many to learn in one life. Lessons of compassion, hope, faith, nonviolence, tolerance, charity, empathy, nonprejudice, and others can require many, many lifetimes. We are given countless opportunities to pay our debts to others and to repair our relationships with them. Gregg and his supervisor were able to do both. We too can accomplish similar healing, even with our most difficult partnerships. Love and forgiveness, augmented by understanding and patience, can fix all.

Choosing this path of patience and kindness rewards us with incredible blessings. We do not choose this path for that reason, for the reward is in the doing. The blessings come anyway. Through empathy and insight, Gregg and Frank could reunite and prosper. Their relationship reached a higher spiritual octave.

Awareness means seeing from a more complete perspective. Gregg provides a clear example of how this can lead to healing when he is able to see the beatings Francesco had to endure as a child. Now Gregg could comprehend the connection to Francesco's behavior and values as an adult. With this comprehension, Gregg let go of his own judgments and forgave

Francesco. As an additional benefit, Gregg's relationship with Frank, Francesco's current incarnation, was deepened.

As you have previously read on the subject of progression therapy, our future is not set in stone, not some fixed and unalterable pathway extending forward in time. It is a system of possibilities and probabilities, with some outcomes more liable to occur than others. One potential outcome, the probable future, is the most likely to happen, but it is certainly not guaranteed. Gregg's description of alternative choices echoes these futuristic concepts. If, in the 1600s, he had chosen the more gentle and less confrontational approach, his life would have been dramatically different. His future lives, including his present incarnation as Gregg, would also have been altered and improved. His relationship with Frank would have begun at a stronger and even healthier level. Ultimately, the time that it takes is unimportant, for progress is always being made. And with every step forward, the spiritual path becomes more clear.

Cynthia's story, which also explores the importance of the student-teacher relationship, provides another moving account of love's timeless nature.

. A SOUL MATE'S RETURN .

I was privileged to be in one of your training seminars during the summer of 2010. By that time, I had read all of your books to date and was interested to share experiences with those of the same belief system that I had come to as a result of your writings. This belief system would include life as a never-ending cycle of evolution with those we love, who can teach us the most.

I am sixty-one years old now, but I began to have a recurring dream when I was in my late twenties. In it, I was at Mount Vesuvius as a young woman of nineteen or so, in love with a townsman with whom I was forbidden to associate due to cultural prohibitions. As the earth shook and the lava began to flow, I took refuge near the water, under a covering. A man ran into the same cavern: it was my beloved. Without any words, he held me close and I had the knowing that he loved me also, even though it was not allowed. The dream ends there—no pain, no experience of death itself, just the deep understanding that the love I had felt in my heart was mutual.

I have had this same dream every now and then for over thirty years. When I was introduced to your work, the dream's emotional intensity and vividness, as well as its repetitive nature, brought about the realization that this could have been an actual life experience within my soul memory. After reading more of your work, I pieced together the facts that applied to my present lifetime.

At fourteen, I was sent away to parochial school, where I was instructed by a man whose voice I recognized like a bolt of lightning. We became friends, and I was his student for four years of high school. I continued my education and stayed in touch with him. I married another man, and my former teacher came to visit our family for about twelve years, when he was in good health. During these visits, my husband, daughter, and I entertained him and his friends and offered them a home in which to stay. On one visit, my husband and I discovered that our daughter was born exactly fifty years to the day as my teacher.

There had always been a distant attraction for this man, although when I was so young I did not understand it or know what to do with this ancient memory. His voice was unmistakable. After studying with you and witnessing others' stories, I told him of this entire experience, relating to him that I believed I had known him in an ancient time. Not long after my revelation, he became very ill. I came to his aid, calling family members and checking on his care. His medications are now keeping him in balance, and he appreciates who I have become to him: a friend, mentor, and special advocate. Now *I* am in the role of teacher, and we have met once more. There is absolutely no doubt in my mind that we are here again to support each other's joy and growth.

I have also discovered through watching the History Channel that I lived in Herculaneum, a small town near Pompeii that was seriously affected by Vesuvius. Recently, a new discovery was made of several bodies found near the boat docks, the bodies of those who took refuge there, thinking they would be safe. Looking at the maps of the region shown and seeing the remains and where they were discovered, my soul knows that is where I fled and met up with this dear man, whom I have loved for centuries.

At your seminar, I recounted the same story under hypnosis. Today, this man and I enjoy a delightful relationship. I speak to him several times per week. He loves to hear of my daughter's progress as a young woman, and he and my husband have the utmost respect for each other. I feel peace and joy, knowing that we have eternity.

∽ *Cynthia*

The power of a volcano is no match for the power of a soul mate. The love of soul mates is not always romantic. It is eternal and unconditional, it transcends time and space, yet it can be the love of parent and child, of best friends, of siblings, of grandparents or cousins, or many other platonic forms. Perhaps your soul mate is a college professor with whom you take a course, whose passion and knowledge for the subject he is teaching influences your own professional trajectory. Once you finish the course, you move on and so does he; your work together in this lifetime has been completed.

We have families of souls, rather than just one soul mate, and we are being connected all the time. Sometimes it is only for mere moments, yet even this brief amount of time can change one's life completely. Whether you are together for ten minutes, ten months, or ten years is not as important as the lessons that are learned, the directions, and the reminders that occur when these encounters happen. There is a familiarity, a depth of knowing. You relate at a certain vibration that you wouldn't expect from such a short time. Soul mates come together again and again to interact. There is karma or destiny together.

It is good to see how Cynthia and her teacher's soul relationship was so appreciated by the entire family and absent of any jealousy, resentment, or fear.

Unconditional love does not ask for anything in return. This pure love never creates dependencies or debts. It simply exists. An absolute energy, it never ends. It instantly connects lifetimes centuries apart and promises that all loved ones will be entwined throughout eternity.

Witness how Carla, the author of the next story, translated this concept into action as she reached out to her sister with a love that outlasted both time and tension.

. SISTERLY BONDS .

Several years ago, I had the privilege of seeing you at Omega Institute in New York. It was the end of the day and you had time to perform a childhood regression, for which I happily volunteered. I was hesitant to go up onstage and expose myself, but I knew that I was in good hands, and I trusted you. I was also curious to see what experience would show up.

It did not take long before I had a memory in my mind. I was about four years old, and I was holding my two-year-old sister's hand, helping her down the stairs on Easter morning. We were so excited. I remember the feeling of the carpet under my feet, of my pajamas. We made our way downstairs and found lots of Easter baskets waiting for us—along with a baby chick! I was a little nervous about the chick being eaten by one of our dogs, but truly it was quite a happy memory.

As I was coming out of the hypnosis, I became emotional and started to cry. The audience asked why I was upset over such a pleasant memory. You see, at the time, that same sister and I were feuding and not speaking to each other. And all I could remember was that genuine, innocent love that I felt for her. I missed our close bond, which we had shared throughout most of our lives.

The most important thing I took away from the whole process was that only love is real. So, after the weekend seminar was over, I contacted my sister and told her about the experience. We cried on the phone and started laughing, asking each other, "Whatever happened to that little baby chick?" The session with you brought my younger sister and me back together again. Today, we still share that close bond. We both came to another seminar together and did some group regression work, and we realized that we have shared many lifetimes, in many different relationships.

I will always cherish that regression that I did in front of the audience that day. It forever changed my life.

∾ *Carla White*

Such a powerful message is conveyed in Carla's brief account of her childhood memory. Love never ends; it never stops. Its energy is absolute, eternal. An innocent memory of the little sisters at ages four and two reminded Carla of the immediacy and importance of the bonds of love. The temporary feud seemed insignificant in comparison. A phone call was made, and the relationship was quickly repaired. Anger and hurt were forgiven.

Carla's lesson applies to us all. How many passing fights, arguments, and misunderstandings are we allowing to rob us of the joy of loving interactions with the significant people in our lives? Our egos and our pride get in the way. Do we have the courage to pick up the phone and heal our relationships, as Carla did?

Love transcends everything else.

. THE BRITISH PUB .

My husband and I were at the Being Fearless conference in New York City. After the second regression, we awoke and asked each other what we had seen. I mentioned that I was in a pub.

He responded, "A British pub in the 1800s?"

Yes. In a nutshell, he was outside a British pub in the 1800s but could not go in; he could only look through the windows. He described the inside furnishings, but there were no people.

The pub was exactly like the one I was in during my regression, but in mine I was a barmaid (possibly also a prostitute), and he had strangled me to death. We are now divorcing, although not because of this regression.

I was reading one of Dr. Weiss's books at a ball game this summer, and a friend asked about it. I told him of the regression and of being murdered in the pub. He gasped and reminded me that my ex-husband

and I owned a Victorian house from 1887 in Connecticut, and that the only room my husband had wanted to redesign was the "bar room." For some strange reason, I had never put the two things together, but my friend was exactly right. My husband had redone the entire room in the theme of a British pub, complete with a mahogany bar and a British-bulldog dart room!

                                                    ∾ *Bonnie*

Simultaneous recall of the same past-life scenes is a validation of the memory. So is the subconscious re-creation of the actual setting. But there was no violence this time around. Much progress has been made.

Soul relationships are not always harmonious and peaceful. Even soul mates can prove toxic if one soul is not as developed or evolved as the other. Bonnie's account of her past life demonstrates this concept, and the following story provides an additional example.

. TRUST AND DECEPTION .

I trained with Dr. Weiss for a week in New York in 2009, and now I work in Australia using past-life regression. I love this method, and my dream is to make it available to mainstream people who suffer in many areas that could so easily be sorted out, leaving them free to get on with their lives.

I met a wonderful lady in Sydney, Australia, during a facilitator training class that I held the following year. Her case may raise awareness as to why so many women struggle to get pregnant or are judged for choosing not to have children.

Charlotte was the first person to agree to come up and be regressed in front of the class. Her experience began as she saw herself standing on cobblestones, with many shops around her. She was a "grubby" girl of about eleven years old, wearing a dirty dress and apron. This was in England in 1845. I asked her to go to her home, but she couldn't—her home was the streets.

Charlotte could not sense any parents. She went back even further in time to when she was five years old, when an accident had claimed the lives of both her parents, leaving her an orphan. The orphanage was cold and lonely. She had a friend there, a younger girl of about four years old named Sally, whom she recognized as her best friend in her current life. The girls took care of each other.

As the regression proceeded, Charlotte saw herself at nineteen years old and stated that she was in love with a man whom she recognized as her ex-husband in her current life. Pregnant with his child, she was so happy and believed that he loved her very much.

An incredible sadness soon washed over her, and she started crying, "He took my baby! He took my baby." She could only repeat those words over and over as she continued sobbing. The man whom she had loved was married and well-to-do, and his wife was barren. Because his wife could not have children, he set Charlotte up and then took her healthy baby.

I directed her to go to the time that she next saw her son. She easily moved ahead, seeing him as a twenty-year-old man, very handsome and impeccably dressed and coming out of what appeared to be a government building, with large pillars in front. Seeing him took her breath away. He was beautiful, and she was so proud. She then saw his father and, as he knew her, his mother walking behind him. Charlotte did not want to speak to him; she was so ashamed of her appearance, but she felt happy knowing that he had a life that she could never have given him.

Moving forward to her last day, Charlotte saw herself as old in appearance but not in age. She died on the street, where she had lived. Her lesson from that life was not to be so trusting of people.

In her current lifetime, Charlotte does not have children. She also told me that later that same evening, she had called her best friend (Sally from the orphanage), who lived in the United Kingdom, to relay the story. To her absolute surprise, when she was describing the part of the life where her baby had been stolen, her friend said, "That's because his wife couldn't have children."

"What made you say that?" Charlotte had asked her.

"I don't know," the friend had replied. "And yet I just knew."

∾ *Toni Reilly*

Fear of losing a child again, in this or any other manner, can lead to the conscious or subconscious decision not to get pregnant. Was Charlotte repaying a karmic debt from an even earlier incarnation? We do not know. But her lover in that life and his wife, if she knew of his plan, will certainly owe her a debt in future lives. There is no escaping our debts and obligations. We must make it up to those people whom we have harmed in previous lifetimes. As we do, and as we practice kindness and compassion for all other beings, we progress rapidly on our spiritual path. Our vibration is elevated.

There were many opportunities for love and empathy to be expressed in Charlotte's nineteenth-century lifetime. Her lover in that life could have been much more generous and caring. The orphanage could have been more supportive, more nurturing, and not so "cold and lonely." Society could have been more charitable, so that this trusting woman would not have to live and die on the streets. Only Sally seemed to be understanding and considerate.

Our present world has not changed that much. Goodwill, altruism, and loving-kindness must become more universal virtues and be extended to all people. When this happens, Charlotte and the rest of us will be able to safely trust humanity at a much deeper level.

Charlotte and her lover were presented with several meetings to resolve their karma and to treat each other as spiritual beings should. Judi, the author of the next story, was likewise blessed with numerous occasions to develop a relationship with her soul mate. She met Patrick many, many times in her present life—and she will continue to meet him many, many more.

. WISH YOU WERE HERE .

When I was in middle school, I was sitting on the front steps to my porch in Springfield when a boy from my neighborhood walked up the street with his friend, Patrick. Patrick immediately came over, sat down next to me, and started to talk. He was so cute and seemed to really enjoy talking to me. I remember asking what his name was, but I didn't understand what he said. I asked him to spell it, and he spelled it with an apostrophe after a part that didn't make sense to me; from what I recall, it was "P'draig." I asked him where the vowel was and he just smiled.

My friend came down, saying that Patrick's parents were coming to get him. He hadn't wanted to leave, but he could not stay because there had been trouble with his father before. Later, I heard that he had been beaten by his father.

After he left, I asked a neighbor about Patrick's name, and she said he was not from this country, that there were problems with his father's behavior, and that he might have to be sent back to where he came from. From what I recall, the beating was so bad that the police were called. I felt sorry for Patrick, and that evening when I went to bed I prayed that he would be okay. It was the first time I can ever remember praying for anyone.

When I was in high school, there was a boy who would stop by the store where I worked and talk to me every day. He would just magically appear. I asked him his name, and he said, "Pat." He told me he was from Ireland. I used to ask him how long he had been standing there behind me, and he would just smile. We built up a good friendship over the months until he told me he would not be able to stop by again. When he left that day, I cried. I had a thought come to my mind that I would see him again one day and that he would be my husband, and this thought comforted me.

There were so many other things: a boy with whom I felt a strong connection who would always say hello to me after French class, tapping me as he left the room. One whom I would talk to at a place we called "the wall," whose conversations I enjoyed. I remember, in college, weekends at the Jersey Shore and a nightclub I went to every weekend. There was a man onstage working with the sound and lights who would stare at me; I thought he was cute, so I smiled and waved. I always felt that someone was watching me there, so I soon stopped going, but I had the strange feeling that I might have blown an op-portunity that life would have given me to meet the man on the stage, and that there was something more for us. And then, there was the time when my friend mentioned a coworker named Patrick who had been born in Ireland. Even though my friend assured me it wasn't the boy from my memories, I daydreamed that it was he. I baked banana bread and pumpkin pies for my friend to take to work and share with Patrick. Eventually, I forgot about all of this and married someone else.

Thirty years after the last time I saw Patrick, he contacted me via the Internet and asked to meet up. On the initial meeting, I did not recognize him. He asked if I truly remembered him and looked me in the eyes. I recognized those eyes — it was vaguely coming back. Afterward, he said that we should meet for a real date. When we did, I felt such a connection that it scared me. I strongly felt that he would be my husband, but I was scared as my last relationship had been with a man who had left me. We talked, and I realized it had been him all along: the time with his father, "the wall," French class. I asked him about my friend, his coworker, and it turned out that Patrick was the one with whom he had shared all my cooking. It was also Patrick on the stage at the summer nightclub, doing the sound and lighting.

My last day with Patrick was in July 2008. We had a wonderful date, but we were not able to meet up again after that due to our distance. The last week that Patrick and I talked was right before your workshop. He asked me to share my experiences with him when I got back. I also happened to mention that I had asked the doctors to check my heart. That same week, a few minutes before my heart test, I learned that Patrick had died—his own heart had given out. He had fallen down the stairs and had a heart attack either before he fell or somewhere along the way to the bottom of the steps. I never got to say good-bye.

Since Patrick has passed on, he has communicated with me. These experiences show me that love never dies. When I was going to meet up with him on our first date, I had asked God to show me a sign when I met the right person. I then saw a shooting star at the same time that the song "Wish You Were Here" by Pink Floyd came on the radio.

I took that as a sign and shared it with him. He said, "We're just two lost souls swimming in a fish bowl," which is a lyric from the song.

After he died, I asked Patrick to be with me one day as I went to the dentist. I said, "Let me hear that song one more time before I get there." As soon as I pulled into the parking lot of the dentist's office, the song came on. I got goose bumps while listening to it on the radio. I loved it; he was with me. After the appointment, I went home, and as soon as I walked into the house my daughter came out with a painting she had done of Syd Barrett, a founding member of Pink Floyd. I had never shared my story about Patrick with her, or the meaning of the song to us. Next to the portrait were the words "We're just two lost souls swimming in a fish bowl."

~ *Judi*

We are often so tentative with love. We stop, we hesitate, we rationalize, we become afraid, we walk away. But love is not tentative with us. It keeps coming back, trying again, setting up new opportunities. Love is persistent.

Love never dies. We hear its songs whenever we stop to listen. We smell our beloveds' scents even after they have passed on. We see their messengers: the birds and animals, the sky, and other signs. We feel their touch. We receive their signals; we sense their presence.

As Pink Floyd said in another song, and as Patrick would undoubtedly tell Judi himself: "I will always be here. I will always look out from behind these eyes. It's only a lifetime. It's only a lifetime."

. THE SPLIT SOUL .

It is 2001, and I am living with the love of my life. I am breathing love, I am seeing love, I *am* love. I feel more myself than I ever felt. I feel strong, glamorous, and so fortunate to be perfectly complete. I have the most amazing child and the most incredible man in my life. My family is fine. Because I feel invincible, I am successful. I become a little moneymaking machine. Life doesn't seem to get more perfect.

I discover the deepest secrets of my sexuality, and every cell of my body is sensual. I am happy. I am love.

The summer of 2004 comes, and he is gone. He had to choose between living with me, building a life with me and my son here in North America, or moving back to his old country in South America. I need to choose to let him go or choose to keep him. And I have the power to do both. We both know that our love stays the same, because there is no time, no past or future—it just is.

Years pass by. I can't afford the luxury of getting depressed, so I fight it. My income drops drastically. My savings are paying the monthly bills. I am getting sick; my immune system fights against me. I am becoming desperate. Lying in bed, I have time to think and change my priorities. God is with me. I get back to the day-to-day life, but I am not myself again. I thought that he took away my desire and left me empty. My mind was saying that I had to close the door and forget him, my heart was craving for his touch, and my soul was totally and irrevocably in love with him.

Last year, I started to let your CDs guide me into my past lives. My past life is linked to my current one, and I understand that. The most unbelievable fact that I had acknowledged while regressing is that, during a life around the year 1850, I saw myself in the body of the man I love in this life. I was he, the man in this life that made me feel complete and perfect, the man that taught me to love myself, and because of this love I could love the universe.

I was he. I am he.

Back then, I saw him (me!) being totally irresponsible, leaving my wife. No reason, just ignorance and selfishness. My wife back then was a dear friend I lost ten years ago in the current life. She was caring, beautiful, smart, and fun back in that life, the same as she was in this one.

When I regressed back to that time again at your conference in Toronto, the experience was so vivid. I saw myself in his body, not caring about anyone but myself. I saw myself dying alone in a railroad station. What did I have to learn? How to be alone, and how to be responsible. I did not learn that back then. I feel so much guilt for leaving my wife, my friend; it is hard to express in words.

While regressed, my dear friend came to me, along with my uncle. They are both gone in this life, and they both came to comfort me, to calm me down. At the conference I was crying, feeling so deeply guilty; I was crying and could not stop. "It's okay, it does not matter, it's fine. Calm down. It is okay." This is what they told me.

I am learning my lessons, slowly but surely. I am very responsible in this life. I am raising my son by myself, and I work hard to offer him the world. The man I love (who is *me*!) is responsible now too, back home in his country and raising his own children.

We are finally getting it, and we are responsible. And alone. Why alone? Are we a split soul?

∽ Violet

Even after their deaths, our loved ones often help and guide us from the other side, from the spiritual dimensions. Violet describes being comforted by her dear friend and by her uncle, both of whom had died. In the regressed state, when our usual mental barriers are relaxed, such helping visits by our spiritual family are more clearly perceived.

Real and lasting happiness and joy cannot be dependent on others. These are inner states. Lovers may leave, but love cannot. It is our real nature. Violet is learning these difficult lessons, and she is finding an inner love that is permanent. Her karma is to feel the effects of her decisions and irresponsibility in the lifetime of the 1850s. The shoe is now on the other foot. Her dear friend, who was the wife back then, has already forgiven her.

There is metaphor in this memory. Was she her lover then? Or was her subconscious showing her the connections to her present life, the karmic debts, and pointing to the lessons to be learned? Perhaps because she was the man who left his wife in the past life, Violet merged the two male identities into one.

Further regression could bring defining details. Yet the real work is already done.

Mark and Kathleen, a husband and wife whose story ends this chapter, describe their own journeys with the work of past-life regression. Their experiences have helped them to understand not only each other but also other significant familial relationships at a much deeper and more empathic level.

. REGRESSIONS OF RIVALRY .

In my late teens in this lifetime, I was at first baffled by the fact that my otherwise loving and conscientious mother would always find fault with any of my girlfriends, particularly if she thought that a relationship might become serious. I used to tell her to give the girls a chance. Eventually, I concluded that she probably saw my girlfriends as rivals for her only child's affection.

The teen years gave way to the twenties, and at the beginning of a postgraduate academic year's stay in France as an English-language teaching assistant, I met Kathleen. We were both English assistants at two different high schools in the same town. I came from England, Kathleen from the United States. Our relationship did indeed become serious, and we married and decided to make our home in America.

The conclusion that I gave at the end of the first paragraph only begins to explain the turbulence that my mother created on occasions during the sixteen years from my engagement in 1976 to her death in 1992. We were treated to all manner of manipulations in letters and phone calls, and our visits to England to see her and other family members were punctuated by outbursts of temper, usually for reasons that were clear only to my mother. We soon realized that she was trying to drive a wedge between us. The only way for us was to present a united front, which we did. Indeed, my mother remarked on that, and even though she eventually stopped trying to manipulate our relationship, the outbursts continued.

I was able to spend the last two weeks of my mother's life with her in the hospital, where she had been admitted because of the later stages of terminal cancer. Just before I arrived, a cancer-induced stroke took away her power of speech, but not her hearing and understanding. Despite all that had happened during the past sixteen years, I was grateful just to be able to be present with her during her final days.

After my mother's death, Kathleen and I often reminisced about my mother's volatile personality, wishing that our relationship with her might have been more peaceful.

Fifteen years passed. Then, we began reading Dr. Weiss's work and using his regression CDs. From the first session, I found it easy to go to past lives. One of my early recollections was of a life in which I was the manager of a large estate in Derbyshire, England, sometime in the nineteenth century. Imagine my surprise when I realized that my wife in that life was my mother in this lifetime, and that Kathleen was an estate employee, probably a cook or member of the kitchen staff, something that she has been able to confirm in her own regressions. Kathleen and I had felt a strong mutual attraction then but were unable to go beyond a platonic relationship, as I was married.

Subsequent regressions to that lifetime provided more information. I believe that the estate might have been Chatsworth because of an incident that happened in the past life when my wife (my current-life mother) and I were shopping in Buxton, the nearest large town to the Chatsworth estate. She and I were in a store when Kathleen and some other estate employees entered. I turned to greet Kathleen and the others and, when I turned back to my wife, there on her face was the same look of annoyance, frustration, and disdain that I had seen many times on my mother's face in this lifetime, especially after Kathleen and I became engaged.

During another regression to that lifetime, that same look was on my wife's face when Kathleen stopped by our house to inquire about my health after I suffered a respiratory illness that eventually led to my death. I had been helping a local farmer at lambing time, had been caught in a heavy rainstorm, and had contracted a cold, which became bronchitis and then pneumonia. Interestingly enough, I suffered from bronchitis on a number of occasions as a child in this lifetime.

We certainly have our own evidence that souls do incarnate in groups. Whether Kathleen, my mother, and I have been together in additional lifetimes, we do not know. Before we began past-life regression work, we put my mother's reaction to our relationship and marriage down to possessiveness and desire to control. Regressions to that past life, coupled with meditation, reflection, and other spiritual work, have revealed to us how much my mother's reactions were based in fear: fear of losing the person around whom she had built her reality. It would be easy for us to comment that there was no need for her to fear losing her loyal husband in that past life or her son's love in this life, but her fear was real for her, and it manifested itself as described. We are now able to see her actions and reactions with compassionate understanding. We see her as a wounded soul, and we wish her inner peace and healing.

It is fascinating just how many themes and aspects of past lives occur again in present lifetimes. I have visited, in chronological order, lives as the wife of an Indian nobleman, a Roman senator, a European builder in medieval times, a blacksmith, a Royalist cavalryman in the English Civil War, a professional court harpsichordist, a mariner, the estate manager, a French female professional theatrical singer, and a young German living in Berlin just before and during most of World War II (the lifetime prior to this one). Architecture and buildings interest me in this lifetime, as does music. I sing as an amateur in recitals and have recently begun learning the piano. I enjoy being at sea, and in fact Kathleen and I used to give enrichment presentations in maritime history for passengers on cruise ships. In two of the presentations, I sang sea shanties. And my profession in this life? Before I retired, I taught French and German at college for thirty-two years. Although time and effort on my part were needed to learn the two languages, I did not experience any difficulty in learning them to a level of fluency.

Past-life regression is a valuable tool for personal growth. When accompanied by a karmic connection, it can lead to a deeper, spiritual understanding of reality. We are all here to learn, to heal, and to help other souls to do the same. Kathleen and I are profoundly grateful to have had the opportunity to be reconnected as soul mates in this lifetime and to be able to nurture a loving relationship that has been rewarding, fulfilling, and, most of all, spiritually energizing. We have found our compass, and that compass is love.

∽ *Mark and Kathleen*

Love triangles are far more complex and enduring than we realize. Present-life mother and daughter-in-law were romantic rivals in the nineteenth century, and the jealousies from that time were carried over to the current lives. Even though the relationships had changed and the woman who had been Mark's wife reincarnated as his mother, her insecurities persisted. Past-life therapy can heal these emotional wounds, and Mark's mother might have benefited if she had had the inclination and the opportunity to experience a regression to that Derbyshire lifetime.

Many other emotions and feelings may be carried over from past lives. Anger, love, fear of loss or separation, rivalries, mistrust, concerns about betrayal, affinities, a sense of powerlessness, and overprotectiveness are only some of these. The relationship is repaired when the past-life origins of the problems are recalled and released. Then the relationship can be completely fresh, clear, and in the present moment. All the old baggage is discarded.

If relationship problems appear to make little sense given the present-life determinants, and if the problems seem resistant to reason and correction, these are clues that they may be originating from one or more of your past lives.

Our souls are constantly reuniting in order to grow and evolve. To know the past can heal the present and lighten the future.

Mark and Kathleen close their story and this chapter with a wonderfully apt metaphor. "We have found our compass," they write, "and that compass is love." Love is indeed that most exquisite instrument, helping us to navigate the rocky terrain of this earthly plane, guiding us toward the heavens, toward our home. Whenever we become lost in the woods, it reorients us with a gentle touch, realigning us on our path. Its force is magnetic, its wisdom unerring. Love is the device, the direction, and the destination. It points the way and it *is* the way. Love is our true nature. Love is our true north.

. 10 .

Lessons That
Animals Teach

We have been linked to animals and have shared this planet with them since the beginning of human time. We are connected to all sentient beings; the illusion of separateness is what fuels such pain and suffering in our world. Animals have souls too, and they may have their own lessons to learn. The brief but brilliant life of a butterfly may be a quick foray into experiencing the physical world. And to cast off your past with the sudden realization that you were born to fly is to undergo a spiritual as well as physical metamorphosis. The tortoise, in its century-long stay on Earth, may encounter a vast multitude of lessons. Around it the years come and go, teaching of life's impermanence and the truth that everything shall pass. Yet animals are also the instructors. The hummingbird sips the nectar of life, reminding us to taste its sweetness. Dogs are often the embodiment of loyalty and loving service. To watch tiny ants working together tirelessly to build astonishingly intricate cities and civilizations is to understand the power of community and perseverance. All animals have much to teach us about unconditional love, about intuition and instinct, and about living life in a fearless way.

Our pets can help us during our transition after death. They are frequently there to greet us and comfort us on the other side after we die and leave our physical bodies. They also reincarnate, as so many pet "owners" know. They can come to us again and aid us more than once during our particular lifetime. They can reunite with us in our future lives.

Their expression of love for us never ends. They will oftentimes sacrifice themselves for their owners. People tend not to do that for each other.

Animals are ubiquitous and loving beings, helping to herd us back to our spiritual paths if we happen to stray. In that sense, even our birds, horses, and other pets have a bit of the sheepdog archetype in them.

It is a well-known saying that cats have nine lives. Of course they do. All animals and people do—and many, many more than that. What a gift it is to share them together.

. MEMORIES OF MAGIC .

In my years of working as a professional animal communicator, I have been continually touched by the healing impact that understanding our relationships with animals can have. One of the most intense and emotionally complicated bonds I have had is with my horse, Magic. We are close, yet over the years our relationship brought inexplicable challenges that were not easily resolved, no matter how many trainers we went through. One day on my Wisconsin horse farm, when I was struggling to understand the depth of my feelings for Magic, my spirit traveled: first reminiscing in this life about him, and then to an ancient time where Native Americans and horses lived side by side. These visions helped me to understand my present-day conflict with him. Discovering my soul connection with Magic opened a door that brought peace to a grief I didn't even know was there.

My emotions regarding Magic intensified during the summer of 2006. As the heat reached its peak, so did my frustration.

"I am so angry at you!" I screamed, standing next to him as flies buzzed around us, gripping the riding crop over my head and ready to whip his back. "I hate you! I hate you!"

Clenching my jaw, I hit Magic instead on the neck with the flat of my hand. I reeled backward and stiffened my body as my breath sucked into my chest. Hesitantly, I turned my head to face him and saw my reflection deep within his liquid eye. His black-and-white body froze in place like the cold metal gate next to us, yet his skin quivered across the tense muscles on his neck.

I dropped the whip from my hand, collapsing into sobs on the dirt in my barn. "What is wrong with me?" I cried, repulsed and shocked at this intense hostility that I harbored for a horse I deeply loved. I shrouded my head in my sweatshirt and continued to weep.

As I sat there, the familiar horse odor that had saturated the fabric of my sweatshirt transformed into a faint but discernible smell of sweet sage. Sitting up and pulling the sweatshirt off, I flipped it around, examining it for fragments of the herb but finding only tear spots that had stained the cloth black. With the next breath, the wafting fragrance filled my nostrils again. The scent of the sage acted as a conduit to the near past and then to a past life, as images began to unveil in my head. I closed my eyes, following this familiar aroma through time to when I first met my beloved and difficult horse six years ago.

Magic and I had found each other at a stable where I was working. His lanky three-month-old body felt familiar, and when my heart jolted in confirmation, I knew he was the one. Weeks earlier, after praying for direction from my guardian angel about a new horse, she had told me of his coming. She went on to say that we would share an intense connection. Incredibly, we had both survived major fires. The presence of his raw, burnt legs, caused from running through smoldering hay, brought forth the agony of my own car fire, when a semitrailer hit my vehicle and I became trapped inside. I ultimately jumped through the flames as my only escape. I desperately sought to forget this trauma, but I couldn't turn away. We needed each other. Over time, I would help him heal his legs, and he would help me heal deep emotional wounds.

After we had been together for almost six years, the last two felt almost unbearable because of Magic's new sassy and unyielding nature. During brief calm moments, however, he repeatedly told me, "I'm sorry," and "Forgive me." Why would a horse care so much about these topics anyway? I was constantly amazed that I found myself angrier in his presence than with any person or animal I had ever known.

Then one evening after kayaking with my friend Mary, it all began to make sense.

"It's getting dark. We had better get our kayaks out of the water," I remember saying, shivering while looking down into the dank shallow water of Bad Fish Creek. "I don't know why I feel so creeped out here all the time. It doesn't make sense. I've felt that every time I've been here, even though it's been years now."

Together we pulled the boats up the muddy embankment onto the grass. To get them home we would need my truck, which was parked at my horse farm just a short distance away. Walking across my neighbor Doug's hay field was the shortest route. Instead of leaving right away, however, we felt compelled to linger and talk about our favorite parts of the day.

Suddenly, I felt a large, strong, and kind hand against my back. The hand gently pressed against me like a pilgrim touching a sacred site. I was not scared and lengthened my back into this soft, deep connection. My rational mind thought, *It must be Doug.* I turned, but only the muddy edge of the creek returned my look. There was nobody. I flung my head around and blinked my eyes in confusion.

"Mary, a man just touched my back. I swear I'm not crazy."

"I know," she said.

"You do? How?"

"I just saw about twenty people standing behind you. They were dressed—no, you look," she said patiently. "Look in your mind's eye."

Closing my eyes and taking a deep breath, I asked to see who was there. Immediately, there was a large group of Native Americans standing in front of me, emanating love and telepathically sending me these words: "We love you. We are so happy you are here. Please know we forgive you. All wrongs are released."

The man who had touched my back looked wise, like a trusting father. Next to him, a large woman who radiated love was enfolding me in a warm embrace, and each person in turn sent what felt like an incredible hug. "We will send you more visions to bring you full understanding and forgiveness for yourself and your horse," they said.

I knew that they were speaking of Magic. Once again, I had no idea what I would need forgiveness for, and I wondered what Magic had to do with this.

I opened my eyes and walked across the dark field with Mary. My bones vibrated inside my body as I felt myself like a seed sprouting, changing, and growing. I wasn't sure I was ready for this. But seeds sprout and grow, regardless.

Weeks passed before the next full vision emerged during a deep meditation, in which I saw myself in a past life as a Native American woman with my baby and husband.

"Hey, stop that!" I was saying, and I giggled as my husband grabbed me around the waist. I could feel the heat radiate off his taut body as he stood beside me.

"I'm going to get you, Shayna," he teased, as he crouched on leather hides that covered the dirt floor inside our home. His big eyes glowed with playfulness, and he darted between our small daughter and me.

"You are just a little bear, Little Bear," I said. "You think you're so big and strong that you should be called Big Bear. No way! You're always going to be my Little Bear." I continued to pester him as I swooped up Ayasha, our baby, and ran out of our hut into the sunlight.

"Grr," he growled, with his big hands made into claws. "Here I come!" With Ayasha at my waist, we ran through the trees and out into the field. "I'm coming, Shayna. You girls had better run."

As I looked down at my daughter's soft tuft of black hair, we pranced like sneaky cats to hide among our herd of horses. As we moved into the open grass field, a rush of earthen-smelling wind brushed our faces. Ayasha cooed and flung her arms up in excitement at the sight of the paint horses gathered around us in different hues of black, white, and gold.

Nestled in the middle of the herd, we peeked over the white mane of Magic, looking for my husband. I had no sooner mumbled, "Where's papa, Ayasha?" when I heard, "Boo!" and felt warm fingertips grabbing my shoulder. I spun around and he was standing behind us. "How did you get there?"

"You see, my wife, I am a fast warrior."

I raised my eyebrows and nodded. Then Magic's fuzzy black-and-white nose hit me, as if he wanted in on the fun. I grabbed my head, for he wasn't gentle and it hurt. "That horse of yours is rude," I said in irritation. "You should trade him to another tribe."

"Never," he said. "He has power."

"Too much. He's going to hurt one of us," I recalled saying, and then the image faded out.

I opened my eyes as the past life ended. I knew from this little story that I had loved my husband and daughter. My sense of unity in the tribe was deeply rooted to my connection with them. Magic was challenging in that life too. I relaxed my shoulders, knowing that his sassy behavior did not just start with me in this life.

A week later, I found myself focusing on another scene from that same past life, one in which there was a small crowd of people grieving and hunched over by a man lying on the sun-warmed grass. Some of them were chanting quietly as they passed sage through the air. A heavyset woman adorned in a skirt made of leather and beads was off to the side, bouncing a toddler on her hip. Near her, a young woman with dark hair knelt on the ground in a simple buckskin dress.

The smell of sage filled my nose as vividly as it had that day in the stable with Magic. I cautiously moved across the green field to take a better look. *Who are these people?* Then it became clear that the young woman kneeling on the ground, wailing inconsolably, was Shayna. This time, I was a witness to the scene instead of actually experiencing it again.

The sun beat down on her hair, reflecting a halo of bright arching rainbows. Her hands flung out from her chest and then back again, pulling at her clothing. I looked past her to the face of the fallen man. It was Little Bear. I grimaced upon seeing blood flowing out of his head, staining the grass. He was not breathing. Kindness shone out of his face, even in death. Splayed around his head, his long hair, matted and sticky, covered a rock. Red droplets smeared its surface as flies buzzed around it. Slowly turning to the left, I saw a black-and-white horse standing solemnly as leather reins dangled off his head onto the ground. *Magic?* My mind reeled. *Oh, my goodness, were you involved with my husband's death? No wonder I've been angry with you.*

The landscape blurred while I gazed at Little Bear. My breathing became shallow as I bent down and looked right into the woman's face. Suddenly, I became filled with incredible sorrow and grief. This was really my life that I was seeing. The devastation of her loss filled me. Her love was gone, and she felt utterly alone.

Shayna fell back on her haunches as she pulled clumps of grass out of the earth. Gasps from her open mouth were barely audible as I looked around, imploring support. No one could see or hear me. Dropping the dead grass, she stared vacantly, the grief of losing her young husband etched in her eyes. I tried to reach out telepathically and send her the thoughts, *It's going to be okay. You're going to live in a house across this field someday. You're going to make it.* But she could not hear me.

The heavyset woman called to the toddler who had wiggled free, "Come back here, Ayasha!" Oblivious to the tragic sight, she bumbled toward her mother. Shayna spun around and gripped her daughter at the waist. Her hands convulsed, pinching the child's bare skin, causing her to cry. She stared at the screaming Ayasha as she pushed her to the ground. Shayna looked around at the clan, steadying her gaze on each of them, her jaw clamped tight. They all turned away, staring at their feet and shuffling them in the dirt. The same large woman picked up the crying Ayasha and walked off.

Another group of people came running to the scene, attracted by the commotion. "What is going on?" they asked at once.

A tall, slender man with gray braided hair stepped forward. "Little Bear rode on Magic fast and playfully. We were all watching and encouraging him. Then Magic flipped his head in defiance and slipped into a slight gorge, throwing both of them to the ground. Little Bear hit the rock and died."

The new arrivals walked over to Little Bear and paid their respects. I saw my native self get up from her dead husband's side and walk into the crowd, taking her baby from the arms of the large woman.

In silence, she walked away with the child resting on her hip. No one followed her.

Shayna moved across a field of yellow flowers and headed into the woods. The tall, thick-barked trees emitted a pungent earthy smell, and the purifying scent of water filled the air. As she slipped down the grassy twig-covered hill, she used one hand to keep from falling while the other grasped her beautiful daughter.

The sound of rushing water became thunderous. Shayna stepped into the quick-flowing stream, immersed up to her thighs. Struggling against the water's flow while moving deeper into the powerful current, she took the child from her hip and slowly immersed the baby's chubby torso into the swirling water. She took a deep breath and lowered her daughter below the water's surface. Shayna's arms stiffened. Ayasha's tiny body went limp. Shayna turned toward the current, feeling her baby's soft skin for the last time, and let go, watching as her dreams and sweet baby daughter floated into the woods and darkness.

Screaming and pulling at her hair in mad grief, she leaped back up the embankment and ran out of the woods, through the field, toward her husband's lifeless body. The clan, shocked at the sight of Shayna without her beloved baby, frantically searched each other's arms with their eyes.

"No!" someone cried out. "She took the baby with her!"

Hunan, Little Bear's younger brother, grabbed her arms and screamed, "Where is the baby?"

Shayna pulled her arms free and slapped him across the face. He dove at her waist, pushing her to the ground.

The large woman rushed in with intense eyes. "Someone, run to the river!" she yelled. Five natives raced across the field through the woods and down into the creek. They searched in desperation among the downed trees at the creek's edge as the sounds of splashing water echoed hauntingly across the land.

"You're too late," Shayna screamed at them. Glaring at Magic, she cried, "Everyone I love is dead now, and it's all because of that black-and-white horse!"

A wave of knowing that the child was indeed dead flashed over the large woman's face, and she said, shaking her head, "Let her up." They moved away from her in disgust and shock.

The images turned to black as I felt myself being pulled back to my present life. Sobbing, I opened my eyes. I sat in my current bedroom, filled with grief, gratitude, and understanding of why my "tribe" had come back to me. It would not be easy, but I knew that I could now truly heal.

Shame was a thread that had woven itself through my life. No matter how hard I tried, I could never find the source until Magic led me on the path to love, peace, and self-forgiveness.

The love that our wise animals give us so that we may be free is incredible. With my beloved horse's persistence and the beseeching love of my past-life family, I learned that no mistake is too big to be forgiven—even lifetimes away.

∽ *Asia Voight*

In this very powerful narrative, Asia enables us to glimpse an important role that animals play in the lives of humans. Animals teach us about unconditional love, and they often devote their entire lives to this purpose. Their love is not dependent on our behavior. It is strong and unwavering. We do not need to earn it. It is freely given and not arbitrarily withdrawn. We can know this love and feel it at a deep level.

Animals reincarnate, as Magic's story illustrates. Their souls may not be as individuated as those of humans; perhaps their family or group soul mingles more. But this distinction is not an important one.

Guilt and shame are negative emotions that cause us great discomfort and disability. They are partly caused by our belief that we have not lived up to some arbitrary level of thought and conduct. We have disappointed ourselves by not conforming to an internalized and very lofty standard of behavior. Our failure creates anger, and the anger is directed inward. Depression and despair often follow.

This whole process is preventable.

The past is an excellent teacher, but once you have learned the material you need not keep studying it over and over again. Doing so will only prevent your education from advancing. Learn from the past, then let it go. We have all made mistakes in our present lives and throughout all our past lifetimes. Clear awareness of our mistakes allows for correction and the intention not to repeat them. Intense guilt, shame, and anger fog our vision and thus obscure the lessons, which only leads to repetition of the mistakes. These negative emotions block our growth and steal our joy. Nonjudgmental awareness dissolves harmful negativity and helps us to regain our bearings.

Magic returned to teach Asia these lessons. He was the doorway into the past life that contained so much tragedy, loss, grief, and shame. He would have spent his entire life helping her make this connection so that she could begin to forgive herself. He would do this out of love, for the love of our pets is limitless. We may be angry at them, yell at them, and even hit them, and yet they patiently wait for the lesson to unfold. Magic waited six years. He would have waited for all of eternity.

The mechanisms through which animals relay such important messages to humans can take a variety of forms. Magic facilitated a journey into Asia's past that allowed her to come to a transformative understanding. Ozzie, the dog featured in the following story, used a more hands-on approach, so to speak. In his own unassuming way, he managed to both affirm the existence of an afterlife and reassure his owner's friend that her beloved husband, despite his death, had never left her side.

. PROOF OF PRESENCE .

I asked my friend, Hillevi, to share her lovely story. As she tells it:

I was married to a wonderful man named Robert, who passed away. Several years after his death, I visited my friend, Mara, who had met Robert once twelve years earlier. Mara and I lived in different parts of the country, so we did not have the chance to meet or visit each other often.

Mara had offered to give me a reading. She had attended some of your seminars in Florida, and she has had many accurate experiences reading people. I gave her Robert's wedding band. She put it in her hand, and we sat across from each other. Mara had her back to the window, and I had my back toward the apartment. Her Maltese dog, Ozzie, slept next to us on the floor.

We both sat very quietly, waiting for Mara to get messages. She told me the information that she received, and I said, "But how do I really know that Robert is with us?"

Suddenly, we heard a loud bang. I turned around, and on the tile floor behind me was a small, wood-framed photo of Robert. Next to it was Ozzie, who only was twice the size of the framed photo. What was so amazing about this is that the photo of Robert had been in the bedroom, tucked behind some bags and a large suitcase.

What made Ozzie awaken, get up from the floor, go into the bedroom, and bring the photo to the living room? This is something that he had never done before or since.

I went to take a look in the bedroom, and neither the bags nor the suitcase were moved. The floors are tiled, so we would have heard if Ozzie had dragged the wooden frame across it. Instead, he had put the frame in his mouth, carried it fifteen feet, and then dropped it on the floor behind me. How he did this I am not sure, but Mara and I strongly felt that Robert was with us, helping Ozzie to carry the photo into the living room and drop it with a loud bang. This was Robert's way of answering my question!

∾ *Mara Gober*

The instinctual mind of animals is not obstructed by the logical, thinking, analytical functions that the human brain and mind possess. This frees them to be more attuned to communications of diverse frequencies, vibrations, and sources. Perhaps Robert found it easier to connect directly with Ozzie, who then performed a rather complex task of locating the unique photo, bringing it from deep within the other room, and dropping it right behind Hillevi. What are the odds of that?

. . .

Walter Jacobson, a psychiatrist, wrote on his blog about his experience while attending my weeklong training at Omega. During one of the group regressions, Walter saw, in his mind, the image of two cupped hands. But as a self-professed left-brained and analytical person, he found himself unable to recall a past life or any other images during the first few days of the workshop.

On the fourth day, I brought Walter onstage to demonstrate how to perform a regression on someone who was having difficulty remembering his past lives. The cupped hands that Walter had previously visualized were my entry point into his past life. When people have hands they usually have feet, and so I guided Walter to look down at his. He could see them now, clad in men's leather sandals, and he could also see that he was next to a river.

What was the significance of the cupped hands? At first I thought that he must have been interacting with another person, but as we delved further into the scene we realized that his dying dog was lying on the ground beside him. Walter had been gathering the water from the river and holding it up to his beloved dog's face, for the dog was too weak to drink on his own. The gesture was an incredibly compassionate one, and the entire audience of workshop participants was visibly moved by the profound love between man and dog. Not long after, the dog died, and Walter, now left completely alone, was filled with sadness. I asked Walter what he had learned from that lifetime, and his answer was simple and heartfelt: "Love."

More understandings about that lifetime came to Walter after the regression. As he wrote: "The lesson from my past-life regression was not simply about love but about devotion as well. Devotion is a very important part of the lesson I'm here to learn. When I care for my dog, I need to do it with devotion to her needs being met more than my mine. When I care for our horses, the same needs to be true: that I am fully present, fully dedicated, fully communicative, and fully nurturing. And, last but not least, I need to be devoted in my service to others, in the expression of my compassion, acceptance, and forgiveness of everyone whose path I cross, and in my bonding with my significant others."

Upon browsing the Omega bookstore that week and entering its back room, Walter looked down and saw a statue: an exact replica of the two cupped hands that he had envisioned. The sculpture was entitled *The Hands of God*.

Recently, I was reading the local newspaper and becoming dismayed by the relentless chronicling of hatred and violence occurring all over the world. People were being brutally attacked and left for dead in the streets. A teenager was shot and killed in a hate crime, merely because of the color of his skin. Literally right underneath this last article was a piece about two cats, and I silently blessed the newspaper for including this wonderful story of love and devotion.

An elderly Floridian woman had become enamored with and adopted two kittens from the same litter, a brother and sister whom she named Jack and Jill. The woman eventually moved to Maine, but Jack ran away just before she left, and she was forced to leave without one of her treasured pets. A neighbor happened to find the lost cat and called the woman in Maine, only to learn that she had died and that her relatives had given Jill to a local animal shelter two months prior.

The neighbor grew troubled that Jill was all alone, and she scoured the shelters in Maine to find her. After prayers and a painstaking search of hundreds and hundreds of cats, Jill was located. However, the neighbor could not afford the $500 needed to transport the cat back to Florida. As she told the story to her coworkers at the country club, they banded together, along with others who had heard the story, to collect the money on her behalf. Within only two days they had reached their goal, and not long after, Jill was back home, finally and happily reunited with her brother Jack.

Reading this, I was reminded of Walter's memory of lovingly cupping his hands to quench the thirst of his dying dog. We humans are capable of expressing great compassion and devotion to our beloved pets. To expend so much energy and money to reunite two cats is such a noble and tender act. Furthermore, so many had to come together to achieve this goal: not only the determined neighbor but also the patrons, members, and staff of the country club who had pitched in to cover the cost. If only we could treat other people with the same careful compassion that we extend to our pets, then our newspapers would not be filled with accounts of atrocities. The papers would instead feature stories of charity, kindness, and hope. Humans are important too.

People are so wonderfully devoted to their pets, in fact, that they often ask me if we can reincarnate as animals, and if we have inhabited those kinds of bodies before our own human ones. I do believe that it is possible that we have had lifetimes in animal form. It could be that we simply do not remember these lifetimes. During regressions, human memories are more easily accessible, and they are most likely the ones in which traumas and symptoms have their origins. In my own work with patients, I have found that once you become a human, you tend to stay a human. I've personally yet to encounter any people who were sent back to the animal kingdom as a form of punishment for being too violent or too hurtful in their human lives. Rather, there seems to be a progression to the human level, and it is the level where, for the time being, our lessons are to be learned.

We can change our species and kingdom if we choose to, for that may offer us a new avenue for learning. We can explore animal consciousness, or plant consciousness, or even the consciousness of the clouds, as other stories in this book demonstrate. Why should we ever put any limits on our awareness, on our soul?

. GUIDER .

Omega is a truly special place, one where amazing and wonderful things of a synchronistic nature regularly transpire. People meet people they are meant to meet and get messages and answers they dearly need. Miraculous "happenstances" are virtually commonplace there. When they occur, the feeling one gets is, "Wow, of course. This is what was needed, wanted, hoped for, and meant to be." I went there for four consecutive years to learn from Brian and Carole, to regress as many people as I could, and to open myself and embrace whatever miraculous synchronicities would come my way.

In August 2006, before going to Omega, I had recently returned from visiting my brother in Texas. While there, I took advantage of the opportunity to see my friend, Dr. Jerry Casebolt. Jerry is a great healer, a shaman who also happens to be a licensed, experienced chiropractor. People who go to see Jerry must be prepared for something different, something special, in the way of treatment. Chiropractic bodywork, breathwork, deep-tissue shiatsu massage, some Rolfing techniques, guided imagery, hypnosis, and deeply moving and relevant storytelling that mixes archetype, metaphor, symbolism, and allegory—these are all of the tools of Jerry's work, and he uses them brilliantly and seamlessly.

When I went to see Jerry that summer, I had recently snapped my left Achilles tendon, having fallen off of a ladder. Suffice it to say, I was experiencing significantly less range of motion and immense pain. While working on my leg and back, which was excruciating, Jerry began to talk to me, as he always did. First he took me through a full-body relaxation and healing meditation, in which I visualized a white, healing light entering the top of my head, passing through my entire body, and leaving through my feet. He then asked me to visualize an animal coming to visit me, to give me a message of healing. Immediately I saw an immense owl, a great horned owl, and I told him so.

"Good. That is your power animal, and he's here to help you to heal," Jerry said. "What is his name?"

"His name is Guider," I replied. What followed, as Jerry continued to work on me, often burying his thumb or elbow into my body to work out a knot somewhere, was a beautiful visualization of Guider showing me the way to greater awareness, insight, health, and wholeness. It was so beautiful, so real and powerful. I cried.

A few weeks later, I found myself at Omega Institute for the first time, and I was so excited to experience mediumship through psychometry and to conduct my first regression that I remained on campus after class, talking with classmates and doing more regressions, until 9:30 that evening.

It was very dark, and I was exhausted and exhilarated as I walked toward the parking lot to begin the twenty-minute drive back to my hotel in town. I was full of excitement from the day's events, literally spiritually high, and I loved it. In a field in front of the dining hall, I observed a beautiful ceremony. A large group of women, approximately 150 of them, were standing there on the grass in a huge circle, each holding a candle. I stopped and listened from under a nearby tree. They were singing a song in unison, and as each refrain ended two new women from the circle would step into it, move in opposite directions, and stop to hug each and every woman. These are the words they so wonderfully chanted: "Dear sister, dear sister, I must let you know. You have loved me all these years, and I love you so." That was it—such a simple, beautiful sentiment.

I found the way to my vehicle in the parking lot, and I realized that I was singing the song as I walked. Merely doing so made me feel closer to my sisters and brothers. It was a powerful refrain. I began driving out through the heavily wooded area around Omega, and as I left the campus I passed the large circle of women, still continuing that lovely ceremony. I slowed down to observe them one more time and then drove through the deep woods. It was a sweet summer night, and I had the window down. I was alone on the dark road, and as I rounded a tight bend there at the edge of the road, approximately fifteen feet away, looking directly at me, stood the largest, most beautiful owl I had ever seen.

"Guider," I whispered, in awe of the bird's size and beauty. He watched me in the headlights for about ten seconds, and then he opened his massive wings and, with one big swooping whoosh of them, lifted himself to a branch on the very edge of the road. Landing on the end of the branch in a big maple tree, he turned his head, and those large yellow-orange eyes looked right at me.

"There you are, Guider," I said, as I crept forward slowly in my vehicle. I stopped only a few feet away from his tree, and we stared at each other, eye to eye, for seconds.

Guider then simply fell from the tree branch, opened those massive six-foot wings of his, and glided to yet another tree branch on the edge of the other side of the road. Settling there, he turned his big head and fixed those beautiful, luminous eyes on me again. This time, when I slowly crept forward to this great owl, he sat and quietly regarded me for a full minute.

Now I got goose bumps, as I knew instinctively that this was Guider. He had come to see me and to show me the way, to give me a message, to impart some sacred wisdom. Guider would continue to fall and swoop to successive tree branches, all on opposite edges of the road, a total of six times, and I would continue to idle forward to where he was as we stared into one another's eyes, over and over. The experience was mystical, surreal, and profoundly touching.

A car's lights began to loom out of the darkness behind me then and I knew I had to drive, as sitting still in the road was no longer a good idea. As if he understood, Guider fell from the tree one last time, swooped closer to my vehicle, as if to say good-bye, and glided off into the dark forest.

What a truly magical experience. Though there may seem to be, there are no accidents at Omega. The person gets what they were supposed to get. That day, I had performed my very first regression, something I had yearned to learn. The person I regressed had remembered a life long ago as a Native American. This had held great personal meaning for her. Native Americans have long known of the importance of a visitation from a power animal. And, that same night, I was gifted a wonderful visitation from mine. Guider seemed to be saying, "Welcome. You have found your right path. Now follow it, helping others along the way, to where you will find your true self."

As Brian would so often say that week, "There are no accidents. We are all connected."

ᘯ Michael Brown

And, as Carole would say, "Sometimes miracles happen." If our hearts and minds are open and loving, we will find our right path and our true self. There will be many signs illuminating and confirming the way.

I too have seen this group of women in the field. Sometimes they are all wearing white dresses or robes; with the white candles surrounding them, this is a marvelous sight in the dark of night. Their song is melodic, addictive. I hear the words "You have loved me all these years," and the millions of years connecting all our existences and incarnations come to my mind. How many thousands of sisters we have had over these lifetimes.

As Michael began singing the simple words of that sweet song, his heart opened even more. He felt a connection with all his sisters and brothers, the entire human family. In that mystical and pure state, he was ready to meet Guider and to receive the confirmation he needed about his chosen path.

There is a goddess in Celtic mythology who often took the form of a large, wise owl. Her all-seeing eyes allowed her to peer into the infinite depths of the human subconscious, of the soul. Her giant outspread wings bestowed healing and compassion upon anyone who sought her guidance as she flew powerfully through the night. She lived in and ruled over that heavenly place where souls awaited rebirth and where poets were said to be learning the wisdom of the stars. It was she who decided whether a soul should be given a new body or sent on to a higher spiritual realm. A symbol of feminine power, she is the deity of karma, of past-life memories, of reincarnation.

Perhaps Michael sensed her archetypal presence in that candlelit field of women as they sang of the ancient bonds of sisterhood. Perhaps he sensed it in Guider, the immense owl who graced his path again and again, or in the stars above on that sweet summer night, where resting souls eagerly anticipated new life. "There are no accidents," Michael said, and he is right. There are no coincidences, either. There is only the universe spreading its loving, angelic wings of comfort around our shoulders, guiding each of us on our way.

. II .

Short and Sweet

The work of regression therapy, with its ever-present themes of illness, loss, grief, and death, can often feel quite heavy. Humor provides a balance. Life lessons are not restricted to difficult experiences; they are also found in the lighter moments. Some may even seem so frivolous that we do not give them the attention that they deserve. But they, too, have much to teach us, and they can be therapeutic in their own right.

One summer, I was teaching a training course at the Omega Institute. The past—and present—lives that we were exploring happened to be particularly stressful, and as a result the week proved to be even more emotional than usual. In the final moments of the last day, as the workshop was coming to a close, a young woman approached me with a very serious look on her face. I stopped to spend a moment with her, sure that she was about to ask me something profound.

In a quiet voice, she asked me the question that had been on her mind. "Do you know who you look like?"

Her question surprised me, but I answered that I did not.

Without a hint of a laugh, she replied, "E.T."

"You mean, the extraterrestrial?" I thought that I had misheard her.

"Yes, E.T."

I was convinced that I had not understood her correctly. "You mean, the little guy who rode the bike across the moon?" I asked, pantomiming pedaling a bicycle.

"That's right!"

Thinking back on it now, I wish I would have asked her for more details. What about me, exactly, resembled E.T.? In what way did I look like that small alien? But at the time I was too perplexed to even respond, and I just walked away.

Perhaps that brief encounter had transpired in order to provide me with a lesson in humility and ego. Perhaps there was some deeper significance in her metaphor that has not yet revealed itself to me. Or perhaps I just needed a good laugh after a very long week.

Whether humorous or serious, this chapter illustrates how apparently simple events can contain the seeds of deep truths and wisdom. These stories may be small, but their effects and implications are nothing short of powerful.

. APPLES OF ONE'S EYE .

I recently attended your workshop in South Florida. At the very beginning of the event, you were mentioning that you'd sign books at the end and only one per person, for time's sake, and that instead of personalizing each inscription, you would sign "Love, Brian Weiss."

I was sitting in the audience of about nine hundred people and thinking that, during the next break, I needed to phone my son to remind him to pick up our friend's dog from the kennel so that she wouldn't have to stay the following day. I was completely immersed in that thought. Then I came back to what you were saying, which was "For example, if you were to ask me to sign it for Appolonia . . ."

Our friend's dog's name is Appolonia—Apples, for short.

I just loved it.

                                                      Margie Samuels

There are no coincidences or completely random events. Everything has a purpose and a reason, even if we are not aware of it at the time. The name "Appolonia" popped into my mind, and it became my example. I guess

Apples really wanted to leave the kennel. Something or someone impressed that name on my consciousness, and it came through very clearly. As a result, Appolonia has more than a personalized inscription in a book—she has an entire story.

From apples we move on to celery.

. CELERY CLAIRVOYANCE .

I attended your wonderful workshop in Los Angeles a few years ago. When we did the energy exercise in the afternoon, I partnered with Lisa, a woman sitting in front of me. I exchanged my wedding ring for her watch. Even before you started counting, I had a vision of a dolphin, halfway out of the water, which was very playful and cute. I tried to ignore the vision as I felt it had come too suddenly to be valid, but the dolphin wouldn't go away.

When hearing about it, Lisa had a big smile. "This is my favorite animal!" she exclaimed.

I was pleased and relieved that I had done a good job.

I waited to hear what she had seen about me. She looked confused and almost apologetically said, "Even before we started, right in my face, I—I saw a big, green, juicy bunch of . . . celery!" She stretched her hands far apart and said, "I mean, really big!" This sounded pretty funny, but I felt somewhat disappointed. I hated celery and couldn't think of any deep or noble meaning behind it.

I got home around seven that evening and was treated to a big, cold glass of juice. My husband recently had become a juice fanatic, creating his own recipes with fruits and vegetables. I started telling him the story with Lisa, and as I mentioned the celery, my husband ran to the refrigerator like a madman and came back with the most plump and juicy bunch of celery that I've ever seen. That very afternoon, at the same time that I had been doing the psychometry exercise with Lisa, he had been getting his juice ingredients at the market. He couldn't resist buying the celery bunch, being so impressed by its unusual appearance and size. We have been married for twenty-two years, and the wedding band that I had handed to Lisa has his name engraved on it.

I will never look at celery the same way again.

∾ *Sophia*

The proof of our incredible psychic and mystical nature does not always have to be grand and cosmic. A magnificent meteor shower or solar eclipse has the same importance as a bunch of celery. We just need to know that we are gifted spiritual beings with intuitive abilities far beyond our everyday comprehension. Whether we learn this from heavenly visions or earthly vegetables does not matter.

In the world of psychic phenomena, just like in the realm of subatomic physics, the usual limitations of space and time are transcended. We are capable of knowing events that are happening simultaneously even if they are geographically distant. Sophia's husband was eyeing the celery stalks around the same time that Lisa saw them "right in front of [her] face" at a workshop miles away.

Sophia's story also emphasizes the truism that sometimes we do not recognize the importance of an event at the time that it is happening. Eventually, its significance will come to light. Sophia was disappointed by Lisa's vision of the celery until that evening, when her husband recognized the connection to the purchase he had made hours prior.

Dave was likewise disappointed with his psychic perceptions until his psychometry partner revealed how perfectly accurate they were. His story follows.

. HUNTING FOR MUSHROOMS .

I was one of the audience members in your Tampa workshop, where a curious small thing occurred while we did the exchange of articles. My wife and I switched our belongings with people we did not know, and my partner was a Chinese woman. She gave me her bracelet, and in the exercise I kept thinking of mushrooms. *How silly,* I had thought.

She had envisioned a perfect scene from a family farm we owned in Pennsylvania, and all I could come up with was mushrooms.

It turned out that she was an avid mushroom hunter. Her father-in-law, who sat next to her, had given her a mushroom kit, and she was feeling very annoyed with herself that she had not utilized it yet!

∾ Dave

Be it celery or mushrooms, the important part is the exchange of knowledge, memories, and experiences through the flow of energy. Once we let down the veil of our conscious minds, we allow this flow to occur. We become aware that we are connected and that we know so much about each other. It is difficult to be prejudiced or violent when you can so clearly see and feel the energetic bonds that unite us all.

In his book *The Hidden Messages in Water*, Dr. Masaru Emoto demonstrated how words, too, can transmit this energy flow and consequently influence the molecular structure of water. Marylyn and her mother also witnessed firsthand the transformative power of words and books. Their story, next, shows what happens when we read with our spiritual eyes.

. READING BETWEEN THE LINES .

Near the end of her life, my mother could no longer read regular-sized-print books, only those in large print. At that time, I had a copy of your book *Many Lives, Many Masters* in regular-sized print.

One day, we were sitting together on the sofa, and I was finishing reading your book, one of my favorites. She took it from me and started to turn the pages. She had never done anything like this before. Because I knew that the print was too small for her to see, I asked if she would like me to read it to her.

"No," she replied, "I can read it myself."

I knew that she couldn't, but I sat there and watched her go slowly through your book, looking at each page carefully. Finally, she reached the end and returned it to me. She had a beautiful look of peace on her face. I knew that she had read your book simply by turning the pages. And I had the distinct feeling that she knew that I knew. It was a moment of wonderful connection between my mother and me.

∽ *Marylyn Calabrese*

There is an energy in books, one that often transcends the print. Sometimes, when I autograph one of my own, I have the conscious thought of putting my energy into it along with my name. Marylyn's energy was in her book, and perhaps her mother could feel that as well.

Whatever the mechanism, a beautiful connection ensued.

Amy writes about another moment of connection between a child and a parent: this time with my son, Jordan, and his own son.

. HEROES .

My brother, Jordan, tells a story of driving in a car one sunny afternoon near his home in Philadelphia. His son, Travis, who was seven years old at the time, was sitting in the backseat. They were leaving a busy shopping center that had only one exit lane and a streetlight at its end. There were many cars waiting to exit along with them; the traffic was heavy, the line long. While they waited, Travis looked out the window and saw a man standing nearby, collecting money for charity. When he asked Jordan what that was all about, Jordan, seeing the information on the man's vest and signage, replied that the money went to children with cancer.

Travis listened, and then he asked if they could give the man a dollar.

"Oh, I don't know, Trav," Jordan said noncommittally. The thought hadn't really occurred to him; he was, as we all are, accustomed to seeing people collecting money for one cause or another on a daily basis—on the street, on the television, in the mail—and giving to some but not all as request after request piled up. Would one dollar really be of much help? Who knew where that money went, anyway? He wasn't even sure he had a dollar on him, and to check would have meant unhooking his seat belt, reaching into his pocket, fiddling around and taking everything out, perhaps some change falling onto the floor; it just didn't seem worth the hassle. At a red light with so many people behind them, any delay caused by stopping would surely have resulted in shouting and horn honking. And, sure enough, at that moment the light turned green and there was nothing more he could do, so he said something like "Ah, well" as he began to drive away, thinking nothing else of it.

It was only when they had finally left the shopping center and made the difficult merge into six lanes of congested traffic that Travis said, "Oh, but Dad, we could be heroes."

And so, after the long wait to get onto the street where they now were, there was no other option but to make a U-turn and drive back to the shopping center just to go all the way around again and sit in the traffic again and wait at the light again so that they could, this time, hand the man some money.

Looking in the rearview mirror as he drove off, Jordan saw Travis excitedly pumping his little fists in the air and whispering, "Yes!"

∾ *Amy Weiss*

To be a hero doesn't require great action and thousands of people. Simple acts of kindness qualify too, and the results of these radiate outward to all of the earth and beyond. Charity and kindness can never be minimized. Everything is energy, and the energy of compassion encompasses all the others. A resonance is established, just like the ringing of a bell that sends a storm of beautiful sound waves into the atmosphere, just like a stone thrown into a pond that sends ripples to the entire shore. Acts of kindness can ripple to the shore of our soul's universe. And, sometimes, children can be our best teachers.

Jordan's story is of a special moment while driving in a car with his son, who had an important lesson to teach him. Upon hearing it, I couldn't help but think of a similar experience that I had, one generation ago, when Jordan was the child and I the father driving him. That time, the lesson had been for me. As adults, we tend to forget those beautiful, wise insights into the world, but our children will always be the vehicle for reminding us. I tell this story in my book *Through Time into Healing:*

Several years ago, after a ten-hour day of seeing patients, I was beginning to relax by meditating in a reclining chair in my office. After only a few minutes, already in a deep state without any particular thoughts in my mind, I heard a booming voice inside my head. It was like a telepathic trumpet, and it shook my whole body.

"Just love him!" the voice thundered. I was instantly wide awake. I knew the message meant Jordan, my son. At this time, he was a typically rebellious teenager, but I had not been thinking about him at all on this day. Perhaps, subconsciously, I was wrestling with how to deal with his behavior.

One very early and dark morning a week later, I was driving Jordan to school. I tried to get a conversation going, but he was particularly monosyllabic in his responses to me that day. Jordan was just plain grumpy.

I knew I had the choice of being angry or of letting it go. I remembered the message "Just love him!" and I chose the latter.

"Jordan, just remember that I love you," I said as I dropped him off at school.

To my surprise, he replied, "I love you, too."

It was then that I realized that he hadn't been angry or grumpy at all, he just wasn't fully awake yet. My perception of anger had been an illusion.

I continued driving in to the hospital, about forty-five minutes away. As I passed a church, the sun was just rising above the treetops, and a gardener was leisurely mowing the grass.

Suddenly I had a feeling of great peace and joy. I felt immensely safe and secure, and the world seemed to be in perfect order. The gardener, the trees, and everything else I could see were luminous and glowing. I could almost see through them; everything had a transparent golden quality. I felt connected to everyone and everything—to the gardener, the trees, the grass, the sky, a squirrel climbing a tree. There was the total absence of fear or anxiety. The future seemed perfectly clear . . . perfect.

I must have seemed strange to the other rush-hour commuters. I felt a kind of detached, universal love for them, too. Even as other drivers cut in front of me, I just waved them in and smiled. I wondered why all these people were rushing so much. Time seemed to stand still and then disappear. I felt incredibly patient. We were here to learn and to love. I could see this so clearly. Nothing else really matters.

The luminosity and transparency of objects continued as I drove to the hospital. So did the state of detached loving-kindness and great peace and joy. So did the feelings of patience and happiness and interconnectedness with everything else.

This state stayed with me as I began my workday. I was unusually intuitive with my patients that morning, especially with two new patients I had never seen before. I could perceive light in and around people: everyone seemed to glow. I could really experience how everything in life is connected. I knew with certainty that there was no such thing as danger, no need for fear. Everything was one.

Jordan's presence that morning, with our simple connection of love and a more complicated lesson on assumptions, had opened my heart, sparking a completely transcendent experience in me—one that expanded up to the sky, down to the tiny blades of grass, and everywhere in between. Clearly, he already knew how to be a hero.

. 12 .

Spiritual and Mystical Experiences

Mystical or spiritual phenomena present people with a glimpse of the other side—of the "real" world. They can occur through meditation, prayer, nature, near-death experiences, or in many other ways. Occasionally they occur during sleep, in dreams, and in that period of time just before falling asleep or awakening, before consciousness is reached. Those habits and patterns that bring us to such transcendent moments may work well for one person but not as well for another. It is important to find the path that works for you. The use of drugs, whether hallucinogenic ones or other types, can provide a superficial encounter with these higher levels, but there will not be a complete understanding of its nature. For this reason, among others, I do not recommend using drugs to bring about these states.

The glimpses that such otherworldly experiences provide us are extremely valuable, for they offer insight into the true nature of mind and of being. Such insights show the permanence of existence beyond the body, beyond the brain. They allow us to reach enlightenment. They show the beauty and the wisdom of the process (or the Tao, or the flow), which is always there, which is always right. This process is guided, perhaps, by a divine presence, often reaching down to us through an act of grace to nudge us back to our destiny and to help us with the lessons that we came here to learn. The stories in this chapter present a wide variety of such experiences, from the earthly to the distinctly unearthly, yet all the roads lead back to the same place: a life-transforming recognition of our soul's essence.

Some features of the mystical or spiritual event are a feeling of oneness with all that is, of an energy that connects everything. There is a sense of timelessness, of infinite patience. With the understanding of such an occurrence comes an increase in one's ability to reach out and help others without expecting anything back in return, and to approach each person and each situation with grace, kindness, and tolerance. There is peace. There is joy and happiness. Frequently, there are also increased intuitive abilities and a knowledge of things that are unknowable by use of the five senses, which may include psychic and healing abilities. This is true for all great spiritual traditions.

The most significant characteristic, however, is love. It is an unconditional love, rather than one that is romantic or specific. One realizes that this kind of love is everlasting, eternal, and not subject to the laws of human nature or of the earth. It can never be lost; it is a universal constant. To illustrate this, imagine a mother's love for her baby, or a person's love for a dear pet. The baby or the pet does not need to perform in order to win love and acceptance; it is there no matter what the child or the animal does. It is deeper than that. It is profound. It has no conditions. It knows no limits.

And neither do we.

. INDRA'S NET .

One night during the professional training that I attended at the Crossings in Austin, Texas, I had a dream unlike anything I have had before or since.

In it, I was one of millions of octagonal disc-shaped objects, which traveled at light speed to and from Earth's surface to an outer universe above it. As we left Earth with information about this planet, we would approach a vortex-type opening, shaped like a funnel, and we would begin a swirling, circular pattern as we entered it. Once we passed through the long tube into the universe, we would straighten out and, upon coming out at the other end, would intersect and join with others in what appeared to be a blanket made up of millions of us. We then discharged our information and swirled back down to Earth through the vortex, going the other way and retrieving more information. This pattern repeated over and over.

I woke from this dream in the process of doing a very specific hand motion, which at the end of the dream was being given to me as a means of communication with the blanket or net above Earth. There was one motion that tied my visual and emotional content to the net, and one motion to disconnect. I have used these hand motions ever since to connect with this net and disconnect from it, with the purpose of providing the net with the human experience.

It was clear to me that the net held and does hold all of the knowledge of the universe, and that what I am to provide it is the emotional component. As an example, if I am having a thought that I find disconcerting, I will connect and let the net feel that emotion. Then I disconnect.

At first I only connected on good things, but I soon recognized that the net was nonjudgmental and not an assessor of good or bad thought. Thus, I began and still do communicate anything that I find to be unusual, good, or bad about the human condition.

Now, I must add that I work with the severely mentally ill (particularly the schizophrenic population), and I would likely say that someone was psychotic or delusional for engaging in such things as I am describing. However, the dream happened, the information was received, and, right or wrong, I feel obligated to do as it revealed I should. Trust me, I'm sitting here shaking my head as I write this.

The morning after I had the dream, I awakened and relayed it to my wife. Let me interject at this point how the whole ordeal was feeling. Have you ever jumped off of a cliff or high dived into water far below? The first time I ever did, I felt exhilaration coupled with complete helplessness upon having left the board. This is how the events of the week with Dr. Weiss felt at that point. I had been on a perfectly sound diving board and had bounced up and down a few times; however, upon finally leaving the board, there was no turning back. Emotions were running the gamut from complete and utter wonder to panic, and everything in between.

That day, I was in search of some coffee on a break and went around to the back side of the building, where I stumbled across Brian and Carole as they too were taking a break. Carole kindly said that they were interested in my experience and asked me to relate it to them.

I did so, briefly, as I felt that surely they heard this stuff all the time and that what I considered life-altering for me was probably common news to them. However, they took honest interest, and Brian mentioned having heard of something in India's history about a net above the world. This, of course, turned out to be Indra's Net, and the descriptions that I have read about it on the Internet are quite similar to my experience. Brian also remarked that the communication process with the net was a gift given to me. I had not thought of it that way; I saw it more as an obligation. Now I realize that the two are not mutually exclusive, and that an obligation can indeed be a gift.

The seminar gave me immediate empathy for Brian and the emotions that he must have felt while keeping the regression information quiet in the early years. Like him, I did not tell many people about any of my experiences, particularly of the net—until now, of course. Interestingly, those I have told about it have often responded with an awareness of something beyond the limits of Western organized religion, and I have been grateful for their position. I wish to say that the seminar and this experience rocked my safe little boat, and I know now that it needed to be rocked, for which I am beyond grateful. I have a long way to go, but at least I have no fear of the path anymore.

ᨱ *Raymond Wilson*

As Raymond progresses rapidly on his spiritual path, he is simultaneously sharing the details of his experiences and thus helping many others on their own paths.

On that day in Texas, when Carole and I were taking a break on the back porch, Raymond came looking for some coffee. He then proceeded to accurately describe the image and concept of Indra's Net, about which he had never heard or read anything. In his earnest manner, a portion of his mind thinking that he must be weird, he described a twenty-five-hundred-year-old concept about the holographic interpenetration and the interconnectedness of all things and all beings. Although Raymond is an incredibly down-to-earth person, what he relayed was as far from Earth as possible. He had no idea that these ancient Hindu and Buddhist concepts and images were being validated by the findings of modern particle physics.

The "weird" part was Raymond's ability to tap into the ancient images so clearly, just as he had been able to see and draw the millennia-old Shaivite symbol of Nikhil's regression to his princely coronation. The *truly* weird part was probably the shocked look on my face as I realized what he was so accurately describing.

At the conclusion of that Texas training, I had dictated some of my recollections. I found a snippet about one of Raymond's regressions, a cosmic conscious memory. I remembered that he had been part of a "quilt consciousness" overlooking the earth of the distant past or future. He was not alone in this quilt; he knew he was with other spiritual beings, and that they were all somehow interconnected. Raymond was neutral about this planet's capabilities for nurturing the growth of souls. Earth was black and icy, yet when he was sent down to determine the texture and nature of its covering, he discovered that it was not solid ice but something softer, more flexible. And knowing that it did have the potential to sustain spiritual life, he and the entire consciousness were happy.

He then, basically, went through the life cycle of evolution. First, he was a kind of one-celled being; as he became a tiny organism in the ocean, like a sea snail but smaller, he grew very excited. This organism extended its flagella, or protuberance, above the water level. This was an extremely important evolutionary step, which thrilled him and the overlying consciousness. It's not clear if this experience was the beginnings of evolution on Earth, or if it was in the distant future as a regeneration of this planet was occurring.

Raymond sent in his own account of the experience, clarifying my initial impressions:

As the regression began, I began flipping through eons of time and through great quantities of lives. This moved at a lightning-fast pace. It was most similar to the films that used to be shown in high school, with frames that flashed by as the end of the film strip went *click, click, click* at rapid speed. The other comparison would be to a television back in the day, one on which you could adjust the vertical control and the screen would roll quickly with a bar in between each scene. This is how my regression occurred.

In my mind, I knew that each frame was a life and that I was going backward. The film slowed and came to a stop in a primordial ocean with darkness and kelplike vegetation that was rooted deep into the sea floor. I was a single-cell-type creature with a single hairlike appendage, and I was on the stalk of one of these kelp. I could note light above and was working my way toward it. Upon reaching the surface of the water, I raised my flagella into the air, and in that moment I knew quite distinctly that what I had just done was new and very important for the future. I did not know specifically of what importance; however, it seemed to be tied to evolution, and there was a clear feeling of new life and development. I felt safe and quite independent, and I was unaware of any other life forms around me.

Upon the end of the regression, I had no question that I had been in the oceanic soup before human life. I still do not know how to interpret this, but I knew that it was important at the time, and I hold it so now.

Our bodies may be constrained by this physical dimension, but our minds and souls are not. In both his dream and his regression, Raymond allowed himself to venture beyond and above the earth; doing so literally afforded him a universal perspective onto existence. The same was true for Marcia, the client featured in the following story. To heal her human life, she needed to uncover its decidedly nonhuman origins.

Our souls are as vast and limitless as the stars.

. THE MISSING PIECE .

Marcia, an elegant and attractive South American woman in her late forties, came into my office for her first session one dreary winter afternoon. Although she enjoyed children, Marcia had never wanted any of her own and wondered if this had anything to do with a past life. She also often experienced indigestion; it didn't seem to impact her life in any major way and she was already under a physician's care, but she was mildly curious whether this too could be traced back to earlier times. All seemed relatively well, and I felt confident that, with hypnosis, we could explore the straightforward issues with which she'd come to the session.

We were ready to start when Marcia off-handedly mentioned a recurring dream she had had. In it, she was an otherworldly being from a beautiful planet with three suns. There was always someone she was leaving behind, someone who could not follow her; she could never see who it was, and she awoke each time with overwhelming sorrow. As Marcia spoke, she sat on the couch, looking not at me but outside the window, far off into the distance. She was not depressed, not at all, but as she described the dream an ancient, ineffable sadness seemed to be slowly unfolding within her, a paper-thin flower opening its leaves. There was a longing, a homesickness that was all the more confusing and poignant because she had no idea where this home even was. Marcia was successful, she enjoyed her life, and she had a very happy marriage with a husband whom she loved. Yet she felt that there was some kind of missing piece—some kind of missing peace. Was it a soul-mate relationship that she was beginning to recognize? Its presence was starting to be revealed to her in dreamy fragments, but these were, as is often the case with dreamy fragments, so hazy and vague that they only left her feeling unfulfilled. I can't remember now if she spoke about not feeling exactly like she belonged here or if that was just what was so obvious from her eyes, from the way she looked out the window at something so far beyond this office, this world.

I regressed Marcia and she easily went back into a lifetime that addressed her lack of desire to have children. It seemed to provide her with the answers she was seeking and she was content enough, so we moved on. Immediately and without any prompting, Marcia moved ahead into another lifetime. In it, she was an otherworldly being from a beautiful planet with three suns. I asked her to look down at her body, but she quickly corrected me: "Bodies are not important." Her people were visited by a group of tremendously wise, ancient beings from another land, one that was completely devoted to healing and whose origins they could project with their eyes. Marcia clung to them, absorbing their wisdom and knowledge as they taught her how to heal others using metals. "They are so much higher than us. We're peasants compared to them," she explained, referring to the visitors' depth of intelligence as well as love. They were, as she put it, "working on what is going to become the human body." Marcia, drowning in the profound love and spirituality in these beings' eyes, thought about leaving her planet and becoming human. "My people are the last of a long, long line, and we are the only group of beings that can transition into humans," she said. "The others are creators." Marcia trusted them so fully, and she was always up for an adventure, but she loved her home very much and she knew, without being aware of any details, that the missing piece from her dream was a part of her life there. She was thrilled to feel its presence around her again and to realize that they were, at that moment, not yet separated. This was something she could never leave behind.

At once, Marcia became dejected. A warlike people had invaded her planet, imprisoning people's essences inside statues and idols and causing terrible destruction as they seized control. With resignation and because she now possessed knowledge of healing, she said, "Now I have to go to Earth. I need to help." She mourned how Earth, the project of those exquisite healers with eyes full of bottomless love, had not turned out the way it was supposed to. "It wasn't going to be like this. It is very, very different than what I had expected it to be," she said.

I asked Marcia again about the entity that was visiting her in her dreams. This time, there was no hesitation. "We are two of one. You can choose either to be a whole one or to be two of one. This is chosen just for the experience—not in the human sense, but more like a mirror, something so that you can see the face of you. It is part of me, yet it is separate from me." She sighed. "It was the stronger part. I was more like the dreamer." *Interesting*, I thought. *Throughout light-years and lifetimes, ever the dreamer.*

Marcia's voice was thick with regret. "I came to Earth on an impulse decision! Just to help. And now I'm stuck. And I'm forever separated from this piece. My piece." It could not follow her to Earth; she could not return to it. The grief over any separation is intense, but an eternal one seemed unbearable. I was used to working with clients who had lost loved ones to illness or death, divorce or distance. As difficult as those events were, we could work with them. But I was at a loss for what Marcia was experiencing: the endless separation from one's *self*. I pictured her sitting in my office only an hour earlier, staring out the window; now it was painfully clear what she had been searching for. I pressed her for details about the piece: Was there anything she could do in this life that could help her to reconnect with it, or to cope with the separation? "Just keep the memories," she said dully, clearly not believing this herself. Even though Marcia desperately wanted a better sense of what this other part was, it eluded her. Not only was she unable to see it, without it, according to her description, Marcia would never be able to see herself—the very face of her.

I hated to end the session on such a palpably sad note. So I led Marcia into one of my father's healing visualizations, in which she visited a temple with crystals. I thought that it could help clear up the emotions generated by her regression, as well as give her insight into her indigestion issue, which she had requested. This meditation doesn't require the client to speak, so I instructed Marcia to take a few deep breaths and listen to my voice. Her face and body visibly relaxed. There is a point in that meditation in which a wise teacher or guide joins the client, who then visualizes a large movie screen appearing that can help illuminate some of the sources of her physical condition. I paused here for a few minutes so that Marcia could spend time watching the screen, and although she was silent, she was clearly in a deep state, engaging in the visualization. I sat back in my chair, finally taking a few deep breaths myself. It had been a long, exhausting day.

Then, suddenly and without warning, Marcia's entire being exploded into joy. Tears were streaming down her face but she was laughing. I bolted upright in the chair. What had happened? Reluctant to interrupt such an obviously emotional experience, I waited for her feelings to die down, but they seemed only to intensify. "What are you experiencing?" I finally asked. It felt as though I weren't speaking to a client but to a glowing ball of energy.

It took a moment before Marcia could translate whatever she was feeling into ordinary, earthbound words. "My guide," she said, "he's going to show me! On the movie screen!"

"Show you—the origins of your indigestion symptoms?" I asked, not understanding why this would spark such a strong reaction in her but more than happy to go along with whatever was happening.

"No, no." Marcia was almost literally jumping for joy as she sat up in the recliner. It was as if a completely different person were sitting there in front of me. She had come into my office somewhat quiet yet content; she had plumbed the depths of existential grief and sorrow as she explored what it meant to become human; but now she was radiating waves of bliss, her arms spontaneously lifting themselves up in front of her, giving the impression that she was floating. It was unlike anything I had ever seen before: happiness, transcendent and pure, bursting inside and through her. She looked like a child with her excitement for what she knew was about to happen next, but at the same time she seemed beyond physical form, neither adult nor child but simply soul, lovely and huge and dreamed up in delight by the beautiful-eyed beings she cared for so dearly. Marcia held her hands up to her heart, as if it were too big, too deep, too boundless in this moment to be contained inside a mere human body, this tiny, temporary shell. "He's going to let me see, just this one time, my entire self. He's going to show me," she whispered, "the missing piece."

I did not say another word. It was difficult not to ask Marcia questions about what she was discovering, but I recognized that doing so would have only satisfied my intellectual curiosity while interrupting her blissful reunion. For healing to occur, she did not need to describe to me what was happening; she only needed to be there, to experience it. Many years ago on another planet, Marcia had lost her piece. That very day on this planet, she had found her peace. And that was all that mattered.

∾ Amy Weiss

Existence is so much more amazing and miraculous than we can begin to know. New universes are bubbling up into creation all the time. Energies and forces exist far beyond our comprehension. It is as if we are trying to hear a dog whistle but the sound vibrations speed away silently, outside our aural range. And then there are the nonphysical realms too, beyond number, stretching to infinity.

Our souls can plumb these realms. We have lived on the world of three suns, and we have been the wise ones, also. But we have forgotten our origins. How to fathom timelessness, eternity? Our souls know. We all have a missing piece. It is waiting for us at the end of our spiritual journey. It is at home.

Death is often described as passing through a doorway into another dimension—a higher one, with many levels—that is brighter, greater, and much more vibrant. Consciousness becomes expanded and multisensory. It is akin to graduating from the limitations of the old black-and-white televisions to the three-dimensional, high-definition colors of modern ones.

But reincarnation is not limited to the earth. Souls attend schools throughout all the universes. It appears that souls in every universe and every dimension are the same. Souls are souls. Physical bodies, however, vary tremendously despite the similarity of the souls within. After death, when all souls enter those higher, multilevel state(s), they are drawn to the plane or vibration of most comfort to them. It is there where we come together once again. Advanced learning takes place. Reincarnational planning is begun.

It is also there where Marcia could possibly meet once more with the entity from her dream. Even if karmic gravity pulls them once again to different worlds when it is time for them to reincarnate, this separation will only be temporary. When liberated eventually from the cycle of rebirths, they will never again be separated, never pulled apart by the forces of incarnation.

Of course, since fundamentally all is one and everything is connected, separation is only an illusion. All souls come from the one indescribable source. But our illusion is very ancient and very strong, so if our reunion with our closest soul mate, our other half, is temporarily delayed, it is good to know that it will be inevitable—and eternal.

Can those beings in the higher states appear to us while we are in physical form? The next two stories suggest that they can—and do.

. ROADSIDE ASSISTANCE .

The discoveries that you have made, which I have read about in your books and learned about in your Chicago workshop one recent summer, are helping to alleviate my fear of driving in cars. I'm a terrible passenger. I'm a better driver because then I'm in control and can take precautions that some people think are excessive.

In fairness to myself, I once was hit by a semitruck on the expressway going eighty miles an hour. Miraculously, I was not hurt. My car was totaled; I didn't get a scratch. I'm quite certain that "something" held me in my seat. I remember, a fraction of a second after I put my head down and said aloud, "This is bad," seeing my body shake back and forth, and wondering how I was staying in my seat. And then it was over and I was fine.

I was on the other side of the expressway in oncoming traffic when my car finally stopped spinning and came to a halt. A man ran up to my window and said, "Put it in neutral," which I did. He pushed me to the emergency lane, and a moment later cars came rushing by me on the expressway. And then he disappeared. No car drove away; no one was walking anywhere near me. He was just gone.

Reading your books has allowed me to view that incident differently—with less fear, absolutely. Knowing that I have a lesson to fulfill in this lifetime has helped me to accept more of the "why" in my life.

Robin

Robin's story reminds me of many others, including the one by Asia that directly follows it, where in conditions of extreme danger an angel or divine figure appears and moves the person to a place of safety. I'm not sure if Robin's "angel" was a heaven-sent being or simply an ordinary person coming forth to aid another in distress. Is there really any difference between the two?

The real moment of impact for Robin and Asia occurred not when their vehicles collided but when they came face-to-face with an essential spiritual truth. We are always protected, always cared for, and always safe from harm. It does not have to take a crisis to realize this. Sometimes, it only takes a story.

. GUIDED BACK TO LOVE .

Growing up in a conservative Christian family meant that beliefs that were different from my parents' were routinely abhorred. Detested. Even a mere thought that might deviate from the family norm created a palpable fear inside me. As the youngest and only girl in my family, I knew and experienced things that were way outside my parents' Christian mind-set. At the age of three, I delighted in communicating with angels, animals, and spirit guides. Widening the split between my spiritual world and my parents' Christian heritage was my strong impression of past lives. Early on, I would look at people and see their faces change, sometimes so much so that it took me a while to recognize them. I did not understand this strange phenomenon at the time and thought it might be bad or "ungodly" because no one else seemed to experience it. Maybe there was something wrong with me. Afraid of being flawed, I fiercely desired to know the truth, but I would not get any answers until many years later during a near-fatal car accident.

In the winter of 1987, a semitrailer crashed into my van, trapping my twenty-three-year-old body inside. Searing flames breathed down on me. Panicked, I tried each door, only to find them bent and ungiving. I was choking and on the verge of fainting when my guardian angel appeared. Brown, wavy hair encircled his face, and his skin was as soft and smooth as the maroon, gray, and blue robes that flowed around him. Miraculously, he guided me out of a partially open window and through the flames. I survived—barely. With 72 percent of my body burned, along with "multiple complications," I was placed on the ICU's most-critical list for two months. Each exhalation could have been my last.

Suddenly, the alarm on my respirator blared as swarms of nurses and doctors ran to my aid. "Code blue!" they yelled in a frenzy. I was dying. My spiritual body floated out and crossed through a doorway into an expansive starlit sky. There, a woman and two men who called themselves Ascended Masters greeted me. Dressed in comfortable, neutral-toned linens, they emitted wisdom and kindness. They said that they knew all about me and, as representatives of God, were here to teach me about my life and to guide me back to Love.

"Your spiritually connected childhood has been forgotten, and your adult years have so far been marked by fear," said the elder male Ascended Master. I nodded.

"We have teachings for you about regaining that oneness. We will show you your other lifetimes to assist you."

"When you say 'other lifetimes,' do you mean past lives? I was raised in the Christian faith," I stammered. "My minister professed that there is only one life, and then heaven or hell."

"That's not true."

Throwing my hands up to my mouth, I smiled as a profound understanding began to settle in. "Is that why I saw people's faces change, and sometimes entire scenes play out around them? Were those scenes their past lives?"

"Yes," the female responded.

"I didn't make that up?" I let out a huge sigh. *Nothing is wrong with me and I'm not crazy!*

At that moment I looked down, unconcerned, at my burned body, lifeless on the hospital bed. The doctors and nurses continued their attempts to revive me. Only a few minutes had passed, but it felt like hours. I focused my attention back on the Masters.

"It's time to start our lesson," said the Ascended Masters. "In a moment you will see and feel how similar lives, one lived in fear and one lived in love, profoundly influenced you and those with whom you had contact. This experience will guide you out of fear and toward the deliberate choosing of love, thus transforming your life."

The Master raised his arm in an arch, and several holographic screens enclosed me. "Are you ready to see your other lives?" he asked. A man appeared on the screen, jerking around sacks of grain in a mammoth underground vault. As he counted the bags, his long robe dragged on the dirt floor. He pursed his lips while marking the number of sacks. "Not enough to go around," he said, shaking his head and pounding his fist on the nearby table.

A moment later, the door opened and a young woman with her hair wrapped in fabric collapsed at his feet. She squeezed her hands together and pleaded, "My family is starving! Please help us! You are our last hope." She raised her clasped hands high in the air as she wept, and her eyes intently searched his face for a humane response.

"I have nothing for you. Leave!" The man stood up and flipped his robe behind him. The hard edge of the fabric whacked the floor, sending a fine swirl of dust onto her face.

"No, you don't understand. We will die without your grain," the woman begged. She grabbed the bottom of his vestment.

"Get out!" He pushed her off of him and into the wall.

She stumbled out the door toward her waiting family. Her child ran to her and threw his arms around her waist, but she knocked him to the ground, sobbing and yelling at him to stop.

The screens lifted. Spinning around with outrage, I said, "What a horrible man! How could he have treated me like that?"

The three of them scanned me with a gentle smile and replied, "You were the man."

The intense sensation of a burning steel rod pierced my stomach. I tried to swallow. "Well—well, there wasn't any food for her. I must have needed the grain for someone else, or to replant the crops for next year's harvest, or . . ." Defensively, I babbled on until I screamed, "I had to say no!"

With kindness, they said, "It's not that you said no, but that you said it with a closed heart."

"Oh." My shoulders slumped. "I don't think I know how to say no in a loving manner."

"Actually, you do. We will watch a similar scene from another life where you said no yet remained in a loving heart."

I shivered and turned back to the screens, where I saw another young woman, this one with hair to her waist. As she stepped into the room where a man sat with sacks of grain, she cried, "My family is without food. I beg you for help!" Buckling at the man's feet, she reached both of her hands up toward his face.

He bent down and cupped his hands around hers. "No, I am sorry," he said. His voice was firm but soft. "There is no grain to give to you or your family." Gently, he helped her up and to the door. Once she was outside, her young child ran to her, and she embraced him.

The screens moved away, and I said, "It is possible to say no with an open heart."

"Circumstances outside you do not have to lead your heart. Instead, allow your heart to lead in all circumstances."

"I see that when I lived as the fearful man, I created a wave of fear in the woman, which then went to her family. Instead, when I gave love to the other woman, she gave love to her family."

"Exactly. We are all connected. The well-being of the individual is woven into the well-being of all things. Whether we give love or fear, everyone and everything is affected." They added, "We would also like you to share with others what you've learned here. They don't need to have a near-death or death experience to receive spiritual life healing. It is available to everyone who desires and asks for it. With direction, anyone can learn to see and feel their own past lives and learn from them."

The Ascended Masters told me that they would be back to teach me more, but for now it was time to return to my body. The doctors revived me. I felt heaviness and pain, as if I were wearing a wet suit that was filled with boiling water, trapping my frail body inside.

As the weeks passed, the Ascended Masters continued to visit and guide me. They helped me find the perseverance to make a complete recovery.

These spiritual teachings became an anchor in my life. The Masters showed me how all of us are able to unite with the divine and heal what feels broken. We don't need a near-death experience to have our truth revealed to us. All we need is to find a way to release our fears and open our hearts. For me, it took a dramatically close wake-up call. For you, perhaps these shared words of the Masters are enough.

Asia Voight

Many people who have had near-death experiences become more intuitive, have psychic dreams, and often lose their fear of what happens after death. They know.

The overwhelming majority of us will not have a near-death experience, but we can learn the same lessons nevertheless, as Asia points out. We can do this through meditation, through practices of spiritual contemplation, and through past-life regression. The methods may be slower or different, but the results are the same. We see and feel the interconnectedness of all beings and of all things. We understand the need to give and to receive love, and in the process of doing so we let go of doubt and fear. In realizing our true nature as eternal beings, we can reduce or even eliminate our fear of death and dying.

Among the beautiful and wise thoughts and teachings in Asia's story, one quote from her Masters instantly grabbed my attention: "Circumstances outside you do not have to lead your heart. Instead, allow your heart to lead in all circumstances." How true this is.

More than thirteen hundred years ago, the Chinese philosopher Huineng wrote: "When we are free from attachment to all outer objects, the mind will be in peace. Our essence of mind is intrinsically pure, and the reason why we are perturbed is because we allow ourselves to be carried away by the circumstances we are in. He who is able to keep his mind unperturbed, irrespective of circumstances, has attained enlightenment."

Our hearts and our minds can transform all outer circumstances, bringing love and peace even in the most difficult of times. Fear eats at our stomach, our immune system, our health. It constricts our heart. But fear is sustained by our dependency on outer things, people, and situations. If we are content with the inner state of loving-kindness and serenity, which is independent and self-sufficient and not buffeted by the vicissitudes of other people's opinions and behaviors or the false security of our possessions, then we will be at peace.

Like Asia's story, Michael's, which follows, sheds light on the near-death and after-death experience. His visions and emotions after leaving his physical body in his past life are consistent with so many other accounts of this nature. They tell of a magnificent recognition of oneself as a spiritual being on a journey that lasts much longer than the human body. Deep within the horrors of a long-ago war, Michael discovered his own pure essence. He discovered peace.

. KNIGHTS OF LIGHT .

As a past-life regressionist and spiritual counselor for the last seven years, and a crisis counselor, diagnostician, and psychotherapist for the last twenty, I have taken hundreds of people back to their past lives. Many of the sessions have been profoundly moving and healing. But my favorite of all was one in which I was the client and the facilitator was Dr. Brian Weiss. I had not asked for the experience, and it was completely unexpected when Brian offered, a wonderful surprise. The fact that it was to be onstage, under the lights and in front of so many people, was a bit daunting, but there was no way I was going to pass it up. Brian and I had spoken a number of times, privately, mostly about our work. I don't talk about it much, but he was aware that I was living with chronic pain in my back.

I had regressed many people by then but had never been regressed myself. I felt both excited and concerned. I knew that I was almost as left-brained and empirically based in my thinking as Brian. That fact, and the chronic pain I experienced constantly, made it seem unlikely that I would be readily induced into trance. Moreover, I knew every word of Brian's induction. I knew where he was going to try to take me, and exactly how, with what words. As I stepped up on the stage, I whispered to Brian, away from the microphones, "Please don't get discouraged if you can't take me there. If this doesn't work, it will be my fault, not yours." Brian looked into my eyes and said, "Let's see what happens," as calmly as if he were saying, "Isn't it a beautiful day?"

He made no attempt to perform anything remotely like a standard induction. He simply began talking to me, as if we were sitting together on a park bench. I remember thinking, *When is he going to hypnotize me?* The words he said were not at all what I expected. "Tell me a few things about your childhood. What was that like?" he asked.

Sitting next to him on the stage with my eyes gently closed, a wonderful, early memory did come to me, one I had completely forgotten. Merely by talking, Brian was able to transport me to a beautiful memory, with inordinate clarity, from my childhood.

As he took me to a past life, I became conscious of how incredibly quiet it had gotten in the room. I began to feel an enormous wave of heat flowing toward me from the silent audience. There was an intense feeling of prayer and goodwill in the room, as I began searching in all directions (with my eyes closed) for an image to appear. An air of expectancy seemed to be building. Seconds turned into minutes as I searched for an image, and I could actually feel the crowd right there with me, willing me into an experience, group-praying that the images would come. Just as I was about to say, "I'm sorry, Brian, but I see nothing," I saw the dirty face of a young boy, perhaps twelve to fourteen years old. I immediately felt—knew, somehow—that I was this young boy. I was standing just a few feet inside the shade of a forest, talking to a knight who was in the forest with me. I was putting a bridle and a saddle on the knight's horse. The knight's armor was laid out all around on the ground next to me. Next to the armor I saw a curious little set of steps, just three steps, with a halter attached to them at the back. These steps could be put on one's back, like a backpack.

The heat from the crowd had grown increasingly intense, and the quiet in the room was deafening. "It is the Middle Ages," I finally said, and a huge group sigh of relief rose up from the audience in front of me. They had all been attempting to assist Brian and me with their focus, their own healing intentions and prayers, and now they realized I had made it there. I could see myself very clearly in a life long, long ago.

"I am a young page," I explained. "I am wearing crude sandals, made of rope, with leather on the bottoms. My hair is straight, dark brown, and looks as if someone put a bowl over my head and cut around it. My face is dirty, and I am wearing what looks like a burlap potato sack, with holes cut in it for my arms and legs. I have a rope belt tied around my sack-dress at the waist. Just outside the forest, to the left, is a huge, open field, and men are assembling there. There are knights on horseback, and many more are walking, with various weapons and shields." Some simply had large axes and crude clubs and maces. Others had swords and knives with them. Still others had long bows and crossbows. All were coming together, mingling and talking, there in the field. Thousands were arriving from every direction. On the hill to our right was a large, beautiful castle with tall turrets.

I was now finished putting the bridle and saddle on the horse, and I was standing on the top step, putting chain mail down over the knight's upper body. There were tears welling in my eyes as I heard myself begin to speak. "They say you will not return, that you are going to die."

"Who said that?" he asked.

"Everyone. They say that the army you go to fight is ten times the size of ours, and that you and most of the others will die."

The knight looked directly into my eyes as he said, "Do not fear, for dying is easy; it is living that is hard. To die valiantly on the field of battle with my friends is an honor, and it is a destiny we all know awaits us. I am not afraid, because I know that our souls live on and go up to heaven when our body dies. We never truly die."

By this time I was crying silently as I began to slide his armor over his head. Tears were running down my cheeks. "Don't go. You don't have to go," I whispered. Still crying, I began placing his helmet down over his face and head. I positioned the steps next to his horse, and he slowly and carefully walked up them. Swinging his leg over the side of the saddle, he said, "Remember what I have said here today. If I do not return, we will meet again in heaven." With that, he turned his horse toward the quickly filling field of men and rode out of the darkness of the forest toward them.

Brian moved me ahead in time, and I saw four men walking into the castle courtyard, carrying a knight. He was lying on his back, on his shield. I did not want to believe it was he, but I knew that it was. I began running, chasing them into the castle, and arrived as the knight was being placed on the ground. They removed his helmet, and the men began feeling around his waist belt and retrieved a small, leather pouch. Opening it, they pulled out a small note on a crude piece of paper. What they read aloud from the note instantly made me both happy and sad. "To he who finds this note, it is my last wish that my horse, my sword and armor, all of my personal property, and my station in this life go to my page." Of course, that was I. I was distraught that I would not see him again in that life. I appreciated all that he had done for me, but I also began to realize, then and there, that I might be looking down at and realizing my own future. *Yes, knights fight and knights die,* I thought. I was crying openly as the men handed me his sword and began stripping the armor from his body and handing it to me. There was no sensation of celebration. I had lost my dear friend and was being filled with a sense of duty, a duty that I had doubts I could perform.

Moving forward in time to see more of my life as the page, I found myself in the castle courtyard, now taller and a little older. I wore a simple, long shirt, with no armor at all. I was fighting with a man much larger and stronger than I with big wooden swords. I was attempting to block his unrelenting blows but failing miserably. Every three or four blows, the man would strike or plunge the dull, wooden sword into my body. Each time he did, I heard him shout, "Dead! You are dead!" It was a lesson in humiliation, humility, and patience. It seemed effortless for him to continue "killing" me, over and over, with different swipes and blows to my body. The images began rapidly shifting, and I grew taller and more broad shouldered in each as other men continued to train me to fight. Fear, trepidation, and anxiety tugged at me each time I "died" there in the courtyard, as I sensed that one day before long my adversary would not be my friend, and the swords would not be made of wood.

Brian smoothly took me forward in time again, and I was now fully grown, standing in chain mail, a handsome man in my early twenties. The armor now fit perfectly. I stood inside the courtyard of the castle and a page stood in front of me on the set of steps, sliding my armor over my head and upper body. With tears in his eyes, he begged me not to go, just as I had done so with the knight when I was a page, and I repeated the very same words to him that I had heard so long ago.

Soon I saw myself on a large, broad, open plain. The land was flat and dusty. I was in the thick of a massive battle. I was on my horse, and there in front of me on his own horse was a huge, powerful knight, much larger than I. He was clearly very experienced, as he was raining relentless blows down upon me with a massive, heavy sword. The fighting was extremely loud now, close and intense, and I could hear men swearing, groaning, yelling, and screaming. The battle seemed to be coming from everywhere, from all sides: the clanging of metal against metal, the frightened cries of horses and men, the dust continuing to rise. I was growing weaker each time I fended off another blow from this man's sword. Just then, on my left, I saw a tall man coming up from behind me on foot. I had enough time to notice him in my peripheral vision as he lifted a sword to strike me. With one swift, slashing motion, I swung my sword down toward him. It cleaved his left shoulder and arm completely off, and he fell back to the ground.

At that moment, I saw an amazing thing. The man whose entire left shoulder I had severed was wobbling to his feet and coming up behind me. With the last bit of energy he could summon, his right hand laid his blade flat, down onto the back of my saddle, with the tip against the center of my spine, under the back curvature of my armor. He leaned all his weight against the tip, and I felt a burning sensation as his sword entered my body. Helpless, I began to convulsively twitch and shake as I watched the entire blade emerge from my lower belly. Mortally wounded, I found myself lying in the dust, the sword sticking out of my lower abdomen. There, only a few feet away from me, lying on his side, was the man I had just killed—the man who had just killed me. The sheer madness of war could be heard all around us. The screams of the swords, the horses snorting and rearing up in pain and terror, the wounded men scattered all over the ground. Many were calling out, calling for their mothers and wives, swearing, screaming, crying, "Please kill me. Please kill me, I beg of you." Curiously, I could feel no pain and no fear, only a warm calm coming over my entire body. Perhaps I was in shock. I looked over at the man who was dying on the ground just in front of me. He was silent, staring at me as I stared at him. The two of us exchanged these last gazes silently, looking into one another's eyes, blinking in the dust, knowing that each would be the last person we ever saw in this life.

And then, I became aware of a subtle stirring inside me, and I felt a very odd but pleasant sensation. I had closed my eyes, and I was gliding, floating out and above myself, feeling completely weightless. I gazed down at myself—not at the body lying on the ground but at the thing that rose from it, which could somehow look down and see the former me, my shell. I was an intensely bright, white light, so powerfully strong that it was difficult to behold. I was only about five feet above myself, and I glanced over to where my adversary had been lying. He too had become a luminous white cone, hovering just above his own body.

With joy, I explained to Brian that my adversary and I were now two cones.

"Cones?" he repeated.

"Yes, we look like cone-shaped white lights." Both of us began to rise slowly over the field, and I could see that thousands of men were still fighting and that the battle had stretched nearly a half mile in every direction.

As we went up a bit higher, I began to witness something deeply moving and truly incredible. All around and through the battlefield, I could see countless brilliant cones of light slowly rising upward, rising from the dust in every area of the battle. We were all ascending, becoming farther and farther from the conflict below, our souls weaving into the air in an indescribably beautiful movement. It was such a stunning contrast from the horror and chaos of the war beneath us.

"Are there any lights that are bigger or brighter than the others?" Brian asked.

"No. We look exactly the same."

"Any lights going down?" he wondered aloud. I could feel his fascination, his keen interest in what I was seeing.

"No. We are all the same and we are all going up," I responded. "There is what looks like a giant funnel that has formed in the center of a very large cloud, and we are all floating toward its center. I feel wonderful, as if I am swimming in an ocean of love. I have never felt so wonderful. No pain at all. I feel better than I ever did in my body—completely untethered from it, free of it. No pain, no worry, only great peace and bliss."

"How many other lights are ascending with you?"

"Hundreds," I whispered. "There are hundreds of cones above us, and hundreds more coming in from below."

I felt us all begin to float into the funnel, and I described what this was like. "The funnel's end is large, but there is a narrower, more luminous tunnel attached to it as you enter, filled with an extremely strong white light. There are about thirty cones crowded in there with me, and we are all the same light as the tunnel." I was in absolute awe. I was later shown a photo of that moment, taken by someone in the audience. I was looking straight up, above me, my head rocked back, and my expression was just that: one of complete, revelatory awe.

"We have come to a great room. It is incredibly bright white in here as well, the whole room, but this room seems limitless—it has no walls. So many beautiful white cones are floating, hovering, all around. There is great peace here, as well as the sensation that enormous, limitless love surrounds us. Two brilliantly lit, very wise-looking old men with white robes and long beards have come for someone. They are leaving with a group of about thirty cones, getting smaller and smaller as they disappear to the right. I wonder where we go from here?"

"Do they come for you?" Brian asked.

"Not yet, but I am calm and patient. There are so very many of us. It is so peaceful here, and I know that they will come for me when it is my time," I replied.

As we waited, Brian asked, "What do you think you learned from that life?"

"That war and killing are madness. That no one wins, and all on both sides lose. Every time a man on either side falls on the battlefield, misery befalls their families and their loved ones, who grieve very deeply. The men who die need not be grieved for. They are experiencing pure love and bliss as they are welcomed back to the resting place. But the grief, pain, and depth of the sorrow it causes their loved ones and so many others is incalculable. Every time one man falls, someone at home loses a son, a brother, a husband, a father, an uncle, a nephew, a friend. Their grief and pain run deep, and the hole that is left in their lives is never filled—until we meet again in heaven. Then we can lay down this burden of grief that we felt would never fully abate, and we can see and embrace our loved ones who have gone before us in the peace and serenity of the resting place. Love is the constant, most important thread that runs through the tapestry of all of our lives. It is what makes living so very sacred and special. To share our love and be loved—nothing else is remotely as important."

I opened my eyes as I was brought out of the trance and looked out at the audience. Many of them were crying and smiling at the same time. Those, I thought, are tears of joy. They were happy and thankful for what they had just witnessed, as was I. I had never anticipated that such a joy and blessing would come my way.

Brian asked if the area in my back where I was stabbed is the area where I experience the most back pain. I replied that it was the exact same place. Since that day in the summer of 2009 I have had a noticeable reduction in the pain. Approximately one-third of it is completely gone, and I now have hope that even more of it will recede in the fullness of time.

Clearly seeing and experiencing your life and death from over five hundred years ago is a truly amazing experience. You are changed. Your eyes are then fully opened to the truth of what we are. We go through a universal metamorphosis, over and over again, until we learn our lessons here on Earth. When we "die," the caterpillar becomes the butterfly, and we float up and out of our body and straight back to our loved ones, and our rightful resting place, in heaven.

∾ *Michael Brown*

Michael's description of the funnel into which the knights' souls entered, the tunnel connected to it, and the clustering of the hundreds and hundreds of light cones is so wonderfully reminiscent of Raymond's imagery in the first story of this chapter: "We would approach a vortex-type opening, shaped like a funnel. . . . Once we passed through the long tube into the universe, we would . . . join with others in what appeared to be a blanket made up of millions of us." And, of course, Raymond's description itself is wonderfully reminiscent of a concept that has existed since the second century. Voices from across the globe and across the ages speak to us again and again of the spiritual immortality that belies our physical mortality.

We are the light, not its shadows. To picture this, think of the sun. We are as powerful and resplendent as that glorious star. Here in physical bodies, we have forgotten that we *are* the light—the sun—instead believing that we are only its reflections, the shadows that it casts. We are exquisite beings of pure and brilliant light, swimming in a sea of bliss. The recognition that we are light is, literally, enlightenment.

When we leave the body, everything is clear. We are bathed in a state of absolute and constant peace, no longer afflicted by the temporary emotions of fear and despair. There is no pain, only a sense of well-being. And when the glowing and wise old men with the white robes and long beards come to take us home and joyously reunite us with our loved ones, we will finally be completely healed. We will be whole again.

This peace does not need to be something we obtain only when we rise from our bodies and leave the earth behind. The earth needs it too. Peace must be found within ourselves and throughout the world, not only at the individual level but also at the international one. What if we finally decided to stop engaging in wars? What if our countries cooperated instead of competed? And what if, as this next story by Bethany suggests, our political structures and systems were to be founded on and motivated by love, instead of power?

There is nothing more powerful than love.

. GLOBAL KARMA .

During a meditation at your July 2010 course, I channeled a little note about world leaders and group karma.

There is a separate plane in the spirit world for governments, where great minds can enter and negotiate with world leaders who have passed away. They can change the things on the ground for good, but they are only allowed to change what is from the heart. They can negotiate and whisper in the ear of their ancestors, and they love this. In such a way, they can create the most magnificent change in thinking.

They can converse and work for a peaceful outcome, which isn't based on power but on love, balance, and making things right.

The world leaders all have their guides, but they don't often listen to them. Yet this is changing for the better. If these leaders started doing regressions, it would help and then filter down to create a massive change, releasing a lot of energy and karma and healing on a huge scale. This is true even for dictators considered to be cruel and brutal—if they started regressing, healing, and raising their vibration, then the whole situation that they created would be released.

All the leaders are in a little pocket joined together by group karma, and as soon as one begins, they will all be released into a higher vibration here on the ground as well as in the spirit world. Therefore, the trouble that was their energy will be released peacefully and without any further ego.

If people were trained to do hypnotism and regression as part of a treatment for terrorists, it would create a shift on a massive scale. It would prevent future situations from happening. They can regress them to get to the karmic root cause and then heal it. This can even be done to the people who work for them, so that healing can occur *up* the line.

Even the leaders considered to be "evil" have had many spirit helpers who were trying to release healing energy. This would have been their other path in life, had they not chosen the paths they did.

∽ *Bethany*

Of course politicians and world leaders are spiritual beings. We all are. We have the same spiritual helpers and advisers as they do, whether guides, Masters, angels, wise beings, or whatever we want to name these emanations of the divine. Many governmental officials, however, are close-minded about the spiritual realm. Ego and pride prevent them from opening up to the possibilities.

Unbeknownst to Bethany, I have been working for many years with politicians and leaders from all over the planet. We work confidentially. Progress is slow, but it is steady. There is hope.

This development is not limited to the political sphere; it encompasses many other traditionally left-brained and logical professions too. In the next story, an attorney relates her own account of overcoming her doubts and awakening to her higher nature. "When we are open," she writes, "there is always a way for the universe to show its truth."

Let her words be a way.

. CLOUD CONSCIOUSNESS .

We are all spiritual beings living in human forms. Under hypnosis, we are able to tap into our inner selves and to know our true nature better. One may question the validity of images, past lives, or future lives that are revealed. At first, I also had doubts. Nevertheless, when we are open, there is always a way for the universe to show its truth. This is a step in my own process of awakening, which has transformed my life. Dr. Brian Weiss's hypnosis program has not only benefited individuals in their healing but has also opened up a deep ocean of knowledge about the universe, which is beneficial to human evolution at large. My own hypnotherapy subjects have taught me about the coexistence of multiple dimensions, how our thoughts create and affect realities, the law of karma, the possibility of change, and the interrelatedness of all beings and events. As Saint Augustine said, "Miracles are not contrary to nature, but only contrary to what we know about nature."

Before I learned hypnosis from Dr. Weiss at Omega Institute in 2005, I had an unbelievable experience in Hong Kong. Out of curiosity, I had my first hypnosis session with a psychic called Jacqui, who was recommended by my friend, in April 2005. While I was expecting to experience some past lives, to my surprise I witnessed and felt myself as part of the clouds with consciousness. I was without any gender but in a white, transparent form.

When Jacqui asked who I was, I answered calmly, "I am a goddess."

She asked me what I was doing, and I replied, "I am flying amongst the mountains, making sure that the plants have sunlight and rain."

"How do you know that you are a goddess?"

"I am elevated in the air, and I see tiny people from the ground asking for my help. Some are bowing to me, and some are simply praying. But I can only motivate other people to help them. I cannot do it directly, for it will scare them."

As a lawyer, I have never thought of saying or experiencing something like this, and so my logical mind thought it must have been just a dream. Jacqui told me that it was not, but rather that it was an example of devic consciousness.

"What is devic consciousness?" I asked.

She radiated a beautiful smile, looked at the top of my head, and hugged me. "Of the angels. I see many angels over your head."

I later browsed the Internet for the term. One article that resonated with me said that our evolution may be in biological form like animals; in devic form, like natural forces (the winds, the clouds, and the rain); and from other stars (souls with higher wisdom from other planets). These evolutions are interchangeable.

With what I learned from Dr. Weiss, I became aware of my true self and my abilities, and I have used these skills to help others awaken, know their life purpose, heal themselves through understanding the law of karma, and, above all, raise the consciousness of many people. All these are beneficial to mankind.

In one regression that I conducted, a woman called Mei described being in a forest—being "back home." She felt incredibly happy there. I asked her what she saw.

"Many transparent white beings. Millions. They are smaller than a rose. They have transparent wings."

"Are you one of them?"

"Yes," she whispered. "I've no sex; I'm neutral. My name is Arono."

"Do you belong to a particular tree or plant?"

"No. We work together as a group. When we see that a tree needs energies, we give energies to it collectively. We protect nature."

I asked her if she had any messages to relay. She replied, "We are of a higher vibration that gives energies to the trees and plants. We form a supportive network of energies to merge with the vibration of the earth. In this network, there is no competition, only cooperation and happiness. We work together. We communicate through telepathy. We are all transparent; there is no hiding, no cheating, only honesty and peace. Our energies are pure."

"Are you different from the clouds?"

"I could be clouds," she said. "It is just a thought form."

I asked Mei if she knew anything about the year 2012. She responded, "About that time, there is a change on Earth: climate change, energy change, wind, rain. We need to cooperate. Humans need to cooperate with us."

I questioned what could be done.

"Learn to look at your inner self," she said. "Look at your heart. Keep aware and change. There is no law and written contract. You can manifest. Ten to twenty years ago, many Masters came to Earth to help. They are higher beings; most of the babies these days are higher beings. They are happy and content, and many of them are psychics. Parents have to learn from their babies. They have special vibrations never known on this earth, and they've come to help. The parents live in a competitive world, but these babies are noncompetitive. They can feel the inner heart of adults. They've come to awake our inner ability." She added, "I remember that my mission is to deliver a message from the Source."

I brought her toward the Source, and then asked her to describe it.

"Golden light," she said. "It is a sense of Being. I can't see the vibration. It can be big, it can be small. Being can happen without a physical body. The Source is where all the universes come from. It is just knowing, a consciousness, expanding energies. In human language, it means 'light in a space.' But there is no dimension. It only exists."

"What messages does it have for you?"

"When we change, the world will change. We don't need to work so hard. In a hundred years' time, humans will not need any devices. Not many people can align with the energies from the Source. I can hold the original vibration, absorb it, carry it, and affect humans with it. My vibrations will affect the vibrations of my surroundings. People come to you because they are attracted to your energies. They are just like clouds; we are like a tree. People come and rest under our shadow, and they go. Just give them energies. When we need energies, absorb it from the Source and give to the rest of the world. This is what receiving and giving means. The energies from the Source are abundant. I am the Source and part of it. It is expanding, and so am I.

Assist others. When we are confused, go to the Source, restore, and feel the energies. Feel stronger. Help others to find their true self, because not everyone can align with the Source. Be patient with humans. Bitterness is normal. We have to learn the emotions of being human, but we should not allow ourselves to be trapped by these emotions, for we are just here to learn. You choose your partner just to experience love. Learn about human relationship and vibrations. It is all part of the learning process."

One morning, I had a whim to browse through a book by Sri Aurobindo, an Indian yogi and saint. In one chapter, he mentioned that "all natural forces are personal." In other words, all natural forces have consciousness. If we recognize them as fellow conscious beings, just as we ourselves are, we can communicate with them. The scientists cannot control weather because they treat it as simply a dead object. The shamans and people who understand nature relate to it in a different way. They personify the forces, regarding them as friends, and these consciousnesses respond favorably. In fact, many children personify the sun, moon, flowers, and trees and regard them as benevolent companions. Perhaps we are all born with this kind of intuition and kindness. I believe that there are many people who can influence environmental events with their beliefs, and that a collective mind will have exponential effects.

Many natural disasters are about to happen for the purpose of great transformation and purification in the near future. If our collective minds believe in and communicate with these physical forces, we will reduce a lot of casualties caused by such disasters. Instead of using scientific equipment to fight against them, we could simply handle them by acknowledging their consciousness and treating them as friends. From ancient knowledge and channeled messages under hypnosis with higher spiritual beings, I have learned that only love and compassion will raise the vibrations of people and the land and lessen the effects of these disasters.

Dr. Masaru Emoto, an internationally acclaimed researcher on consciousness in water, has discovered evidence of how our thoughts will affect the shapes of water crystals. There is evidence of nonlocality of changes, of how our thoughts travel and instantly affect the quantum field. I met Dr. Emoto at a conference, where he joked with me about influencing the earthquakes. I told him that it would be easier to mobilize the wind and rain first. I know that he is more in-depth than what he has disclosed to the world. His research has been criticized by some scientists who say that it is pseudoscience, that there is no 100 percent proof, and that it could be affected by many other factors.

May I ask: When scientists make certain propositions before doing their "controlled" experiments, can they conclude that there is a 100 percent proof while ignoring all other factors happening simultaneously in this universe? Perhaps my legal training teaches me otherwise; a lawyer's standard of proof is less than that of a scientist. We do not need 100 percent proof; we only need to prove "on a balance of probability" or "beyond reasonable doubt." An open heart to accept the existence of certain phenomena without negative criticism is a great leap forward to human evolution.

$\sim$ *Lingki*

If we are all precipitations from a higher vibrational state, a Source energy, then we are all sentient beings and are all connected. Lingki is expressing this concept in her thoughts and words, which are echoed by the astounding revelations of modern physics. We are, at our core consciousness and physicality, some flux of particle and wave, and as we change polarities, some identical flux of particle and wave at the other end of the universe may be experiencing an instantaneous complementary shift of polarity in reaction to our change.

We inhabit an amazing cosmos where miracles occur constantly, just beyond our everyday minds.

. . .

The concepts of religion and spirituality can coincide, but they are not synonymous. Religion can indeed pave the way for great acts of love, charity, and compassion—or it can be used as an excuse for separation, violence, and cruelty. At the heart of all religions, however, is love. The next few stories demonstrate how religion can be the avenue to greater spiritual wisdom.

. DAY OF ATONEMENT .

One of my favorite "experiences" was on Yom Kippur about ten years ago. I am not Jewish, but I find this to be one of the most meaningful religious holidays. I envisioned myself standing on a stage in a large auditorium. Facing the empty seats, I began to pray that all those whom I had injured or wronged at any time in my existence would please come to the auditorium and take a seat. I wanted an opportunity to express my deepest remorse to them all. Instantly, the seats began to fill up, until the auditorium was about three-quarters full. I was astonished and ashamed to see so many people there.

Then, I began to talk about my regrets, my spiritual search, and the growths that I felt I was making, and I apologized to each person for any wrongdoing for which I was responsible. I asked them to forgive me if they could. After I had spoken and thanked them for coming, they all stood up in front of their seats, held hands, and sang, "Let there be peace on earth." When the last note faded, they all disappeared as quickly and quietly as they had come, leaving me standing there on the stage in awe.

Donna West

When repentance is heartfelt, and when forgiving and being forgiven is sincere, then the slate is wiped clean, the auditorium is emptied. When there is no urge to hurt anyone or anything, there will finally be peace on earth.

. ANGELS AND DEMONS .

I was at one of your conferences in November 2010. After lunch, I returned tired and with a headache. I was very concerned that falling asleep was unavoidable and feared that I'd be the snoring person whom someone would have to wake. After settling down on the floor, I thought, *Oh no, I am going to fall asleep. I did not go to this conference to nap.* Much to my chagrin, I was dozing in and out, but I did manage to go somewhere. I was in a hall with books, and I heard Dr. Weiss say something about pulling out a book from a shelf. One floated into my hands and opened to a page with a golden shimmering name written in large script at the top of the page. The name was Lucifer. It was not the most comforting thought, but I was too tired to judge or block the information.

In this life, I was educated in Catholic schools from grade school to high school. At the age of approximately nine, sitting in my classroom, I can recall being taught about Satan and hell. I simply did not agree with the view of the nun. Wisely, I did not speak my views. I did believe in God. I knew the tale of Christ but could not identify with him, and I did not go to church unless my mother made me.

As an adult, I am very spiritual but not religious. I believe in and communicate with Christ, God, and the angels. I have read sections of the Bible, although my views are not necessarily in agreement with it. I have come to understand that Lucifer was misunderstood in the Bible, but that he did start the ball rolling in a negative direction—a perspective I had blocked for years.

Here is what I was "told" during my regression at your workshop: Lucifer was the closest to perfection, but he was informed that he could not return to the Ultimate Source because of the great separation. As a "whole" group of souls, we decided to separate from God. Lucifer was heartbroken over the separation, then he became angry, and out of anger (or vanity) he tried to hurt God by hurting himself. It was a temper tantrum of biblical proportions. Lucifer was not the evil Satan as portrayed in the Bible. I do not believe that he sits on people's shoulders and tempts them into wrongdoing, contrary to the beliefs of some my friends. However, we are all responsible for our actions—even angels.

Because of my fatigue, I could only witness what came to me that day. The next scene was short and in "high definition," with vivid colors. Looking down, I saw (my?) white, male, bare feet, which were clean and pristine, walking on pretty grass. I looked up, and a voluptuous woman with long, curly, blond hair was walking toward me. *Eve?* I thought. I believe this Eve was the one from the biblical story of the Garden of Eden.

In my view, Adam and Eve were angels. In a story that was channeled through me, I learned that a normal human body could not survive the change to Earth's heavy dimension. This is partly the reason angels were called upon for the job. This deviated from the biblical story. The Tree of Knowledge was a choice; it was not forbidden. It was God's gift to understand what love is *not* and to lead us to better understand what love *is*. Adam and Eve left Eden and went on to other places out of necessity. They did not leave because God yelled at them to get out.

The guided meditation at your workshop allowed me not only glimpses from a book in the heavenly hall of records but also possibly a past-life regression to witness Eve. Information regarding Adam and Eve and now Lucifer continues to present itself in some form or another and keeps calling for my attention.

ᘒ *Helen*

During times of fatigue, just as in dreams, our everyday waking consciousness is less vigilant. It does not filter so strictly, which allows the subconscious mind to emerge. In transcending the rational and literal training of her Catholic schools, Helen could experience a deeper and richer meaning to the characters, stories, and legends.

Sometimes, ignorance or unwise decisions are mistakenly viewed as evil. We learn and grow from all our choices, both good and bad. To understand love in all its manifestations, even by appreciating what love is not, seems like a divine gift. To be yelled at does not.

Could you truly appreciate light if you never knew darkness?

. MICHAEL'S MESSAGE .

I went to a full-weekend workshop at the Agape Spiritual Center in Los Angeles in early 2002. That Friday evening, as Brian began the first regression, I went immediately into a meditative state—from zero to sixty in nothing flat! I recall taking myself into my grove, where I "go" when I meditate, and suddenly there was my grandfather. He was laughing and waving for me to come after him, so I followed and found myself at the staircase. I said, "But, Grandpa, you are getting ahead of Brian!" He just laughed as he glided down the stairs, and naturally I followed, yelling for him to wait up the whole way. When we reached the bottom, there was a door; he opened it, pulled me in, and then smiled and disappeared.

I cannot even describe the colors that I saw when I looked toward the light inside the door. I do not believe there is a human word that can encompass the beauty and serenity. I knew nothing but the names of the archangels; I had never studied about them or looked into their attributes. Yet somehow I knew that I was standing in the presence of Michael. I can still see him in that somehow colorless and color-filled light; I will never forget that moment. He stood, simply leaning with his forearms on his sword with his wings folded behind him.

I, being as quiet and demure as always, said, "Well, that isn't a very angelic pose." He flipped the sword up and extended his wings, holding the sword aloft for a moment, and then flipped the sword back down and gave me a sardonic look. I felt him say, "Better?" with a chuckle, and I said, "Much."

I have no idea how much time passed before I heard Brian say, "Look at what is around you."

"Shouldn't you be showing me something?" I asked Michael, and I received an amused look as he pulled one wing in to show me myself in a glade in the woods, surrounded by animals, happy and alone as I took care of them. Then the wing moved back out, and once again all I saw was Michael.

I heard Brian tell us to go to the end of the life. "Well?" I said to Michael. Once again a wing moved, and I saw myself as an old, old woman with a walking stick, making my way into a city in either ancient Rome or Greece. I knew I was dying, and all I wanted was to reach the temple. When I did, I sighed, sat down on the marble steps, and died. It was so peaceful—no pain. I just needed to be at the temple when I died, and I was, so I was content.

I asked Michael if there was anything I needed to know, and inside my mind I heard, "You are protected when you need to be." I then heard Brian counting upward from one to ten to bring us out of the trance. I came out of the regression, and I have never since felt what I did at that moment. I have never before nor since experienced that kind of peace.

ᘉ *Faith Susan*

In my view, Michael's sword, which represents wisdom, cuts though and ends ignorance and fear. Without fear, we are able to embrace our spiritual nature, letting go of ego, pride, and jealousy. Without fear, we can love freely and practice compassion at all times. We will not be hurt. We do not have to suffer.

Faith's grandfather was the transitional, loving, and familiar being who led her to a higher state of awareness. Michael met her in the light, just beyond the door. Her fears dissolved; there was only peace.

Each one of us is protected when we need to be.

Angels, guides, and gods belong not only to the Judeo-Christian tradition but to many of the world's great religions and cultures. During a group regression, a workshop participant named Keith recalled a very spiritual and emotional moment that had occurred when he was quite young, and as he spoke he described what he saw with childlike terms. He was a little boy when he witnessed the appearance of two guides or apparitions in his room. One was an old Chinese man with a long white beard, and the other was a kind of angelic figure. They took Keith to a much less dense place, a "floating" place, where people were coming and going with information and knowledge. Earth was far off in the background, and he could see how these people were arriving at and leaving it. They were not doing so in their physical bodies, but rather in their spiritual bodies—their energy bodies. Keith watched as they were drawn to this planet by ties to other souls.

As he reexperienced this childhood memory, Keith was able to glimpse the bigger picture. He sensed how we come to and leave this denser world, and how we return to the "floating" place. We come to this school to learn our lessons, and then we return home. His account reminded me of another story, one of a young boy and a bearded Chinese man, which I recounted in my second book, *Through Time into Healing*.

Born with congenital heart defects, a young boy required open-heart surgery at ages three months, two and one-half years, and again at five years. The boy nearly died several times during the operations, and his doctors did not expect him to survive. When he was eight years old, he revealed to his mother that while still unconscious after one of the surgeries, he had been visited in the intensive care unit by "eight Chinese guys" who conveyed information about his recovery. The boy observed that one of the Chinese men "had a sword that he was always twirling around." This man frequently cut off his beard with the sword, but the beard grew back almost immediately. The boy described all eight "Chinese guys" in detail.

In researching her son's startling story, his mother found the physical and philosophical representation of her son's "eight Chinese guys." They are the Pa Hsien or Eight Immortals, Taoist representations of historical figures who have attained immortality. As her son described, one of these is Lu Tung-Pin, the patron saint of barbers, who was granted a magic sword as a reward for overcoming ten temptations.

The boy claims that he is still visited by the "eight Chinese guys," who continue to provide him with information. This is his direct mystical experience of truth and guidance, which he accepts completely, joyfully, and unquestioningly and which provides him with comfort in traumatic and frightening moments. Unencumbered with an adult's mental filter of what is "right" and "wrong" to think and believe, this child is able to accept both a direct source of guidance and a direct experience of spirituality. Unlike his very curious and well-intentioned mother, he has no need to research the facts.

Another spiritual figure regarded by the Taoists as an Immortal is Guanyin (or Qwan Yin), who is also venerated by Buddhists as the embodiment of mercy. A quintessential source of infinite and unconditional love, she graced the author of the story that you are about to read with her presence and, in doing so, changed her life forever.

It is said that, in the belief system of Chinese Buddhists, the mindful state of feeling at peace with oneself and with others is Guanyin. The very principles of loving-kindness and compassion are Guanyin. To feel, behave, and think in accordance with these values is Guanyin, and the person who does so is Guanyin.

The world in its current state could use more Guanyin.

. THE GODDESS OF COMPASSION .

I had been working and living in the hospitality industry for three years in Beijing in the early nineties. It was a fantastic experience and while it was a hard existence living there, I also loved it. A few years later, a job opportunity presented itself in New Zealand, and I jumped at the chance to travel to a new culture.

I was pretty burned out after my experience in China, so I decided that it was time to begin changing my career from stress-inducing to stress-relieving. I made a step to follow what my guidance had shared with me, and that was to learn hypnosis. I totally enjoyed every moment of my studies and became qualified as a hypnotherapist, successively integrating neurolinguistic programming (NLP) and Emotional Freedom Technique (EFT) into my work at my clinic in Dunedin.

Over a decade later, the relationship with one of my soul mates came to an end. I made the difficult decision to leave. I was going through deep, challenging issues at the time. I was filled with doubt, fear, and uncertainty, and I questioned my decision to leave the relationship.

I decided to go to Dr. Weiss's course at the Omega Institute in Rhinebeck, New York. Every day that week, we experienced two past-life regressions, one in the morning and one in the afternoon. I shifted

and released many things. Some of the regressions were profound
for me, and one linked directly with my time in China. During that
regression, facilitated by Dr. Weiss, I uncovered a lifetime in which I
had been a helper and student of a goddess. Her name was Qwan Yin,
the goddess of compassion. I immediately knew her and recognized
her energy signature. I was overwhelmed with joy in the regression to
see her, to feel her energy, and to be with her again.

It became clear during the regression that I had lived a very peaceful
experience with Qwan Yin and had spent a lot of time around her,
studying and being in her energy. In that life, when I was lying on my
deathbed, she came and stood beside me. As I was going through the
transition of dying, just before my soul left my body, she placed her
hand gently over the center of my chest. A golden light and energy
expanded through my whole heart. The feeling was extraordinary—
like I had come home. I wept. I felt so much peace and love. She said
to me, in the final moments of that life, that she would be "forever
with me, in my heart, for the rest of my days and for eternity." I was
overcome with emotion. It was an extremely powerful experience that
day, and it still moves me to tears. Reexperiencing that life reignited the
feeling in my heart, too. It was so beautiful. I felt as if I were floating in
a perfect dream state.

The regression was then brought to a close, and we were allowed
time to integrate. The understandings that I gained after it were
incredible. I felt I had been searching for the same deep companionship,
friendship, understanding, gentleness, and peace my whole life. It was
not a dream. I had already experienced it in that existence, and now I had
proof that this kind of relationship was possible in my present life too.

My inability to let go of my soul-mate relationship in New Zealand
now made sense. I still wished and hoped that we could have had a
similar connection to that which I had experienced with Qwan Yin, but
it was not to be.

I also began to understand the three years that I had spent in China.
How I had loved the Chinese people and their food, felt at home there,
and picked up the language, and how much I had adored exploring
the old parts of Beijing. I had been brought up a Christian in this life,

although I later felt little resonance with some aspects of that faith. But I had images and statues of Qwan Yin everywhere. The understanding and connection had not been made in my heart, mind, and soul until that regression with Dr. Weiss. Lying there in the hall after the regression, I reflected on the fact that two of my best friends in primary school in North Wales were Chinese twins. It all made sense, as did my deep connection with the goddess Qwan Yin.

I understood why I had been totally drawn to this goddess. She had vowed to remain on this planet and not ascend until all beings on Earth experienced compassion in their hearts. This was her mission. My work in this life involved the combination of EFT, NLP, hypnosis, and other spiritual tools. I instinctively knew very early on, when working with clients, that for deep healing to occur at a profound soul level there had to be compassion and forgiveness—not only of others, but also of self.

So many threads began to come together in my mind in an extraordinary way that day. This experience shone a new, humbling light on the tapestry of my work, life, and existence.

What is also interesting is that I am back in China again. I am currently writing this while visiting Shanghai. I visit twice yearly, teaching EFT and other spiritual techniques. I am about to embark on a new journey, developing and teaching courses that will incorporate a number of spiritual techniques including, of course, past-life regression. I feel strongly that I am being guided by Qwan Yin, who I know is with me now, always, and forever. I am grateful that your skill and tools have exposed this link within me, with ancient China, the goddess Qwan Yin, my journey, and my work.

            Michelle Hardwick

Qwan Yin has many names and manifestations. As the bodhisattva of compassion, she exists in every culture and religion, helping us through our pain and suffering in this physical dimension until we all reach a state of deep peace, unconditional love, and enlightenment. At that point, our incarnations can end and we may choose to stay in the spiritual realms. If we can conceive of and feel divine energy entering our hearts, just as

Michelle felt Qwan Yin's, we would be able to fully comprehend that beautiful promise: "I will be with you always, to the end of time." This is the same promise Michelle heard: "She would be forever with me, in my heart, for the rest of my days and for eternity."

Love is forever. It surrounds us at all times.

Like Michelle, I have had my own past-life connection to China. On a trip there several years ago, I was meditating early one morning with monks in the Wu-Tai mountain area, deep within the country. During the meditation, I had an image of myself as a general of some sort, a leader of people. The memory seemed to be several thousand years old. I was sitting on a white horse, up on a hill, overlooking a vast field. From this elevated vantage point, I could look down at the valley below and see all my people, the people that I was entrusted to protect and take care of, to safeguard. My heart was so filled with love and compassion for them. I felt especially blessed to have such a position of responsibility and privilege, and I wanted every single being in that vista to feel the way that I did, to have a heart overflowing with kindness, caring, protectiveness, and the sense that we were all linked together.

I could see myself sitting on the horse and wearing a kind of primitive armor, with a breastplate made of horizontal bars of bamboo wood. I remember feeling that the horse was meaningful too, and that he and I were also connected. At that moment, I vowed to bring this sense of deep and compassionate love that so filled my heart to all the beings in this entire area and beyond. That became my goal.

It is a vow that I continue to make on a daily basis, one from which this book—as well as all my work—is born.

In some of my regressions or meditations I will have mere glimpses of past lives, while at other times it is more like a movie, in which events progress from past to present to future. But in this one glimpse—for I did not see the whole lifetime—the feeling state was far more significant than any details. What was important was to take that vow, to wish that all the other beings in that entire land could feel the same way, and to know that I would do everything in my power to bring that about.

I had this experience and wrote this account before ever hearing Michelle's story, yet how alike they are. Michelle wrote of Qwan Yin: "She had vowed to remain on this planet and not ascend until all beings on Earth experienced compassion in their hearts. This was her mission." That had been my mission as well. Perhaps, at that long-ago moment on the hilltop as I looked over my people, Qwan Yin had placed her loving hands on my own heart, just as she had done with Michelle.

As I mentioned above, some regressions are powerful not for the concrete details they provide but for the deeply transcendent emotions they generate. Your subconscious mind knows where it must go for healing, and you can trust it to lead it to the experience that you most need. When this happened to Nathaniel, the author of the next story, his life did not merely transform—it began.

. THE NATURE OF LOVE .

I will never be the same after seeing you at your San Francisco workshop. Not long ago, I was given a diagnosis of terminal emphysema and congestive heart failure. My life, needless to say, is filled with constant physical pain. I came to your event expecting to uncover a past life but, much to my surprise, I did not go to one, nor did I go to my childhood, as you had instructed us. Instead, I found myself leaving my body behind, floating above it into a universe that was filled with infinite beauty and love. I can only describe it as a wonderfully deathless near-death experience. It was the first peace I had known since my diagnosis, and its memory carries me through the difficult days that lie ahead.

There is no death. I know this because I went there, to this place of unconditional love, and I came back to tell its story. The veil that separates us from being constantly aware of this love was parted for me that day. There is never any reason or anything to fear. There is only love, a love that is indiscriminate and absolutely universal.

Contrary to what I had always believed, no judgment awaited me. Love does not know how to judge; it embraces, without any limits or conditions. We are judged by people all day long but never by God, whom I believe to be the source of this love.

My pain was gone. Love can heal, also. I had not had a painless moment in recent memory. The relief that I experienced during the regression defies description.

Do you know what hate feels like? Ten thousand pounds upon our shoulders. Every time that we are judged or we judge others, another pound is added, until our bodies are so heavy that we cannot move. When we speak of the weight of the world bearing down upon us, this is what it means. And yet I never realized what a burden I had been carrying my entire life; I had become used to it. That day at the workshop, it disappeared. I soared without meaning to. There was simply nothing to hold me down. And we do not even need to do anything special to fly—just transform ourselves from beings of hate into beings of love. It may sound lofty, but it could not be simpler or more instantaneous. The key to happiness and freedom has been in our hands our entire lives. We just never thought to look down to see what they held.

Our bodies are delicate; they ache, they age, they die. To have a body is to have suffering. They are important, for we come into them and into this planet to learn, but there are great growing pains in the process. Once we throw the bodies off, we realize that we are more than we ever imagined we could possibly be.

When I had found out that my death was approaching, I feared what came next. But now I know what comes next. We go to the afterlife, we are healed, we are loved. It is pure bliss. It is the exact opposite of fear. How did we manage to get it so backward?

Afterward, I returned home, but the memory of that experience has stayed with me to this day. The pain returns from time to time, but I can tolerate it now. Just knowing that this place awaits me, that it awaits us all, gives me great comfort. I feel that when I die, I will return to that state of bliss that I experienced during those life-changing moments at your workshop.

I have told other people about what I learned that day. This has become a purpose in my life: to help others. We all have this purpose, actually. We are all important, every last one of us. Although we may behave badly out of ignorance, or fear, or judgment, we ourselves are never "bad." That is not a word that can ever describe a soul.

If, for just a few short moments, everybody could feel the love that I felt, there would be no more war, no more violence. Why would anyone want to hurt a soul? I know all these things now, and although the end of my life may be approaching, it is, in a sense, just starting. I am at peace.

ᘯ Nathaniel Peterson

"Love does not know how to judge," Nathaniel states. "It embraces, without any limits or conditions." We know this innately but we keep forgetting, and we suffer because we forget. We have been taught metaphors to help us remember. The sun shines on prisons as well as churches; the rain falls on weeds as well as flowers. But we still forget. We allow ourselves to be judged by others, accepting their projections and distortions, and in doing so we lose a bit of our confidence and self-esteem.

Instead, we should fill ourselves with self-love. We should remember our true nature as an immortal, spiritual being, an eternal soul who is always loved and who is never alone. The Zen monk Thich Nhat Hanh wrote, "The wave does not need to die to become water. She is already water." Nor do we need to die to become the spiritual beings that we already are.

Nathaniel has lost his fear of death. He has glimpsed the other side of the veil and found it to be pure love. He can fulfill his purpose and squarely face his prognosis. Death is not a mystery to him.

Our lives always hold a deep meaning and a profound purpose.

"Although the end of my life may be approaching," says Nathaniel, "it is, in a sense, just starting." The outlook that has resulted from his workshop experience has given him a new life, one that, even if it is indeed nearing its end, is much more peaceful and satisfying. But what if what we have always thought of as the end is actually just the beginning? Jade, in the final story of this book, depicts this glorious possibility.

. THE END IS ONLY THE BEGINNING .

I attended one of Dr. Weiss's past-life regression seminars in 2010 in Denver, Colorado. Only seven months prior to this event, I lost my sweetheart, Christian, to a sudden and unexpected death. It was the worst thing I had ever experienced, and it left me a basket case, with so many painful thoughts and questions. At the same time, I had also spontaneously remembered a tragic past life with Christian and me that had ended in a similar fashion, which left me feeling even worse.

Because I was so distraught about these losses, Christian's aunt told me about Dr. Weiss and recommended that I go to an event, saying that maybe I would find some answers or at least feel better. I looked him up and read his books, and they gave me some peace of mind. But when I found out that he was going to be as close as Colorado, I took the opportunity to travel and attend his event. My experience there has helped me so much by changing my perspective.

It was the first regression of the day after Dr. Weiss had introduced himself and prepared us for what might be expected and experienced within the context of our time with him. When he put us into a deep state of hypnotic regression, of course I expected to go into a past life, just as I had done times before while listening to his regression CD.

I remember that he had just come to the part where he gives the suggestion to go back to the earliest childhood memory, which I did. Like a child, I found myself in wonder and anticipation of the adventure I would soon discover when he took me back to a previous life. What past-life clues and remnants would I uncover? What would they teach me about my life and myself?

I can't be exactly certain of the words he spoke at the moment of crossing over that threshold between this life and another one, but what I heard was to "step through the door and into the light." I did so with no hesitation.

To my delighted surprise, I found myself being drawn into a tunnel of beautiful light. When he asked us to look down to see what type of footwear and clothing we were wearing, I was taken aback to see that my feet were bare and that I was wearing a long, robe-like gown. In an instant, I realized where I must have been, and although it didn't make much sense to my brain I went with the experience. It was as real as if my eyes were wide open.

Within the tunnel of this warm illumination, I saw the figures of beings. I did not see their faces, but I could feel strong presences. The predominant presence I felt was the spirit of my mother, who had crossed over nearly forty years ago, when I was just a girl. There were others, too, but I was so enamored by the energy of the light that I could not shift my focus away from it.

I became aware that I was weightless, and I was experiencing this wonderful new floating sensation. Every part of me felt as if it were being immersed and bathed in the sweetest, most cleansing energy. It was as though I had died and gone to heaven. The bliss was consuming, and there was nowhere that love was not. I remember thinking that I could stay in this loving light forever. Feeling so peaceful and fulfilled, I knew there was nothing that I could ever want or need again.

Next, without knowing how I got there, I went from floating in the tunnel to some sort of transition area. It seemed like a hospital, except there was none of the equipment that you would normally see in a hospital on Earth. I knew what it looked like because I was in two places at the same time: I was both consciously observing *and* experiencing what was happening while I lay unconscious.

I saw myself lying on a flat, illuminated surface, which, for lack of a better word, I will call a bed. This bed was most curious. I could both see and feel its amazing pulsating energy. I could feel its subtle vibration. It appeared to be made of smooth, crystalline rock, which radiated brightly as it so amazingly energized my spirit and soul. It had a magnetic quality about it, and like the light in the tunnel, the bed was alive with intelligence.

I could feel that something extremely special was happening to me. It seemed to have a healing restorative quality and effect about it. I watched while the unconscious part of me lay there lifeless, while my sweetheart, Christian, who had passed only seven months earlier, was trying to rouse me into the awareness of this heavenly realm.

Although there was a very conscious part of me in that heavenly realm, another part of my consciousness was still lagging behind, maybe in the bliss of the tunnel or, perhaps, still in the life that had been departed. Interestingly enough, the conscious me somehow knew information surrounding my death. I knew that it was sudden and unexpected. I knew it had something to do with my throat area; I got the impression that the cause of death was asphyxiation. I may have choked, but the point that fascinated me was that the sleeping one I was observing on that bed did not yet know that she had left the earthly realm.

In her life, what had surfaced as previous past lives for her were many memories of dying horrible deaths while staying in the body until that last terrifying gasp of air. But this time was different. Because her spirit had left before seeing the face of death, there was no struggle, not even a hint of pain or fear involved with the process, so there was no realization yet of a passing. The body just died without drama, and now she found herself experiencing this incredible peace and freedom.

From the perspective of the sleeping beauty lying there, I had the sensation of being in a deep dream state from which I was ever so slowly waking up, as if from a strong dose of anesthesia. As I was coming to, I could hear my beloved Christian speaking faintly at first, his words then growing louder. I heard him say, "Sweetheart, wake up. It's me. Come on, love, wake up. I'm here with you." As I heard these words in the far-off distance, I was confused about where to focus my consciousness. Which was the dream, and which the reality of my situation?

I could both see and sense the presence of other loved ones with me, all of my beloveds watching over me with great care and attention, awaiting the reunion of that very moment when I would wake from my slumber and open my eyes to be greeted and welcomed into the overflowing joy that love is. It reminded me so much of the mood of anticipation and excitement that is present when a new baby is about to come into the world.

As I mentioned before, I was encountering this whole scene from what seemed to be two quite different perspectives. It was fascinating. But what I am realizing is a possible third perspective. I experienced them both, and now another one is writing the both of them. Perhaps they are all aspects of me, only separated by diverse events in time.

It was only because of the particular spirits who had previously passed before me that I believe that I was witnessing the actual death of my current earthly life. But, as I said, it seemed to be more about a birth into a wonderful new existence, one to which I needed to adjust and acclimate, rather than a death.

I never got to wake up from my unconscious state to see what happened because it was at this time that Dr. Weiss began the process of bringing us back from our hypnotic state and into the awareness of this earthly life. After I returned, it took me a few minutes to begin to realize the implications of what had just occurred. In fact, several weeks later, I am still trying to comprehend them. However, despite my lack of full comprehension, this incident has given me so much more than I could have ever thought to ask for.

It gave me the personal comfort of knowing that Christian will not only be there to greet me when I cross over, but that our love continues on. It has also helped me to deal with my fears about my own eventual passing. By previewing and experiencing my death, I realize there is nothing I need to be afraid of when it is my turn to walk through death's door, for beyond that threshold is unimaginable freedom and bliss. I am forever thankful that I was given this wonderful opportunity. It has truly been a gift.

ᐁ*Jade Kramer*

What if death is really just a birth into a beautiful realm of peace, a realm in which, as Jade says, there is nowhere that love is not? What if our departed loved ones gather with great anticipation to welcome our birth on the other side, to be reunited once again? Then, like Jade and Nathaniel, we would lose our fear of death, and we would embrace life with more joy and more purpose.

In my book *Same Soul, Many Bodies,* I document numerous precognitive dreams and journeys to the near and far future. This is entirely feasible because, as modern physics describes, time is relative and quite different from our conscious perceptions and understanding. It is possible to see the future.

Recently, a woman responding to an interview of mine with a description of her own near-death experience unknowingly echoed Jade's words. "I realized that life is like a dream," she wrote. "When you are born, you wake up into mortality in this physical body. When your physical body dies, you return to immortality. I'm not afraid to die anymore. It is like going home." We sang this truth as children, yet as adults we have forgotten. Life is but a dream, and how merrily we must partake in it as we sail down the stream of time.

The author Katherine Frank writes about time as a deep pool rather than a fast-flowing river. What if time is indeed more like a lake than a swift stream, having depth instead of flow? All our memories, thoughts, and actions are stored there and can be retrieved by entering those deep waters. They do not flow away. They are never lost. We can enter the water whenever we wish. And when we are finished with time, we walk out of the lake and sit on its shore, as everyone we have ever known and loved comes to welcome us back and the brilliant light restores our souls.

Both Jade and Nathaniel, and countless people across the world who have shared their experiences with me, call this shore bliss. It is bliss. It is the Source. Every word and every page of this book tells its story. It is the breath from which the cosmos is created. It exists before and beyond all dimensions. It precedes all space, all emptiness, all matter, all forces, and all energies. It is the timeless precursor of all that is. It is the origin of the field and of all intention. It is love itself, and it is that which begets love. It is known by many names but is beyond knowing.

It is our true home.

It is where we take off our bodies and our masks one last time and cast them into the eddy of eternity. It is where we finally realize that most transcendent truth of our soul's everlasting nature, of its journey into the beautiful dream which is life. It is where, after thousands and thousands of dreams, we awaken, and it is where, after thousands and thousands of births, we are born.

The end is only the beginning.

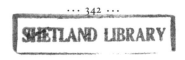

Acknowledgments

Our deepest appreciation goes to Gideon Weil, our extraordinary editor at HarperOne. Gideon's masterful insights and inspired vision for this book, upon reading its first draft, resonated deeply with both of us, and we knew that we had found the perfect collaborator. Thank you also to production editor Suzanne Quist, assistant editor Babette Dunkelgrun, and the entire HarperOne team for their skillful work on this book. We appreciate everything they do.

We are very grateful to Tracy Fisher, our remarkable agent at William Morris Endeavor, whose help has been invaluable throughout the years. She has expertly guided this project since its inception. Our thanks also extend to her assistant, Pauline Post, for all her efforts and enthusiastic support.

We are indebted to all of the organizations that have hosted our events over the years and provided the source for many of the miracles described in this book. In particular, Omega Institute has offered constant support and an idyllic healing environment for our larger workshops and retreats. Special thanks to Carol Donohoe for facilitating these fantastic events at Omega. Hay House has expertly organized most of our full-day seminars, as well as some longer ones. We especially want to thank Reid Tracy, CEO of Hay House, and both Mollie Langer and Nancy Levin, who have tirelessly helped us to touch the lives of thousands of workshop participants.

For his wise advice and input as well as his story, our thanks and love go to Jordan Weiss.

We would also like to acknowledge the loving and loyal S., whose biting commentary literally shaped the pages of this book.

This book would not exist without the sixty-eight wonderful contributors who shared their words with the world. Our own words cannot express how grateful we are to you. Thank you to Renata Bartoli, Ph.D.; Wayne-Daniel Berard, Ph.D.; Bryn Blankinship, CMHt, CI; Lori Bogedin; Kaaran Bowden; Michelle Brock; Michael Brown, MSSW; Marylyn Calabrese; Maria Castillo, LCSW; Cherelle; Valarie Coventry; Horace Crater, Ph.D.; Cynthia; Dave; Eileen de Bruin; Nikki DeStio; Rev. Cindy Frado; Mara Gober; Susie Gower; T. H.; Michelle A. Hardwick; Melanie Weil Harrell, M.A., CH; Jessica; Judi; Mira Kelley; Jade Kramer; Patricia Kuptz; Jeannette; Chris Johnson, M.Sc.; Lee Leach; Michelle Lin, D.D.S.; Nina Manny, C.Ht.; Donna Offterdinger; Judith Oliver, D.V.M.; Nathaniel Peterson; Christy Raile, M.S.N., ARNP, CRNA, HHP; Toni Reilly; Heather Rivera, R.N., J.D., Ph.D.; Margie Samuels; Sandy; Aviva D. Shalem; Faith Susan; Terri; Tong; Gregg Unterberger, M.Ed.; Asia Voight; Dr. K. C. Vyas; Donna West, Psy.D.; Carla White; and Jennifer Williams, LCSW. Some of the story authors wished to be credited with a pseudonym, and although we have not listed their names above, we are equally thankful for their contributions.

Space constraints forced us to leave out some marvelous and very moving stories. To everyone who sent in a submission that, unfortunately, we were not able to include in this book, our deepest appreciation extends to you as well.

And to all the people across the globe and across the decades who have attended our workshops, read the books, worked with the CDs, and shared your stories with us throughout the years, our sincerest gratitude goes to each and every one of you.

ABOUT THE AUTHORS

As a traditional psychotherapist, **Dr Brian Weiss** was astonished and skeptical when one of his patients began recalling past-life traumas that seemed to hold the key to her recurring nightmares and anxiety attacks. His skepticism was eroded, however, when she began to channel messages from 'the space between lives', which contained remarkable revelations about Dr Weiss's family and his dead son. Using past-life therapy, he was able to cure the patient and embark on a new, more meaningful phase of his own career.

A graduate of Columbia University and Yale Medical School, Brian L. Weiss MD is Chairman Emeritus of Psychiatry at the Mount Sinai Medical Center in Miami.

Dr Weiss is the author of many books. His first book on the subject of past life regression, *Many Lives, Many Masters*, became an international bestseller. He is also the author of *Only Love is Real, Messages from the Masters, Through Time into Healing* and *Same Soul, Many Bodies.* Dr Weiss conducts national and international seminars and experiential workshops as well as training programmes for professionals.

Amy E. Weiss graduated *summa cum laude*, Phi Beta Kappa, from Columbia University with a BA in psychology. She received a Master of Fine Arts in fiction writing from Washington University in St Louis, where she won the Carrie S. Galt prize for fiction, and a Master of Social Work from Barry University. A certified hypnotherapist and award-winning nature photographer, she lives in Miami, Florida.

www.brianweiss.com

Also by Dr Brian Weiss

Books

ELIMINATING STRESS, FINDING INNER PEACE (book with CD)*

MANY LIVES, MANY MASTERS: The True Story of a Prominent Psychiatrist, His Young Patient and the Past-life Therapy That Changed Both Their Lives

MEDITATION: Achieving Inner Peace and Tranquility in Your Life (book with CD)*

MESSAGES FROM THE MASTERS: Tapping into the Power of Love
MIRRORS OF TIME: Using Regression for Physical, Emotional, and Spiritual Healing (book with CD)*

ONLY LOVE IS REAL: A Story of Soulmates Reunited

SAME SOUL, MANY BODIES

THROUGH TIME INTO HEALING: How Past Life Regression Therapy Can Heal Mind, Body And Soul

CDs

REGRESSION THROUGH THE MIRRORS OF TIME

REGRESSION TO TIMES AND PLACES

SPIRITUAL PROGRESS THROUGH REGRESSION

Card Deck

HEALING THE MIND AND SPIRIT CARDS

*Available from Hay House

Hay House Titles of Related Interest

THE HIDDEN POWERS OF YOUR PAST LIVES:
Revealing and Healing Your Encoded Consciousness, by Sandra Anne Taylor

IN THE SHADOW OF THE BUDDHA: One Man's Journey of Spiritual Discovery & Political Danger in Tibet, by Matteo Pistono

PAST REALITY INTEGRATION: 3 Steps to Mastering the Art of Conscious Living, by Ingeborg Bosch

PAST LIVES, PRESENT MIRACLES: The Most Empowering Book on Reincarnation You'll Ever Need... in this lifetime!, by Denise Linn

REAL PEOPLE, REAL PAST LIVES, by David Wells

SOUL SURVIVOR: The Reincarnation of World War II Fighter Pilot, by Bruce and Andrea Leininger

WISHES FULFILLED: Mastering the Art of Manifesting,
by Dr Wayne W. Dyer

YOU CAN CREATE AN EXCEPTIONAL LIFE: Candid Conversations with Louise Hay and Cheryl Richardson,
by Louise Hay and Cheryl Richardson

JOIN THE HAY HOUSE FAMILY

As the leading self–help, mind, body and spirit publisher in the UK, we'd like to welcome you to our family so that you can enjoy all the benefits our website has to offer.

 **EXTRACTS** from a selection of your favourite author titles

 **COMPETITIONS, PRIZES & SPECIAL OFFERS** Win extracts, money off, downloads and so much more

 **LISTEN** to a range of radio interviews and our latest audio publications

 **CELEBRATE YOUR BIRTHDAY** An inspiring gift will be sent your way

 **LATEST NEWS** Keep up with the latest news from and about our authors

 **ATTEND OUR AUTHOR EVENTS** Be the first to hear about our author events

 **iPHONE APPS** Download your favourite app for your iPhone

 **HAY HOUSE INFORMATION** Ask us anything, all enquiries answered

join us online at **www.hayhouse.co.uk**

 292B Kensal Road, London W10 5BE
T: 020 8962 1230 E: info@hayhouse.co.uk